FRACTURED
FEMINISMS

FRACTURED FEMINISMS

Rhetoric, Context, and Contestation

edited by

LAURA GRAY-ROSENDALE
and
GIL HAROOTUNIAN

STATE UNIVERSITY OF NEW YORK PRESS

Published by
STATE UNIVERSITY OF NEW YORK PRESS, ALBANY

Cover artwork by Steven Rosendale.

For information, address State University of New York Press,
90 State Street, Suite 700, Albany, NY 12207

Production, Laurie Searl
Marketing, Jennifer Giovani

Library of Congress Cataloging-in-Publication Data

Fractured feminisms : rhetoric, context, and contestation / edited by Laura Gray-Rosendale
and Gil Harootunian
    p. cm.
Includes bibliographical references and index.
    ISBN 0-7914-5801-6 (alk. paper) — ISBN 0-7914-5802-4 (pbk. : alk. paper)
    1. Feminist theory. 2. Feminist criticism. I. Gray-Rosendale, Laura. II. Harootunian,
Gil, 1957-

HQ1190.F715 2003
305.42'01—dc21

                                                                        2003042559

10 9 8 7 6 5 4 3 2 1

To Steven and Max—

To Sarkis, Dante, and Dylan—

For all of your laughter, love, and support.

Contents

Acknowledgments

Many thanks to Priscilla Ross, our editor at SUNY Press, for her early and continued support of this project. SUNY Press remains consistently at the forefront of critical inquiries that help further the discipline of rhetoric and composition. We are very grateful that Priscilla and SUNY Press continue to be concerned about feminist theoretical as well as practical concerns alongside crucial challenges to them. Laurie Searl, Senior Production Editor, was tremendously helpful throughout the process. We also very much appreciate the efforts of copyeditor Camille Hale. Thanks also to the contributors featured in this book whose work truly cuts against the traditional grain of what it means to engage in feminist scholarship, thereby putting pressure upon and expanding the genre. Their research recommends new perspectives and visions for feminist thinking in the future, and we are energized by the directions they take as well as the perspectives they consider. Thanks also to Cori Brewster, Laura's research assistant, whose diligence and thoughtful intelligence on related projects helped support us in the timely completion of this book. Additional gratitude goes to Cheryl Glenn for her excellent suggestions about the project in its beginning stages as well as to the SUNY reviewers of this text for their very thoughtful commentary. Finally, we thank each other for the chance to embark together on this intellectual adventure, one very close to both of our hearts. In working together we have supported each others' ideas as well as come to question our own assumptions about our roles as feminist theorists and practitioners in the academy. Our energetic and ongoing dialogue is what has made this book come alive for us both, bringing these ideas to their current form.

Framing Feminisms

Investigating Histories, Theories, and Moments of Fracture

LAURA GRAY-ROSENDALE AND GIL HAROOTUNIAN

We begin this introduction with a framing discussion, providing a summary of the diverse theories that have impacted the history of feminist philosophy. We make note of both the differences and the critical commonalties that exist between feminist positions. After moving to a discussion of the history of rhetoric and composition's uneasy relationship to such feminist theories, we explore the latest trends in feminist thinking and rhetoric and composition as a discipline as well as the connections between such trends and the unique offerings of *Fractured Feminisms*. Finally, we furnish a rationale for this volume and present an overview of the compelling texts you will find here. We indicate how they extend and augment the decisive conversation about potential links between feminisms and rhetoric and composition.

OF FEMINISMS: LIBERAL, CULTURAL, SOCIALIST, RADICAL, AND POSTSTRUCTURALIST

Our histories of feminisms are records marked by metaphorical as well as literal investments in contradictions, conflicts, and complexities. As a result, there should be little surprise at the number of recent feminist texts that reference differences of opinion within feminist circles, including titles such as Marianna Hirsch and Evelyn Fox Keller's *Conflicts in Feminism;* Elisabeth Bronfen and Misha Karka's *Feminist Consequences;* Esther Ngan-ling Chow, Doris Wilkinson, and Maxine Baca Zinn's *Race, Class, and Gender: Common Bonds, Different Voices;* Frances E. Mascia-Lees and Patricia Sharpe's *Taking a Stand in a Postfeminist World: Toward an Engaged Cultural Criticism;* Elizabeth A. St. Pierre and Wanda Pillow's *Working the Ruins: Feminist Poststructural Theory and Methods in Education;* James Sterba's *Controversies in Feminism;* and Ewa Plonowska Ziarek's *An Ethics of Dissensus: Postmodernity, Feminism, and the Politics of Radical Democracy.* In fact, Mascia-Lees and Sharpe, among other feminists, reason that now principally feminists find themselves in a historical moment of unrest, "a context in which the feminism of the 1970s is problematized, splintered, and considered suspect, one in which it is no longer easy, fun, empowering, or even possible to take *a* feminist position" (3). Instead, multiple feminist positions frequently exist simultaneously, actually disrupting and challenging power relations appears daunting, and we speak of *feminisms* over *feminism.*

In spite of such conflicts as well as because of them our histories of feminism are also marked by countless potentials and possibilities. While the number of definitions for and past chronicles of feminism, aimed at struggles for social justice, equality, and working in favor of political enfranchisement and economic parity, seem positively mind-boggling, familiarizing oneself with such perspectives is crucial. And yet, in spite of such exhaustive attempts to account for the contradictions and contestations within and between various feminist philosophies, any such definitions or histories are never finally able to apprehend the full complexities of feminist thinking and its practices. As a result, inevitably such efforts to relay definitions and histories of feminist groups are overly reductionist and simplistic, at times unwittingly perpetuating such divisions.

All the same, when framing a project such as *Fractured Feminisms,* we find it a necessary rhetorical device—remarking upon various approaches within feminist philosophy becomes an indispensable exercise, supplying critical context for those relatively new to the conversation and advancing common ground to feminists who might identify with different groups while still sharing the unifying goal of struggle on behalf of women's equality. Doing so also divulges the similarities and overlapping investments of feminists who have historically been considered part of distinctly separate groups. The framework that we supply in this introduction is a rough sketch meant to tender provisional characterizations of diverse feminist groups. In doing so, we acknowledge that many feminists hold positions that make use of multiple feminist viewpoints, incorporating the ostensible contradictions between feminist theories into new cohesive programs for change, ones that notably acknowledge internal contradictions and see them as intrinsically valuable.

Most such histories of feminist thinking, including Valerie Bryson's *Feminist Debates,* Josephine Donovan's *Feminist Theory,* Mary Evans' *Introducing Contemporary Feminist Thought,* Anne C. Hermann and Abigail J. Stewart's *Theorizing Feminism: Parallel Trends in the Humanities and Social Sciences,* Ruth Robbins' *Literary Feminisms,* Sue Thornham's *Feminist Theory and Cultural Studies: Stories of Unsettled Relations,* and Chris Weedon's *Feminism, Theory, and the Politics of Difference,* commence with definitions of enlightenment liberal feminist political thinking, which finds its roots in the 1600s and extends to the present. As these histories elucidate, this group of feminists historically fought against the notion that individual rights should only be extended to men. Instead, they have made a case for women to be regarded as autonomous, self-determining individuals who should have equal access to education, political office, pay, and rights. Liberal feminists importantly declare that "women's rights are a form of human rights, and that feminism must not be anti-men; male abuses of power must be resisted, but men, too, can learn the benefits of living in a sexually egalitarian society" (Bryson 11). Liberal feminists regularly affirm that women should be encouraged to enter paid employment and should have more visible roles in public office. Since many of these stances have become accepted as commonly held beliefs at this historical juncture, particularly in American culture, they are often no longer taken to be solely feminist demands. Generally speaking, there is less dispute than in the past about women's right to own property, to sell their labor, or to have access to legal frameworks that protect them.

However, liberal feminists have been criticized for accepting a set of principles that is essentially male because they do not object to the tenets of liberal individualism, ignore the troubling power relationships that pervade male-female relations, and overlook the larger social and political structures as well as biases that deny self-determination and equal competition to women (i.e., critics indicate that basic structures of oppression such as race and class inequities remain intact). Other feminists have justifiably critiqued this position because it works within male-constructed structures rather than searching for ways to overhaul them. Likewise, continuing to separate the public and the private spheres, many feminists have suspected that within liberal feminist thought the power relationships of family structures are not open to necessary dispute and challenge.

Liberal feminism is often connected loosely with the ideals of cultural feminism. While some envision cultural feminism as an extension of such liberal ideology, some scholars detach cultural feminism from liberal feminism. As Linda Alcoff describes it, "cultural feminism is the ideology of a female nature or female essence reappropriated by feminists themselves in an effort to revalidate undervalued female attributes" (408). Going slightly beyond the fundamentally rationalist and legalistic thrust of enlightenment theory, cultural feminists make a significant case for extensive cultural transformations.

Valuing the intuitive, nonrational, and collective approaches to life, they often espouse the significance of feminine qualities and impart alternatives to traditional views on marriage, religion, and the home that have been oppressive to women historically. Some cultural feminists champion the creation of a matriarchal society based on pacifism, cooperation, and nonviolent settlement of differences. Supporting women's self-reliance and separatism unified by a belief in common female interests and principles, they frequently indicate that conventional modes of the feminine might advantageously be brought into the public sphere. In short, they hope to transform ideology and work toward pacifism and maternal thinking, arguing for special legislation designed specifically for women.

Of course, various criticisms of the cultural feminist position have been avowed as well. Since cultural feminists place such a great emphasis on differences between men and women, the issue becomes how one makes sense of such distinctions: Are they biologically or culturally determined? If one specifies that these divergences are primarily in the genes, other feminists stress, this can destablize and undercut human freedoms. If one proposes that these differences are products of social environments, other feminists intimate, then they should be subject to change and mutability. Of late, cultural feminists have tended to be more leery of biological determinism because they suppose that it has been employed historically to construct a model of female inferiority. Instead, they tend to argue on behalf of female traits and values being adopted in the public realm by men and women alike.

While also believing in equal rights and opportunities for all individuals, socialist feminisms have had yet a slightly different focal point. They have been predisposed to incorporate those positions ranging from reformist social democracy positions to revolutionary Marxist communist beliefs. All of these viewpoints hold in common the notion that capitalism has been traditionally oppressive to both men and women and that feminists should fight for greater economic equality as well as a less exploitative social system. With a concentration on working-class groups rather than on an elite minority, socialist feminist methodologies proffer a collectivist possibility, expose where and how gender and class divisions operate to oppress women, and work to abolish or reduce the division of labor. Their aim is to minimize private ownership and maximize the satisfaction of human needs over profit. The critical concentration on historical specificity of any situation, the material conditions of women's labor, and the political possibilities to which they give rise have made such approaches crucial for the development and progression of feminist theories. Such theories have led to a deeper exploration of how feminism might function in women's daily lives with an eye to shared structural subordination and marginalization across other cultural differences. Fighting against the alienation that comes from working within the strictures of corporate capitalism, such feminist analyses have called upon

men and women to subvert prescribed social roles and to concede how the
class system oppresses men as well as women.

The socialist feminist view has also received substantial criticism from
diverse feminist quarters, however. Some affirm that it can seem overly dominated by masculinist assumptions, especially those drawing from Marxist
thought, and thereby represents a new source of patriarchal control rather
than a foundation of liberation for women.[1] Socialist feminism has also been
criticized by liberal feminists because (1) economic failure and loss of individual freedoms could result, (2) the historical problem of socialist men not supporting women's rights fully might continue, and (3) women in communist
societies have often not necessarily attained the desired control over their
material conditions. As such, some feminists have deemed that socialist feminisms cannot adequately conceptualize gender inequalities.

One critical extension of and challenge to the liberal, cultural, and socialist positions has materialized from the radical or women-centered approaches.
Such strategies make a case for the centrality and validity of women's experiences and ideals over those imparted by patriarchal culture. Male domination
not capitalism is at the root of women's oppression, they maintain, and women
and men have distinctly different styles and cultures. Consciousness-raising
groups surface from this strand of feminist thought as well as the understanding that the personal is always already inevitably political. These groups
promote the sharing of experiences in small and supportive groups that scrutinize trends and patterns of domination across women's experiences. As such
they uncover the ways in which women are conditioned to maternal traits, caring for others, flexibility, noncompetitiveness, and cooperativeness. Some who
occupy this position presume that gender characteristics are biologically given,
while others advocate that such characteristics are socially produced and open
to change.[2] In either case, such feminists often accentuate the idea that
women should work together in common sisterhood to defy patriarchy. Politics, then, is redefined by radical feminists to comprise personal and family
relationships, and many radical feminists have historically formed groundbreaking campaigns to secure greater access to the means of reproduction.
They have confronted pornographic representations, attained more abortion
and birth control services, revolutionized laws concerning violence against
women, and worked to end discrimination against lesbians.

Some feminists have found the position of radical feminists objectionable
because it implicitly can signify that there are no regions of women's lives for
which they should not be held accountable to feminist standards: that there is
no aspect of women's lives that is not intrinsically political. Other feminists
have contended that the concentration upon the personal ends up in little
more than self-indulgence and depoliticization of feminist work, leaving the
dominant culture uncontested. Still other feminists have counseled that this
approach is ahistorical, universalizing about women's experiences based on the

experiences of white, Western women. This can lead not only to forms of racism but also to the inference that innate female essence does in fact exist, a biologically determined, true womanhood to which all women must ascribe. Still other feminists recommend that men are painted falsely as the "enemy" in such a view and that, as a result, complaining and whining seem to be the main outcome. In this way, they reason, such feminist work has sometimes led to revictimization rather than endeavors to labor against victimhood in collectively empowering ways.

Perhaps the most recent trail offered for the radical feminist perspective has emanated from feminist poststructuralists, those feminists who elect to confront how oppressive power relations that maneuver through language systems, institutions, and ideologies construct and shape women's identities and their senses of what is possible. Poststructuralist feminists repeatedly specify that the subject or self is not determined by biology but is instead constantly impacted and fashioned by larger social discourses and cultural practices. Poststructuralist feminists affirm that empowerment can occur through disrupting the structures of dominant linguistic and political principles. They also often acknowledge that such contestations can be provisional only because power structures are continually in flux and subject to alteration.

While frequently valued by some feminists for the diversity and provisionality it seems to embrace, poststructuralist feminism has also been contested for its proposition that the workings of macrostructures overdetermine women's situations, neglecting the potentialities of women's resistance to such structures. In fact, some have designated that poststructuralism undercuts feminist opposition to dominant Western intellectual thought that has depended on universality and neutrality in terms of epistemology, metaphysics, and ethics. Others see the spotlight on diversity as simply a new form of liberalism—much like the championing of pluralism or free speech, this time exploiting philosophical jargon to get its points across. Arguing that this is once again the adoption of a masculinist language, critics of poststructuralist feminism at times also find it to be oddly nonpolitical, converging on textual analysis over and against tangible political reforms. This can lead to a preoccupation with discursive structures alone and retains the possibility of becoming problematically self-referential.

Various feminists of color have made the valuable critique that in its endeavors not to focus on essentializing women's experiences, reducing women to their biological status as female, it has turned out to be harder and harder for women who are already situated on the margins to obtain a voice and to have their experiences of oppression validated and acknowledged. [3] Rather than submitting a vigilant analysis of patriarchy and how it operates, such feminists recommend, poststructuralist feminist thought rests at the level of intellectual analysis: If "woman" is no longer thought to be a stable category comprising a shared identity, how can one fight on behalf of women's rights?

This can lead to the impression that collective struggle itself is thorny if not impractical because alliances can only be construed in tentative and tactical terms, ones that take into consideration the historical and cultural specificity of women's experiences.

In response to such problems within the poststructuralist framework, a number of feminists have espoused positional definitions of identity, indicating that identities must be recognized as relative to shifting contexts that engage interactions with others and with ever-changing economic conditions, cultural and political institutions, and ideologies. These feminists endorse the notion that such identities can still be actively utilized as locations through which meanings are constructed and from which women can resist oppressive relations (Alcoff, De Lauretis, and Riley). Other feminists have granted that perhaps we are operating in a postfeminist age, an era when matters of equality seem to be a constructive part of discussions of cultural issues, but perhaps not the only salient part (Mann, Mascia-Lees and Sharpe, Modleski). They pose vital questions about how feminists can have agency in a world that oftentimes no longer acknowledges gender as the key term that it once was.

Despite the specific differences in the positions held by liberal, cultural, socialist, radical, and poststructuralist feminists as well as feminists who ascribe to some combination of these stances, ones that are necessary to explore, undoubtedly there are critical commonalties. These similarities make it promising to converse about feminist practices not in spite of such differences but because of them—to talk about feminist divergences productively between and through such differences. It seems we share certain provisional goals: conviction in the critical cultural and social value of women's work, words, and cultures; assistance for cultural, ideological, structural, and linguistic modifications that will enhance women's productive growth and development; and valuation of differences themselves not only as a starting point for feminist conversations, but perhaps as the ultimate goal of feminist practices. While our thoughts may deviate concerning matters of biology and culture, language and social structures, or separatism and collectivity, our interests and goals still remain remarkably similar.

RECONSIDERING THE RELATIONSHIP:
RHETORIC AND COMPOSITION MEETS FEMINISMS

Many rhetoric and composition feminist scholars have embraced such positions—the liberal, the cultural, the socialist, the radical, and the poststructuralist—as well as continue to extend various combinations of such intellectual tenets in their teaching practices and in their scholarly efforts. While Jane Gallop and others have convincingly reasoned that feminism was institutionalized in the early 1980s at the very same time as multiethnic and poststructuralist issues were crossing the threshold of the academy, as *Is Academic Feminism Dead?* by the Social Justice Group at the Center for Advanced Feminist Studies proclaims, feminist philosophies have had only marginal victories. In many feminist environments we still witness the alienation of working-class people in favor of the promotion of a middle-class ethic, the overworking of faculty of color, and the failure to take oppositions to the system seriously. Likewise, in the past the discourses of feminism and rhetoric and composition have had an influential but perhaps uneasy partnership. This has been due in part to the fact that throughout much of the 1970s and 1980s rhetoric and composition was preoccupied with instituting its own disciplinary prominence and practices. In order to do so, the discipline necessarily had to concentrate much of our energies on the research methods, analytic tools, and spheres of expertise that were distinctively its own, even if the discipline had always been somewhat interdisciplinary in approach. All the same, occasionally this has left less time to survey and scrutinize research happening outside our own discipline's boundaries.

The association between rhetoric and composition and feminism began most fully in the 1980s when a number of books and essays in rhetoric and composition, deriving largely from feminist psychoanalytic models (Belenky et al.; Chodorow; Gilligan; Ruddick; Jardine and Smith), uncovered that the gendered nature of our students' written responses indicated a great deal about divergences between feminine and masculine approaches to writing (Caywood and Overing; Flynn). Drawing from the rich traditions of cultural and radical feminisms particularly, some such scholars affirmed that there was a significant link between the nurturing female teacher and positive pedagogical possibilities (Noddings). At the very same time that rhetoric and composition studies was beginning to get wind of the significance of feminist thinking, however, feminist theorists in philosophy as well as other scholarly circles became profoundly engaged in subverting such views of femininity as inherently nurturing; they began condemning such understandings as essentialist because these attitudes depended in large part upon a biological conception of the category "woman." Instead, drawing upon crucial research by Diana Fuss, Chris Weedon, and others, the theorists championed new feminisms, predominantly poststructuralist feminisms, that acknowledged the critical nature of gender "difference" as socially and culturally constructed. Connecting to mounting interest in continental philosophy, they emphasized that it was no longer easily possible to pronounce that a woman necessarily wrote or taught in uniquely feminine ways or a man in principally masculine ways.

The history of rhetoric and composition's affiliation with feminist philosophy, then, has continually been somewhat complicated—encompassing contradictions, splinters, and differences. Looked upon in hindsight, in some real sense rhetoric and composition's deployment of feminist inquiry was progressing rather gradually, not quite in touch with the discourses of feminism that were, from the outside, beginning to contest its very foundations.

However, by the 1990s rhetoric and composition instigated a more complete incorporation of feminist theory into its research, and scholars became attentive to what the charges of "essentialism" and "accommodationism" might necessitate as well as how to strategically evade them. In rhetoric and composition an array of books and essays called attention to the problematic feminized nature of composition labor and how it had constructed the discipline rhetorically in opposition to literary studies (Miller; Phelps and Emig; Schell). Others queried how feminist theory could be more fully integrated into rhetoric and composition studies (Jarratt and Worsham) and how the "feminine" might be revalued as a locus of crucial contestation for the discipline (Emig and Phelps).

To a degree this scholarship began to position gender as well as feminist theory—often poststructuralist, Marxist, or generally leftist—at the center of critical inquiry within rhetoric and composition studies. This innovative work also put questions of feminist theory that were circulating within other academic sectors more directly into play: How could we reconceive "difference" beyond static, binaristic dichotomies? How could we resist marginalizing constructions of "otherness"? In what ways might the perplexing term *feminine* be revalued with positive traits? What would all this entail for rethinking the labor of rhetoric and composition in today's colleges and universities?

In inviting a dialogue on these new matters, rhetoric and composition scholars were no longer just catching up to the efforts ongoing in other feminist theory circles, as had transpired in the 1980s. Instead, such thinkers were offering up many of the same questions being posited by feminist theorists at the very precise moment within other scholarly quarters. In doing so, they began to employ many of the same theoretical models—poststructuralism, postcoloniality, Marxism, feminism—as other disciplines were in order to respond to these inquiries. In implementing feminist inquiry so completely, however, other Burkean[4] questions unavoidably took a back seat: What are the exact functions of the rhetorics of feminisms, and are they indeed sustaining our feminist goals? What are the relative investments and consequences embodied in such rhetorics and the identities they generate? What are the tangible connections between these feminist theories, largely assumed from other contexts, and the inventive praxis of our discipline? When, how, and why do feminist theories fail feminist practices, and in those moments, what new potentialities do we face and must we learn to embrace?

CONTEMPORARY FEMINISMS IN RHETORIC AND COMPOSITION STUDIES

In the past few years a wave of compelling books concerning the potential intersections of feminism and rhetoric and composition studies have been published. Every one of these texts has found an eager audience, though each has also taken its own significant and diverse slant on exploring the contemporary challenge of reenvisioning feminism and its influence on our discipline. These methodologies might be conversed about in a number of more detailed ways. However, illustrating broad trends helps distinguish major movements we have observed in feminist research within rhetoric and composition. Doing so also unveils potential gaps and fissures in our available scholarship to date.

The first approach may be described as entailing decisive reconstructions and reinvestigations into the history of rhetoric. This tactic has encompassed crucial works such as Cheryl Glenn's *Rhetoric Retold: Regendering the Tradition from Antiquity through the Renaissance* and Krista Ratcliffe's *Anglo-American Feminist Challenges to the Rhetorical Traditions: Virginia Woolf, Mary Daly, Adrienne Rich,* among others. A related part of this path has involved a macrolevel investigation into the consequences of feminist inquiry for research methodologies within rhetoric and composition studies, Gesa Kirsch's *Ethical Dilemmas in Feminist Research: The Politics of Location, Interpretation, and Publication* functioning very productively in this vein. Feminist revisions of the history of rhetoric as well as feminist theory's notable impact on research procedures have been very influential for rhetoric and composition studies, reinfusing our conceptions of what constitutes rhetorical history, divulging its gaps and fissures, as well as altering how we conduct and manage research in the discipline.

The second strategy may be characterized as involving rigorous reexaminations of feminism's primary roles in composition theory. This line of thinking can be perceived in the important work of Susan Jarratt and Lynn Worsham's *Feminism and Composition Studies: In Other Words,* Clayann Gilliam Panetta's *Contrastive Rhetoric Revisited and Redefined,* Louise Wetherbee Phelps and Janet Emig's *Feminine Principles and Women's Experience in American Composition and Rhetoric,* and Jan Zlotnik Schmidt's *Women/Writing/Teaching.* Such texts have both appraised feminist theories' impacts on rhetoric and composition studies and supplied fresh theories concerning women's work in the discipline—nascent feminisms that may be a central part of rhetoric and composition's own history. This scholarship has specified not only that feminist theory might be beneficially harnessed for and joined to our discipline but also that it might be a key site for constructing new feminist theories.

A third approach, similarly important in this outpouring of works, has materialized. It utilizes feminist inquiry as a way to study the voices of women who have been historically marginalized. Books taking this route include significant projects such as Jacqueline Jones Royster's *Traces of a Stream: Literacy and Social Change among African American Women,* Harriet Malinowitz's *Textual Orientations: Lesbian and Gay Students and the Making of Discourse Communities,* and Kristine Blair and Pamela Takayoshi's *Feminist Cyberscapes: Mapping Gendered Academic Spaces.* These texts have brought the marginal voices of women in the discipline to the center of inquiry, thereby defying exclusionist feminist theories and practices. They have also given rise to decisive new feminist structures that integrate matters of literacy, identity, and technology.

Each of these recent texts has presented a great deal to the discussion of vital links that might be forged between feminism and rhetoric and composition studies. The works testify that feminist theory and practice are pivotal for the study of the discipline and its methodologies for research. They also denote both the merits of feminist theory for our own research and our need to assemble new theories that materialize from within the discipline itself. They disclose our need to resist exclusionary practices as we continue feminist research and to bring multiple, conflicting voices to our discussions about feminist inquiry and the history of rhetoric and composition studies in practical sites. However, these efforts also oblige us to scrutinize the ways in which the discipline of rhetoric and composition studies has not always had a carefully crafted relationship with feminist studies. Interrogating the relationship between feminism and rhetoric and composition studies, therefore, may be instructive in thinking through both the existing problems and the untapped possibilities that the use of feminist theory promises the discipline of rhetoric and composition research. Such an investigation may also help shed light on where research in this area might profitably turn from here.

FRACTURED FEMINISMS:
THE NEED FOR A NEW CONVERSATION

Rhetoric and composition's relationship with feminism, then, has been marked by a series of problems: (1) our tendency to disregard the current research within feminist theory literature in constructing our own histories and our own understandings of gender relations in culture, (2) our proclivity to accept feminist theoretical models for the discipline while perhaps asking too few questions about their utility for the discipline's own unique structures and needs, and (3) our supposition that feminist theories that seem diametrically opposed cannot speak to each other in fundamental ways within practical contexts. Based on this history, *Fractured Feminisms* avows that the contemporary task of feminist research in rhetoric and composition studies will dictate not replicating these historical approaches but rather working from within them to unearth our own innovative approaches and problems instead. While recognizing historical differences within and between feminist theories, we will also want to acknowledge critical points of synergy, commonalty, and shared purpose. Finally, we must also be thoughtful rhetoricians and not just feminists, avoiding buying into feminist theoretical rhetorics too fully themselves. Rather, we need to interrogate the rhetorics of feminisms much as we would any other theoretical lens.

Instead, by drawing on the influential work of feminist scholars such as Sara Ahmed, Lynn Chancer, Jean Curthoys, Marianne Dekoven, Kathleen Dixon, Rita Felski, Christina Hicks and Kelly Oliver, and Frances E. Mascia-Lees and Patricia Sharpe, Barbara Johnson, Lois McNay, Elizabeth G. Peck and Joanna Mink, Sue Thornham, France Winddance Twine and Kathleen M. Blee, and others who have raised decisive questions about the rhetorical investments of various feminist theories and practices, *Fractured Feminisms* insists that feminist theories, in their various forms, risk becoming problematic new metanarratives for the discipline of rhetoric and composition. As a result, we should reflect on the discourses of feminism in detail and determine when and where they are productive and empowering as well as when and where they may be just as stifling and marginalizing as the patriarchal discourses that they desire to fight against.

Rather than circumvent feminist theorizing in response altogether, we believe such theorizing must be accomplished self-consciously and reflectively, that it is a site we will need to continue to delve into as well as contest. We affirm that such theorizing can be done productively, and rigorously, through an interrogation of theory's enactment in actual and local locations of practice. In doing so, this book extends the ongoing discussion in rhetoric and composition studies while affording a significant addition to existing feminist texts in the discipline. It achieves this by looking, first, at how feminist theory and practice are applied to and materialize from the immediate contexts within which we work, and, second, at how setting up a genuinely recursive cycle of critique and revision of theory into practice and practice into theory enriches each triple-fold. We judge that the local contexts not only serve to expose the value of feminist theorizing for the discipline as well as the problems with it. They also go beyond this traditional limit to generate new insights and ideas about feminist theory in action within our discipline. As such, these local environments disclose new, practice-based feminist theories that emerge from the discipline itself. As a result, *Fractured Feminisms* puts significant pressure on rhetorics of feminism, yet embraces them as well, and finally extends them in ways that will further the critical discussion about feminist inquiry in rhetoric and composition studies.

In feminist and literary criticism circles, a number of recent edited collections have arrived that take up these imperative issues of the crucial, productive differences within feminist inquiry. Robyn Warhol and Diane Price Herndl's *Feminisms: An Anthology of Literary Theory and Criticism*, Judith Butler and Joan Scott's *Feminists Theorize the Political*, and Carolyn Allen and Judith A. Howard's *Provoking Feminisms* are only some of these. Ironically, such scholarly work has not yet been fully surveyed in rhetoric and composition studies, though a substantial audience exists for works investigating the relationship between feminist theory and the field of rhetoric and composition.

THE COLLECTION

Inevitably this book also stems from our own experiences as feminists. Over many years, as students, teachers, administrators, and feminist scholars we have watched feminist theories in action, observing them move and change shape within local sites and practices. At some moments we have been impressed with feminist theories' abilities to give voice to issues and problems central to gender equity issues. At other times we have been disheartened by whom feminist theory authorizes to speak, who turns out to be marginalized in its discussions, and what "conflicts" or "fractures" remain overlooked. As rhetoricians and teachers we sense that it is imperative to evaluate the rhetorical tactics at work in any theories we employ as well as appraise their practical possibilities. We have noticed how, regardless of our theoretical investments and proclivities, our practices of necessity began to at first alter and finally resculpt the nature of our theorizing. We also started to perceive that many such experiences, shared by us, our colleagues, and others in the discipline of rhetoric and composition, were not satisfactorily taken up by contemporary feminist theoretical work. Working in a new generation, we found that the very radical complexities of feminist interactions were slipping through the cracks somehow, relegated strangely to the "silenced other" of our feminist conversations. Not fitting easily into any one of the historical and theoretical categories offered for feminist thinkers, we constructed shifting feminist identities for ourselves in the spaces in between. We realized that our feminist identities shifted moment-to-moment and were very dependent upon the local contexts within which we worked—their conditions, their practices. At times we found it necessary to both deploy and criticize elements of liberal, cultural, radical, socialist, poststructuralist, postcolonial, and standpoint feminisms. We also came to comprehend that part of being effective feminists meant both embracing and questioning the very language and tenets of feminism itself.

As a result, we started to sense that feminist theories themselves would need to be reinformed and reformed and by feminist practices, by the moments in which practices necessarily fracture theories apart, leading us to interrogate those elements we often hold to be sacred—their rationales, doctrines, and purposes. *Fractured Feminisms* is our attempt to position the lens firmly upon this "silenced other" within feminist scholarship—those moments when feminist theories fall apart, rupture, and fragment, compelling us to rebuild new theories and practices as a result. Doing so gives rise to additional ramifications and intellectual insights, laying bare those occasions when theory literally deserts rhetoric and composition pedagogy, the instances in which issues of globalization and multiethnic issues can be refeminized and marginalized despite our best efforts,[5] and the ways in which both troubling and constructive divergences in feminist praxis can transpire not only across cultures or languages but also within a single institution or a specific classroom.

Commonly fractures signify little more than breaks, cracks, breaches, splits, or clefts. We have certainly witnessed such ruptures in the history of feminism and in feminism's relationship to rhetoric and composition studies, as described earlier. As such, sometimes fractures carry a negative connotation, suggestive of moments when things are broken apart and destroyed in such a way that they cannot be reformed. This can reinforce divisions rather than foster dialogue between and across differences. However, in both the history of feminism and in feminist work within rhetoric and composition studies, fractures have been a major resource in our collective memory and have been exercised at key junctures to generate new feminist practices and theories. Fractures clearly also imply a positive potentiality, alluding to the texture of a surface that has in fact been broken and changed into something new, something that continues to transform in shape and substance. Fractures in this sense are not inevitably negative, instead producing new structures, innovative possibilities, even though they arise from and also seek to preserve within them that which is fragmented, broken, or disrupted. As Ruth Salvaggio pronounces in *The Sounds of Feminist Theory*, fractures do not insinuate themselves into feminist discourses. Instead, they are always already present, creating "volatile, transitory, potentially disturbing, and transforming practices within language" (24).

Our collection enters the energetic debate on the integration of feminist theory in the rhetoric and composition discipline through an exploration of theory's enactment in diverse scenes of practice. As such, we look to these flashes, moments that shed bright if brief light on such fractures in feminist theory. As Berenice Malka Fisher contends in *No Angel in the Classroom: Teaching Through Feminist Discourse*, feminist practices necessarily take many, sometimes contradictory forms. By interrogating theory through the lens of multiple and real sites of practice, we hope to have arrived at a diversity that genuinely represents the wide domain of rhetoric and composition in myriad colleges and universities. In providing this cross-section of texts, we aim to realize a truly democratic investigation into the many, many issues and stakeholders in real composition classrooms and programs throughout the discipline. The journey we take introduces us to one female scholar's struggle to adapt feminist theory for male colleagues and students at an engineering school and two other female scholars' endeavors to shape and revise global, Westernized feminist theory in a Singaporean classroom. We also learn of a male scholar's unending challenge of "dressing up" to be a feminist in his classroom, of an African American female teacher's task of teaching as a feminist theorist in a male prison, and of a female scholar's unending work to pilot feminist theory and courses at a Southern community college. These pieces represent only a fraction of the contributions, described below, that make up the necessarily partial whole that is *Fractured Feminisms*.

In section 1, "Theoretical, Generational, and Administrative Fractures within rhetoric and composition," we find contributors who have risen through the ranks to a level of significant leadership, and from this vantage point reflect upon their experiences and knowledge as feminist theorists, administrators, teachers, and scholars. In the main, they have a strong message for us from their investigations: Feminist theory, intended to be radically inclusive and liberatory, can indeed be neither. These authors seek to turn us toward new visions for truly inclusive feminist theories and administrative approaches. In the second section, "Fractured Feminisms in Writing across the Curriculum and Writing in the Disciplines," we learn from feminists who attempt to utilize feminist theories and practices strategically within different disciplinary settings. We discover the varied results they encountered as well as their new thoughts about the problems of feminist theorizing for interdisciplinary surroundings. In the third section, "Fractured Feminisms in the Classroom," feminist thinkers divulge both the problems and the possibilities of their attempts to apply feminist theory to pedagogical venues in rhetoric and composition. The final section, "Fractured Feminisms across Cultures," investigates where feminist theories can be both constructive and counterproductive to dialogues across cultural differences.

Eileen Schell launches the volume by analyzing feminist composition studies' engagement and lack of engagement with feminisms on the left in "Materialist Feminism and Composition Studies: The Practice of Critique and Activism in an Age of Globalization." Eileen, the director of graduate studies in the Syracuse University Writing Program, and a scholar long devoted to the concerns raised in this piece, addresses the emerging work on materialist and socialist feminisms and Red feminisms, probing how and why "left" feminisms have been incorporated (or not) into the feminist scholarship on and feminist teaching in composition studies. She does not advance a particular argument for or against what sorts of feminist scholarship should be done. Nor does she critique the existing left feminist work that addresses labor, pedagogy, and feminist histories of rhetoric and writing instruction. Rather, Eileen's goal is to meditate on exactly how and why these discourses have entered the discipline and the extent to which they are redirecting existing feminist conversations in writing and rhetoric. Eileen is concerned with interrogating the rhetorics of left feminisms as well as the circulation and value ascribed to these discourses in the discipline because, for so long, so few feminist theorists and practitioners in composition have openly identified themselves with socialist or materialist feminisms, though many do so privately or tacitly.

In chapter 2, "When Our Feminism Is Not Feminist Enough," Joanne Detore-Nakamura describes her long journey to pilot courses based in feminist theory at a southern community college. When Joanne arrived at her two-year institution a number of years ago, there were no courses in women's literature, and talk of women's history month raised little more than a puzzled reaction. When Joanne designed and offered a women's literature class, she was told, "Go ahead! No one will enroll anyhow." Joanne did have a few students—six— who made the course both exigent and rewarding. She realized that scholars like Hoff, Sommer, and Wolf, often labeled "traitors" for questioning the widely held tenets that most embrace as central to feminist philosophy, are making arguments that hold true to her students' lives and local understandings in her institution. Joanne then proffers a dual argument: (1) we do a disservice to feminist scholarship by branding feminist scholars negatively for rebelling against the "theoretical" status quo and thereby creating a schism within the movement, and (2) many feminist scholars who teach in private or large public universities are somewhat removed from what women in the mainstream experience. Joanne encounters mainly first-generation college students from conservative backgrounds. Many of these students seize onto only negative images of feminists—those depicted in the popular media and those taken from watching vocal, radical feminists themselves. Having accepted that the women at her site refuse to be labeled feminist and avoid "women's studies" classes for that reason, Joanne was ultimately successful by interrogating, then reinventing, such feminist classes for her individual students.

Chapter 3, Laura Gray-Rosendale's "Different Administrations/ Administering Difference: A New Model for Feminist Administrative Practices in rhetoric and composition studies" discusses the potential relationships between rhetoric and composition feminist administrative structures and other forms. Drawing from her own experience directing the Northern Arizona University Commission on the Status of Women, a state-mandated body working for the equality of all female employees, Laura emphasizes that feminisms need to be redefined in significant ways. Feminist praxis should be conceptualized as having broader applications and functions, ones relevant to those who identify as feminists as well as those who do not. In the commission Laura locates a potent example of an administrative body that depends upon the study of differences and the willingness to perceive feminisms as necessarily constructed through shared practices. After an exploration of the commission's feminist practices, Laura contends that we must survey the alternative administrative and theoretical possibilities these numerous feminist forms proffer to rhetoric and composition studies. Finally, she advances that feminism at its best should no longer simply operate as a set of specific theories or principles ascribed to by a particular group of women seeking very narrowly defined identities and roles.

Section 2 centers on "Fractured Feminisms in Writing across the Curriculum and Writing in the Disciplines." In chapter 4, "Writing across the Curriculum with Care," Bradley Peters considers how the teaching of disciplinary writing forced him to rethink his role in the classroom: To what extent could a man who uses feminist theory bring a new perspective to writing across the curriculum? Brad worried whether he might inevitably reinscribe a system of hierarchy, one that merely invokes new ways of excluding students. Troubled by Godzich's theories and their influences on Writing across the Curriculum, Brad came to believe that the movements in WAC could not answer the question of literacy education so much as they would "promote a new culture of illiteracy." As a result, Brad turned to a deep study of feminist theorists, discovering ways to deconstruct and transform the conservative, severely limited approaches to writing instruction, particularly those operating in his own WAC instruction. He concentrated on giving students the agency to assume any number of possible stances. Brad's hope was that they would be able to identify their situatedness and respond in kind to their teacher's encouragement, connecting their work to an ethic of caring. Yet, the unexpected reaction of Brad's students caused him to explore what it means if certain students insist on apprehending an ethics of caring and a feminist approach as essentially teleological: another means to an end—something that postmodern feminisms might surely resist, and something that implies the substitution of one pragmatism for another. Accordingly, Brad was constrained to enact standpoint theory himself. As a result, Brad began to uncover his own evolving process of theorizing and teaching, helping him to discern his own feminist and pedagogical identity anew.

Linda Bergmann's chapter 5, "Women's Ways Adapted, Adjusted, Lost: Feminist Theory Meets the Practices of Engineering Education," begins with a narrative of trial and error, analyzing her experiences in adapting feminist theory to the exigencies of teaching in primarily technological universities. Linda takes up some of the issues of essentialism, identity formation, and feminist pedagogy as she observes how these "engineering schools" are a particularly hostile environment for feminist pedagogy and feminist theory (indeed, in engineering institutions, application trumps theory almost every time). She describes the strategic adjustments that she has made in her thinking, teaching, and other practices, addressing the larger issue of whether and how these adjustments can compromise feminist theory and practice beyond recognition. At the center of Linda's paper is the problem of instituting, maintaining, and validating feminist pedagogy in engineering schools. The ethos of engineering institutions validates quantitative educational practices or strict grading systems based on earned points, "plug and chug" exercises in using formulas, and so forth. These schools attract male students who fall into the quadrant of the Myers-Briggs scale composed of introverts inclined toward evidence from the senses, thinking, judging. These students like, and often demand, formulaic instructions, hierarchical classroom structures, and right/wrong answers. Feminist approaches to learning—which rely heavily on collaboration, the dissolution of hierarchies, and the encouragement of personal learning—defy both the institutional traditions of engineering schools and the personal inclinations of the students who dominate them. The questions Linda is addressing, ultimately, concern the value of feminist theory in such a hostile environment. She proposes that, if we want the situation of women to improve in our country and in the world at large, we simply cannot graduate class after class of students who have had no contact with feminist theory and practice.

Rose Kamel's chapter 6, "The Overly Managed Student: Gender and Pedagogy in the Science School," investigates the invention of new strategies and the unexpected results that arrived from implementing feminist theory into courses whose primary design was not intended to be feminist. After an administrative decision to cancel feminist courses so that teachers and students would focus on electives in the sciences and social sciences almost exclusively, Rose resolved to use feminist pedagogy to revive and revise the two electives, the Novel and Literature and Medicine. Her approach was dialectical, emphasizing both the lack of agency in women's lives and the way women question and resist their powerlessness. This approach was challenging to implement to students whose majors—science, pharmacy, physical therapy—require them to sit in large lecture halls, absorb information without much discussion, and take electronically coded quantifiable exams. Rose was now persuading them to contribute to small group projects, ones that required peer research into the way that writers objectify women as Other as well as the strategies of resistance and empowerment this reification engenders. Rose found herself, then, employing the teachings about feminine strategies of resistance and empowerment to her students as her own strategy of resistance and empowerment. The irony of this situation revealed to Rose and her students some new and unexpected understandings of themselves as "gendered beings."

Section 3 is "Fractured Feminisms in the Classroom." In chapter 7, "The Challenges of Establishing a Feminist Ethos in the Composition Classroom: Stories from Large Research Universities," Shelly Whitfield, Veronica Pantoja, and Duane Roen describe some of the trials facing a teacher striving to institute a feminist ethos in a composition classroom. Through the lens of Bakhtinian theory, in which conflicting voices compete with one another, Shelly, Veronica, and Duane argue that, in practice, part of the struggle can be internal to the individual teacher in that an internalized *cuzoj* ("the word or world view of another"—*Dialogic Imagination* 427) dialogues with an internalized *svoj* ("one's own word, one's own world view"). As an example of this kind of struggle, they portray the narrative of a teacher whose feminist academic work contrasts with the belief system of her religious institution. However, they deem that such struggles are as varied as the individuals and sites in which they are enacted, and frequently, the struggle between *svoj* and *cuzoj* is more public. Here, the authors reflect on the narratives of some young, usually female teachers who enter the classroom to find voices that are skeptical of or openly hostile to a feminist ethos and theory. Negotiating these hostilities is not simple or easy—even for experienced teachers. Their composite case study takes up current questions on implementing feminist theories into practice sites that host a wide variety of students.

In chapter 8 Gil Harootunian deliberates on theory gone wrong in "Riding Our Hobbyhorse: Ethics, Ethnography, and an Argument for the Teacher-Researcher." Gil explores the upside-down results that occurred when the ethnography, an assignment designed to enable students to explore the questions of gender, race, and class in their culture, was introduced into her writing studios at Syracuse University, an institution that largely attracts middle- to upper-class white students who have a heavy investment in the status quo of their culture. Soon after implementing the ethnographic model designed to disrupt dominant notions of gender, race, and class in our society into her own studio, Gil encountered persistent resistance and heard strange accounts of the teaching of the ethnography in writing classrooms. This prompted Gil to conduct archival research, during which she examined nearly 200 student portfolios in the archives of the Syracuse University Writing Program to discover that many students had turned the ethnography from an exercise in critiquing society, with all its biases and silences, into an exercise celebrating those biases and silences. From this discovery, Gil investigated the ways in which the chain of ethical reciprocity between feminist theory and practice was broken when the SU writing program attempted to "own" the ethnography by instituting it as a standard part of the curriculum. In her chapter she proffers that only when we come to function simultaneously and consistently as feminist teacher-researchers can we avoid the disastrous results of institutional interference in our programs and classrooms.

In chapter 9, "Challenges to Cyberfeminism: Voices, Contradictions, and Identity Constructions," Sibylle Gruber deploys postmodern feminist theories and postcolonial theories to discuss how teachers—especially women—working in our new technologically advanced environments can respond to the potential problems created by the new demands of computer or television-based academic instruction. Sibylle maintains that in recent years, new information technologies have become an integral part in the lives of composition specialists, and many consider these technological advances a necessity in managing their constantly increasing workload. At the same time, however, these technologies also contribute to an environment in which more is expected in less time. Likewise, these technologies partly stipulate how research and education takes place. Through her experiences Sibylle has ascertained that this is especially evident in classroom situations that are mediated by new technologies, such as web-based courses, web-enhanced courses, and distance education courses presented through instructional television. The instructional limitations based on the medium, the software, or the location can lead to pedagogical and methodological compromises as well as to a loss of autonomy, agency, and control over parts of the curriculum. Sibylle ultimately addresses the threat of a deskilled academic labor force which is no longer responsible for all aspects of a course but which only provides a small although important part within an already existing technological framework, leaving the rest to the ingenuity of technicians and their manipulation of machines.

The volume concludes with section 4, "Fractured Feminisms across Cultures." Stuart H. D. Ching commences with chapter 10, "Feminisms and Memory: Patriarchal Genealogy Translating and Translated in the Stories of Chinese/Chinese American Women." Addressing the intersection between feminism and cultural memory, Stuart poses the following question: How can feminist discourses enable students both to adopt new world views and to affirm and appropriate the power of culturally rooted narratives, specifically in cases when these cultural narratives conflict with feminist values? This question seems especially relevant to students whose cultures are situated outside of mainstream consciousness and for whom, because of this historical and political position, cultural extinction is a real threat. Stuart begins answering this query by looking into the stories and actions of the women in his family. Positioned within twentieth-century Hawaii, and within the discourses of American nationalism, the Hawaii plantation labor system, and its colonial legacy, the stories of the women in Stuart's family express competing needs. In one sense, these stories reproduce Chinese patriarchal lineage, examining the demise of culture, affirming cultural memory, and locating the community in an imagined sense of place. Conversely, they also transform place and memory, insisting on feminist translations and revisions of Chinese tradition. The version of feminism that Stuart locates in these stories remains provisionally rooted within *and* partly resistant to Chinese patriarchal tradition. Supporting tradition and transgressing it, this feminism depends on Chinese patriarchal tradition in order to maintain cultural integrity and yet appropriates this tradition in order to define more empowering social roles for Chinese women. Stuart's essay yields multiple discoveries and assertions, particularly that latent feminist narratives exist in all traditionally patriarchal cultures, as they have in Chinese culture. Thus, although the feminist theories informing composition studies may fracture—may even become limited on various fronts—upon entering into conversation with these patriarchal narratives, feminist texts may also illuminate, affirm, clarify, and extend those latent and partial feminist narratives emerging from students' experiences.

Chapter 11, "Composing Self: An Intercultural Curriculum for First-Year College Composition," brings us to the work of M. Diane Benton. As an African American feminist who taught for years in male prisons, Diane contends that we must overturn current teaching paradigms in our composition classrooms. She examines the paradoxes of monocultural and multicultural curricula and the possibilities of a genuinely intercultural curriculum. Diane traces several pedagogical experiences in which she attempts this and describes what she and her students learned as a result. Drawing from recent and historically based research in African American studies, rhetorical theory, and feminism, Diane maintains that rhetorical experiences could and should form a basis for a critical intercultural curriculum in which students might learn crucial forms of linguistic and rhetorical diversity. This intersection has the potential to reveal the juncture of culture and self and thus enable students to compose crucial identities from which to communicate and enter discourse communities.

Finally, in chapter 12, "Looking to East and West: Feminist Practice in an Asian Classroom," Chng Huan Hoon and Chitra Sankaran share with us their story of teaching Feminist Theory and Feminist Discourse, one of a small handful of liberal courses offered in the Faculty of Arts and Social Sciences at the National University of Singapore. They illustrate how the very idea of teaching feminism or gender issues in a Singaporean context presents many immediate problems, challenges, ambivalences, and rewards, all at the same time. Chng and Chitra then furnish an interpretative account of feminism and feminist issues as they are understood and/or perceived in Singaporean society. In a society where a "communitarian democratic" ideology is promoted over "an ethic of individualism," feminist issues are perceived as particularly problematic, and overt sensitivities to gender politics are actively discouraged. The key difficulties and challenges encountered involve decisions over which theory or theories to adopt for their classroom; the problems of appropriating certain theories; how to deal with Singaporean students' lack of general awareness and background knowledge; the kinds of texts and accompanying course materials available for classroom use; the problems of using either "Western" or "Eastern" theories and texts; and the question of local relevance for particular issues and theories. Chng and Chitra conclude with some observations on the lessons learned from having taught such a course in this particular context and on the ways in which the experiences in a Singaporean classroom could inform and reshape existing global feminist theories.

In the end, we believe that this exploration of feminist theory's kaleidescopic manifestation in the many real and diverse sites of practice within our discipline will be of considerable interest to teachers and scholars in rhetoric and composition studies. We imagine it may both assist the considerable feminist research in which scholars are already engaged and help feminists and nonfeminists to interrogate it more thoroughly. With feminism now firmly entrenched in the academy, as Jane Roland Martin contends in *Coming of Age in Academe* and Ann Russo recommends in *Taking Back Our Lives*, perhaps our agendas need to simultaneously become more locally and contextually situated and yet more globally oriented. The over twenty-year history of feminism's educational institutionalization discloses that political practice has become more complicated and open to ready co-optation, theoretical feminist work that is rarely called into question may too often dominate our vistas, and feminist theories as well as practices of various stripes may take on a more fixed quality, no longer as easily open to change, alteration, and reinterpretation. As a result, increasingly we need to further articulate the relationships between feminist thinking and rhetoric and composition studies. *Fractured Feminisms* demonstrates for its audience the necessity and promise of putting pressure upon and then widening the boundaries of our discourse in rhetoric and composition, a discipline whose unique position as a latecomer to the academy, coupled with its huge domain of practice, advances it the rare possibility to self-reflexively theorize itself. More and more in rhetoric and composition studies, theorizing ourselves will entail reexamining the very theories we espouse, closely investigating the identities they supply for us, the rhetorical investments they require, and the ways in which these advance as well as shut down certain kinds of inquiry. This is not an easy task, nor one we can hope to fully accomplish within this text. However, perhaps this book begins to initiate such a discussion about feminist theory for rhetoric and composition studies.

We write from our vantage point now, feeling all of the vitality and trepidation that comes from standing on shifting ground, earth that is moving and re-forming beneath us. We write into, out of, between, and through fractures in our feminist landscape, fractures that expose new formations amidst thick cracks and breaks within old structures. As we do so, we can only envision this text as a partial beginning. And, we look forward to how such a discussion might develop further—in dynamic ways we cannot begin to anticipate—during the years to come.

NOTES

1. For a very useful discussion of such issues see Kate Weigand, *Red Feminism: American Communism and the Making of Women's Liberation.*

2. For a thorough overview of radical feminism and a valuable critique of attempts to separate it from other contemporary feminist thinking, see Denise Thompson, *Radical Feminism Today.*

3. See, for example, bell hooks' work, *Feminism Is for Everybody: Passionate Politics; Talking Back: Thinking Feminist, Thinking Black;* and *Feminist Theory from Margin to Center.* See also Kum-Kum Bhavnani, *Feminism and "Race."* See also Frances E. White, *The Dark Continent of Our Bodies: Black Feminism and the Politics of Respectability.*

4. Kenneth Burke's interest was always on the rhetorical choices one made, their motivations, and their potential effects. In several texts he asked important questions about the degree to which politically oriented rhetorics actually supported their stated goals. See his discussions in the following texts: Kenneth Burke, *A Grammar of Motives, Language a Symbolic Action: Essays on Life, Literature, and Method, A Rhetoric of Motives.*

5. See, for instance, Marianne DeKoven, *Feminist Locations: Global and Local, Theory and Practice;* Jane Duran, *Worlds of Knowing: Global Feminist Epistemologies;* Catherine Eschle, *Global Democracy, Social Movements, and Feminism;* and France Winddance Twine and Kathleen Blee, *Feminism and Antiracism: International Struggles for Justice.*

WORKS CITED

Ahmed, Sara. *Differences That Matter: Feminist Theory and Postmodernism.* Cambridge: Cambridge University Press, 1998.

Alcoff, Linda. "Cultural Feminism Versus Post-Structuralism: The Identity Crisis in Feminist Theory." *Signs: Journal of Women in Culture and Society* 13.3 (1988): 405–36.

Allen, Carolyn, and Judith Howard eds. *Provoking Feminisms.* Chicago: University of Chicago Press, 2000.

Belenky, Mary Field et al. *Women's Ways of Knowing: the Development of the Self, Voice, and Mind.* New York: Basic Books, 1986.

Bhavnani, Kum-Kum. *Feminism and "Race."* Oxford: Oxford University Press, 2001.

Blair, Kristine, and Pamela Takayoshi. *Feminist Cyberscapes: Mapping Gendered Academic Spaces.* Stamford: Ablex, 1999.

Bronfen, Elisabeth, and Misha Kavka, eds. *Feminist Consequences: Theory for the New Century.* New York: Columbia University Press, 2001.

Bryson, Valerie. *Feminist Debates: Issues of Theory and Political Practice.* New York: New York University Press, 1999.

Burke, Kenneth. *A Grammar of Motives.* Berkeley: University of California Press, 1969.

———. *Language a Symbolic Action: Essays on Life, Literature, and Method.* Berkeley: University of California Press, 1966.

———. *A Rhetoric of Motives.* Berkeley: University of California Press, 1969.

Butler, Judith, and Joan Scott, eds. *Feminists Theorize the Political.* New York: Routledge, 1992.

———. *Gender Trouble and the Subversion of Identity.* New York: Routledge, 1990.

———. *The Psychic Life of Power: Theories in Subjection.* Stanford: Stanford University Press, 1997.

Caywood, Cynthia L., and Gillian R. Overing. *Teaching Writing: Pedagogy, Gender, and Equity.* Albany: State University of New York Press, 1987.

Chancer, Lynn S. *Reconcilable Differences: Confronting Beauty, Pornography, and the Future of Feminism.* Berkeley: University of California Press, 1998.

Chodorow, Nancy. *The Reproduction of Mothering: Psychoanalysis and the Sociology of Gender.* Berkeley: University of California Press, 1978.

Chow, Esther Ngan-Ling, Doris Wilinson, and Maxine Baca Zinn. *Race, Class, and Gender Common Bonds, Different Voices*. Thousand Oaks: Sage, 1996.

Curthoys, Jean. *Feminist Amnesia: The Wake of Women's Liberation*. London: Routledge, 1997.

Dekoven, Marianne, ed. *Feminist Locations: Global and Local, Theory and Practice*. New Brunswick: Rutgers University Press, 2001.

DeLauretis, Teresa. *Alice Doesn't: Feminism, Semiotics, Cinema*. Bloomington: Indiana University Press, 1984.

———. *The Practice of Love: Lesbian Sexuality and Perverse Desire*. Bloomington: Indiana University Press, 1994.

Dixon, Kathleen. *Making Relationships: Gender in the Forming of Academic Community*. New York: Peter Lang, 1997.

Donovan, Josephine. *Feminist Theory: The Intellectual Traditions of American Feminism*. New York: Continuum, 1992.

Duran, Jane. *Worlds of Knowing: Global Feminist Epistemologies*. New York: Routledge, 2001.

Eschle, Catherine. *Global Democracy, Social Movements, and Feminism*. Boulder: Westview, 2001.

Evans, Mary. *Introducing Contemporary Feminist Thought*. Cambridge: Polity, 1997.

Felski, Rita. *Doing Time: Feminist Theory and Postmodern Culture*. New York: New York University Press, 2000.

Fisher, Berenice M. *No Angel in the Classroom: Teaching through Feminist Discourse*. Lanham: Rowman and Littlefield, 2001.

Flynn, Elizabeth. "Composing as a Woman." *College Composition and Communication* 39.4 (December 1988): 423–35.

Fuss, Diana. *Essentially Speaking: Feminism, Nature, and Difference*. New York: Routledge, 1989.

Gallop, Jane. *Around 1981: Academic Feminist Literary Theory*. New York: Routledge, 1992.

Gilligan, Carol. *In a Different Voice: Psychological Theory and Women's Development*. Cambridge: Harvard University Press, 1982.

Glenn, Cheryl. *Rhetoric Retold: Regendering the Tradition from Antiquity through the Renaissance*. Carbondale: Southern Illinois University Press, 1997.

Hermann, Anne C., and Abigail J. Stewart, eds. *Theorizing Feminism: Parallel Trends in the Humanities and Social Sciences*. Boulder: Westview, 1994.

Hicks, Christina, and Kelly Oliver, eds. *Language and Liberation: Feminism, Philosophy, and Language*. Albany: State University of New York Press, 1999.

Hirsch, Marianne, and Evelyn Fox Keller, eds. *Conflicts in Feminism*. New York: Routledge, 1990.

hooks, bell. *Feminism Is for Everybody: Passionate Politics*. Cambridge: South End, 2000.

———. *Feminist Theory from Margin to Center*. Cambridge: South End, 2000.

———. *Talking Back: Thinking Feminist, Thinking Black*. Boston: South End, 1989.

Jardine, Alice, and Paul Smith, eds. *Men in Feminism*. New York: Methuen, 1987.

Jarratt, Susan, and Lynn Worsham, eds. *Feminism and Composition Studies: In Other Words*. New York: Modern Language Association, 1998.

Johnson, Barbara. *The Feminist Difference: Literature, Psychoanalysis, Race, and Gender*. Cambridge: Harvard University Press, 1998.

Kirsch, Gesa. *Ethical Dilemmas in Feminist Research: The Politics of Location, Interpretation, and Publication*. Albany: State University of New York Press, 1999.

———. *Women Writing the Academy: Audience, Authority, and Transformation*. Carbondale: Southern Illinois University Press, 1993.

Malinowitz, Harriet. *Textual Orientations: Lesbian and Gay Students and the Making of Discourse Communities*. Portsmouth: Heinemann, 1995.

Mann, Patricia S. *Micro-Politics: Agency in a Postfeminist Era*. Minneapolis: University of Minnesota Press, 1994.

Martin, Jane Roland. *Coming of Age in Academe: Rekindling Women's Hopes and Reforming the Academy*. New York: Routledge, 2000.

Mascia-Lees, Frances E., and Patricia Sharpe, eds. *Taking a Stand in a Postfeminist World: Toward an Engaged Cultural Criticism*. Albany: State University of New York Press, 2000.

McCannell, Juliet Flower. *The Hysteric's Guide to the Future Female Subject*. Minneapolis: University of Minnesota Press, 2000.

McNay, Lois. *Gender and Agency: Reconfiguring the Subject in Feminist and Social Theory*. Cambridge: Blackwell, 2000.

Miller, Susan. *Textual Carnivals: The Politics of Composition*. Carbondale: Southern IllinoisUniversity Press, 1991.

Modleski, Tania. *Feminism without Women: Culture and Criticism in a Postfeminist Age*. New York: Routledge, 1991.

Noddings, Nel. *Caring: A Feminine Approach to Ethics and Moral Education*. Berkeley:University of California Press, 1984.

Panetta, Clayann Gilliam. *Contrastive Rhetoric Revisited and Redefined*. Mahwah: Lawrence Erlbaum, 2001.

Peck, Elizabeth G., and Joanna Mink. *Common Ground: Feminist Collaboration in the Academy*. Albany: State University of New York Press, 1998.

Phelps, Louise Wetherbee, and Janet Emig, eds. *Feminine Principles and Women's Experience in American Composition and Rhetoric*. Pittsburgh: University of Pittsburgh Press, 1995.

Ratcliffe, Krista. *Anglo-American Feminist Challenges to the Rhetorical Traditions: Virginia Woolf, Mary Daly, Adrienne Rich.* Carbondale: Southern Illinois University Press, 1996.

Riley, Denise. *War in the Nursery: Theories of the Child and the Mother.* London: Virago, 1983.

Robbins, Ruth. *Literary Feminisms.* New York: St. Martin's, 2000.

Royster, Jacqueline Jones. *Traces of a Stream: Literacy and Social Change among African American Women.* Pittsburgh: University of Pittsburgh Press, 2000.

Ruddick, Sara. *Maternal Thinking: Towards a Politics of Peace.* Boston: Beacon, 1989.

Russo, Ann. *Taking Back Our Lives: A Call to Action for the Feminist Movement.* New York: Routledge, 2001.

Salvaggio, Ruth. *The Sounds of Feminist Theory.* Albany: State University of New York Press, 1999.

Schell, Eileen. *Gypsy Academics and Mother-Teachers: Gender, Contingent Labor, and Writing Instruction.* Portsmouth: Boynton Cook, 1997.

Schell, Eileen, and Patti Stock. *Moving a Mountain: Transforming the Role of Contingent Faculty in Higher Education and Composition Studies.* Ann Arbor: University of Michigan Press, 2000.

Schmidt, Jan Zlotnik. *Women/Writing/Teaching.* Albany: State University of New York Press, 1998.

Social Justice Group at the Center for Advanced Feminist Studies, eds. *Is Academic Feminism Dead? Theory in Practice.* New York: New York University Press, 2000.

St. Pierre, Elizabeth A., and Wanda S. Pillow, eds. *Working the Ruins: Feminist Poststructural Theory and Methods in Education.* New York: Routledge, 2000.

Sterba, James. *Controversies in Feminism.* Lanham: Rowman and Littlefield, 2001.

Tanesini, Alessandra. *Introduction to Feminist Epistemologies.* Malden: Blackwell, 1999.

Thompson, Denise. *Radical Feminism Today.* London: Sage, 2001.

Thornham, Sue. *Feminist Theory and Cultural Studies: Stories of Unsettled Relations.* London: Arnold, 2000.

Twine, France Winddance, and Kathleen M. Blee. *Feminism and Antiracism: International Struggles for Justice.* New York: New York University Press, 2001.

Warhol, Robyn R., and Diane Price Herndl, eds. *Feminisms: An Anthology of Literary History and Criticism.* New Brunswick: Rutgers University Press, 1997.

Weedon, Chris. *Feminism, Theory, and the Politics of Difference.* Oxford: Blackwell, 1999.

Weeks, Kathi. *Constituting Feminist Subjects.* Ithaca: Cornell University Press, 1998.

Weigard, Kate. *Red Feminism: American Communism and the Making of Women's Liberation.* Baltimore: John's Hopkins University Press, 2001.

Weiss, Penny A. *Conversations with Feminism: Political Theory and Practice*. Lanham: Rowman and Littlefield, 1998.

Welch, Nancy. *Getting Restless: Rethinking Revision in Writing Instruction*. Portsmouth: Boynton/Cook, 1997.

White, Franes E. *The Dark Continent of Our Bodies: Black Feminism and the Politics of Respectability*. Temple: Temple University Press, 2001.

Ziarek, Eva Plonowska. *An Ethics of Dissensus: Postmodernity, Feminism, and the Politics of Radical Democracy*. Stanford: Stanford University Press, 2001.

Part One

THEORETICAL, GENERATIONAL, AND ADMINISTRATIVE FRACTURES WITHIN RHETORIC AND COMPOSITION

Chapter One

Materialist Feminism and Composition Studies

The Practice of Critique and Activism in an Age of Globalization

EILEEN SCHELL

As a doctoral student in rhetoric and composition in the early nineties, my interest in Marxism and materialist feminism was peaked in a course on critical theory. As I read the assigned critical theory texts, I was most intrigued by the theories that attempted to connect the intellectual work of theory to the struggle for material resources. Throughout the course, I attempted to understand what Ernesto Laclau and Chantal Mouffe have deemed the shift from Marxism to post-Marxism, which they characterize as a gradual flow in other directions, "in the way that river waters, having originated at a common source, spread in various directions and mingle with currents flowing from other sources" (5). A year later, as the fall merged into winter, I proposed an independent study on the discourses of radical feminists, Marxist feminists, and socialist feminists that emerged out of the New Left: Shulamith Firestone, Michele Barrett, Christine Delphy, Zillah Eisenstein, and others. The year before my doctoral exams, over winter break, huddled in front of the heat vent in my family's farmhouse in eastern Washington, I struggled through Robert Tucker's *Marx-Engels Reader* and later through volume 1 of *Capital*.

As I began a feminist dissertation on gender, writing instruction, and contingent labor in English departments, I read the work of Stanley Aronowitz, Erik Olin Wright, Nicos Poulantzas, and others who had debated theories of class relations and labor. I realized later that my foray into Marxist theory and materialist feminism was an attempt to connect my class background and upbringing with the discourses on class and labor in the American academy. While other graduate students appeared more than happy to declare the fall of Marxist thought under late capitalism, I was busy trying to obtain an education in Marxist thought.

Being out of step with the heady postmodern and poststructuralist times of the late 1980s and early 1990s seemed second nature to me. Unlike many of my graduate school colleagues who grew up in urban or suburban areas where their parents worked as white-collar professionals, I grew up on an apple and pear orchard in rural eastern Washington State. Growing up as I did on a small farm, I often felt more ties to Marx's descriptions of nineteenth-century modes of production than to the rhythms of the suburb, the commuter schedule, and the urban business day of 9 to 5 P.M. The farm, the seat of production, was also the site of our home, and the migrant workers, those who worked the farm with my family, lived next door in the labor camp, a series of cabins clustered around a washroom. Until the mideighties, the migrant farmworkers my family employed were white, working-class men and occasionally women who followed the crops across the United States: Washington cherries, pears, and apples in the summer and fall, Florida oranges in the winter, and California fruits and vegetables in the spring. In the late seventies and early eighties, the complexion and nationality of the orchard crew shifted. The generation of white, working-class men and women who made their living in farm work retired and/or passed away, replaced by Mexican immigrants drawn to farm labor out of economic necessity and due to the increasing use of global immigrant labor.

On the farm, issues of class, gender, race, and the struggle for material resources were always visible. In the "back room," my mother paid the two dozen workers who helped us grow and harvest our yearly crops; she negotiated bail or work release for workers in trouble with the law, and she, along with my father, supervised the labor camp. I worked with some of the migrant farmworkers in the summers, our work in the orchards often becoming an opportunity to interact across the evident divide of class, race, language, and gender. Ultimately, though, at night I went home to the white farmhouse, and the workers went to the labor camp. Although separated by only a few yards, our worlds were distinct and separate. In the fall, I returned to college and to the possibility of upward class mobility through education; they boarded trains, buses, and cars and made their way to the next harvest.

The life of the migrant workers who came year after year to our farm and neighboring ones was unmistakably harsh and unjust: inadequate or nonexistent health care, low wages, scant or substandard housing. Although it was not evident to me in graduate school or in my first years as an assistant professor, my scholarship on labor issues in writing instruction was directly influenced by my upbringing on the farm, creating in me an abiding interest in work as a site of human struggle and class conflict. As an adjunct and a graduate student, I had ample opportunity to observe how graduate students' and adjuncts' teaching and interactions with students and their personal lives were affected by low pay, short-term contracts, inadequate office space, and lack of insurance. As I sought to make connections between my interest in class, gender, and labor in rhetoric and composition, I turned to the Marxist-inflected work of scholars theorizing the connections among literacy, class, culture, and labor such as James Berlin, Sharon Crowley, Richard Ohmann, John Trimbur, and Ira Shor. However, as I read the work of cultural critics and critical pedagogues in composition studies, I wondered why there were no feminist compositionists who engaged Marxist-feminist, materialist feminist, and socialist feminist ideas in their scholarship and pedagogy. I found traces of Marxist traditions in the work of fellow feminists, but few or none who directly identified with Marxist, socialist, or materialist feminisms. In her review of theories that have influenced feminism and composition studies, Elizabeth Flynn references liberal, radical, cultural, and postmodern feminisms, but she does not mention Marxist, materialist, or socialist feminisms (202). Moreover, in Susan Jarratt and Lynn Worsham's edited volume *Feminism and Composition: In Other Words*, a number of the essays draw on Marxist traditions, but the majority do not identify Marxist, materialist, or socialist feminist theories as significant traditions from which to theorize or practice feminism. In her response essay to this volume, Deb Kelsh critiques feminists in composition studies for failing to adequately engage materialist feminist thought, arguing that feminists in composition studies should work to develop a red feminism, which draws on "classical marxism," a feminism that attempts to "free all objects of patriarchy from exploitation" (107). In what is to follow, I engage with Kelsh's argument that materialist feminisms need to become a more prominent feminist stance in rhetoric and composition studies. I begin by addressing Kelsh's claim that materialist feminism has been suppressed in feminist composition studies. Although I believe Kelsh makes an important point about the problematic stance of feminist composition studies toward Marxist thought, her critique does not address why rhetoric and composition teachers and theorists do not engage these ideas in the ways she suggests we should. I argue that a compelling critique of the absence of historical materialism in composition is one that acknowledges the class contradictory position of the field and the ways in which Marxist discourses are present in limited but nevertheless suppressed ways. Finally, I sketch potential areas of inquiry that feminist scholars in our field can engage in materialist critiques and practices.

CRITIQUING THE ABSENCE OF HISTORICAL MATERIALISM:
COMPOSITION AND MATERIALIST FEMINISMS

I analyze Kelsh's critique in some detail since it is the first feminist essay in our field to discuss how feminist compositionists should take up materialist feminist thought. First, though, a brief word on the historical evolution of materialist feminist thought seems necessary for those unfamiliar with it. Connections between Marxism and feminism were first made by nineteenth-century socialists inspired by Marx and Engels such as Clara Zetkin, Isaac Bebel, and Alexandra Kollontai and also labor organizers such as Elizabeth Gurley Flynn, Mother Jones, and Rose Pastor Stokes (Hennessey and Ingraham 3). This first surge of activity was punctuated later by a second surge in the 1970s in which a critical dialogue between Marxism and feminism took place among the emerging discourses of the New Left. Many radical and socialist feminists reworked significant categories in Marxist thought to account for gender in their analyses of "production, reproduction, class, consciousness, and labor" (Hennessey and Ingraham 6; see also Hartmann). The term *materialist feminism*, contends Hennessey and Ingraham, came from "the shift to cultural politics in western marxism post-1968" with a "growing attention to ideology" (7). British feminists Annette Kuhn, Anne Marie Wolpe, Michele Barrett, Mary MacIntosh and French theorist Christine Delphy used the term *materialist feminism* to reshape marxism to "account for the sexual division of labor and the gendered formation of subjectivities" (7). Hennessey and Ingraham further explain that these theorists preferred materialist feminism over Marxist feminism because they felt that "marxism cannot adequately address women's exploitation and oppression unless the Marxist problematic itself is transformed so as to be able to account for the sexual division of labor" (xii). Thus, the different labels—*Marxist feminism, socialist feminism,* and *materialist feminism*—provide different "signatures" that privilege "historical materialism," which Hennessey and Ingraham refer to as "emancipatory critical knowledge" (4). One of the goals of materialist feminism is to work toward the elimination of capitalism and to alleviate women's oppression under capitalism. While socialist and materialist feminists have often supported reforms for women within capitalistic structures, the overall goal is transformation.

Despite an interest in materialist ideas in activist communities and among leftist academics, there has been a systematic retreat from class analysis and Marxist ideas in the American academy. The turn away from historical materialism has been well documented in a number of collections and single-authored books by Marxists and materialist feminists who work in English studies, sociology, political science, and philosophy. More recently, in rhetoric and composition, a series of JAC interviews with Ernesto Laclau and Chantal Mouffe attempt to take stock of the directions for Marxist and post-Marxist thought (see Worsham and Olson). While Marxist theory has been part of the work of cultural critics in composition who borrow from the Birmingham School, and Marxist theories have been present in work on language theory, ethnographic writing pedagogy, and critical pedagogy, the tendency has been to "tame" or "domesticate" the emancipatory project in those discourses. As Patricia Bizzell argues in "Marxist Ideas in Composition Studies," although we "draw on European and third World Marxist theories of literature, literacy, and education, citing Mikhail Bakhtin, Paulo Freire, and Lev Vygotsky," we have tended to "denature the Marxism of theorists whose work we use frequently, to assimilate the Marxist thinker into a more apolitical discourse that covers the same ground" (53).

Bizzell's critique is one that Kelsh might find compelling as she argues that the omission of historical materialism in rhetoric and composition seems curious since feminist compositionists "always implicitly—and sometimes explicitly—interrogate the division of labor whereby people are constructed to undertake the subsistence care of humanity" (100). Given this acknowledgement, she argues that it seems odd, that "largely absent from the essays I am responding to (essays by Laura Brady, Shirley Wilson Logan, Nedra Reynolds, and Eileen Schell) is an explicit critique of the late-capitalist division of labor that conditions knowledge production" (100). Citing Marx's "Contributions to the Critique of Political Economy," she argues that the omission of historical materialism in feminist composition studies is both contradictory and dangerous and must be critiqued (101).

Hypothesizing the reasons for the omission of historical materialism in composition studies, Kelsh finds several culprits. First, she argues that composition studies and feminists in composition studies have tended to embrace postmodern and poststructural theories that reject historical materialism. Like feminists in literary studies, feminists in composition tend to cite and rely on a tradition of cultural materialism, not historical materialism (101). In the essays she responds to in the volume authored by Laura Brady, Shirley Wilson Logan, and myself, she finds a concern with language issues, with "resignification" and "representation" and not a critique of capitalism. She contends that "[c]ultural materialist paradigms produce models for people for freedom for some people only. Feminisms that advocate local resistance dependent on the materialism of language are unable to provide an effective way to free 'women all over the globe' from exploitation" (105). In other words, "capitalism must be confronted as a ruthless system, not as a system that simply needs to be more open" (105). Kelsh cites statistics on women and poverty across the globe, asking: "How will the many women on the planet whose daily focus is on staving off hunger, on gaining access to food, be helped by feminisms that argue for liberation in language rather than for liberation from exploitative labor arrangements?" (105).

It is interesting that Kelsh points out that cultural materialist theories come from the academic class (literary and cultural theorists) who stands to gain the most from the exploitation of composition faculty (103). These traditions, argues Kelsh, lead feminists in composition to take on compromise positions. Since cultural materialism is rewarded in the academy, feminists in composition and in other fields recognize that to place emphasis on Marxist ideas is to risk "public demonization" for relying on ideas that many consider "dated," "crude," or politically and theoretically ineffectual (103). Feminists avoid historical materialism and Marxist paradigms, Kelsh claims, because they "do not want to lose their jobs, opportunities for promotion, or a chance for inclusion in projects" (103; for a counterperspective on this see Trimbur).

Ultimately, Kelsh argues that the study and practice of theories of classical Marxism should be a direction that feminists in composition studies should pursue in order to engage global feminisms. Although she is careful to acknowledge that the writers in this first section in *Feminism and Composition Studies: In Other Words* make points that are "insightful, carefully thought through, and based on the most-up-to-date scholarship," she ultimately argues that they are too caught up in the capitalism of the American academy, thus performing feminist work that is ultimately limited and local (104). While Kelsh offers a compelling analysis, she critiques the authors for work we did not set out to do, or for work we were asked to do in a volume whose purview was to address Anglo-American feminisms in relationship to the field of composition studies. Yet, at the same time, her point is well-taken: feminists in composition studies need to engage with global feminisms especially in light of the effects of globalization on the world's populations.[1] Her critique, however, does not factor in the specific set of class relationships within rhetoric and composition that makes the embrace of Marxist and materialist feminist theory a troubled proposition.

COMPOSITION, CLASS CONTRADICTION, AND THE RELATIVE ABSENCE OF MATERIALIST FEMINISMS

It is the material base of composition that dictates, to a certain degree, the ways in which complex political discourses such as Marxism can be thought and practiced. As Bizzell argues, there is a tendency in composition theory and pedagogy to "denature" and assimilate Marxist theories into more "apolitical discourses" or to "read out" Marxist influences (52). In our field, the class contradictory position of the first-year composition course ensures that complex political theories such as Marxism or feminisms are assimilated into more manageable pedagogical discourses. As Lynn Worsham points out in her insightful essay "Writing against Writing: The Predicament of *Ecriture Feminine* in Composition Studies," theorists in composition studies have tended to take up radical theories of writing like ecriture feminine "as a source for new textual and pedagogical models and strategies," as applications, not as theories that help us rethink the relations of the field (95). Making radical theory into classroom assignments domesticates and tames that theory, allowing our field's "will to pedagogy" to flourish unchallenged. The result, argues Worsham, is that "[c]omposition theorists will effectively manipulate ecriture feminine to shore up the foundations of their field as a modernist discipline committed to the old dreams of the Enlightenment" (99). In lieu of this commodification, Worsham points to a different mode of engaging ecriture feminine in our field, that of "unlearning," a process "of defamiliarization vis-à-vis unquestioned forms of knowledge" (102).

Like ecriture feminine, Marxist critique has been "tamed" and domesticated (see Bizzell) by a set of labor dynamics that makes radical discourses into pedagogical stances. Since the working lives of most compositionists center around teaching first-year composition or administering the first-year composition program, the theoretical and practical focus of the field reflects those concerns. Only a few compositionists hold positions in which reduced teaching loads make theorizing, research, and doctoral education a prominent focus. Thus, our field's tendency toward domesticating radical thought is intimately tied to the type of labor we perform in the American academy. As many have pointed out, composition studies is built on the material base of undergraduate writing courses. The first-year writing course carries the institutionalized intent of producing students who can read, write, and process information in ways that allow them to join the professional managerial class or, at least, the middle class. As David Bartholomae writes in "Inventing the University," students must learn to write like us, sound like us (presumably white, middle-class academics and professionals) (135). However, as critical pedagogues and feminist compositionists argue, composition as a field offers potential opportunities for resistance and transformation of oppressive cultural, material, and linguistic structures, although there are conflicting perspectives about whether or not such transformation is possible. It is not my intention here to debate composition courses as conservative or liberatory enterprises; such binary views do not treat the "exercise" of composition instruction in all its complexity or historicity: my point is to indicate that our field is "class contradictory" as composition courses reproduce dominant literacies while also serving a critical site of intervention in those theories and practices of language and literacy. Some teachers and scholars in composition argue even further that the composition classroom is a site for promoting social transformation and social justice, where students can deploy their literacy work as a way of taking action on community-based and campus-based issues. Furthermore, for many students deemed "basic writers," the composition course is simultaneously a gate keeping them from the university or a "way in" to an educational system that would have kept them out in previous eras.

Yet at the same time that many of us embrace emancipatory pedagogical discourses and acknowledge working-class origins, we work in departmental systems and institutional structures in which literacy work is considered non-intellectual "remediation" and devalued socially, politically in higher education. As we know, the composition workforce is often made up of part-time and nontenure-track faculty, many of whom are women, and teaching assistants, both male and female, who are positioned in low-paying, low-ranking positions within the hierarchy of the increasingly corporatized American academy (see Downing, Hurlbert, and Mathieu). The instructional workforce at the top layers of the profession is also predominantly a white workforce. At the same time, "basic writing" courses are often disproportionately filled with students of color, international students who are nonnative speakers, and white, working-class students. In this gendered, classed, and raced structure, there is yet another overlay of classed relations: that between literature and composition faculty. The number of credit hours generated by first-year composition at large state universities makes it possible for English departments to fund specialized, low-enrollment courses and to maintain a faculty size that allows for specialized research and graduate education (see Crowley), even, ironically, that of tenured Marxist and materialist feminist intellectuals whose light teaching loads enable them to launch relentless critiques of capitalist class relations from privileged positions in the academy.

Our field's focus on pedagogy and administrative logics is also mirrored in the preparation graduate students receive. Many graduate students and faculty in rhetoric and composition have not had much of an opportunity to study the history of Marxist ideas and may be unfamiliar with these traditions if their course work and preparation has taken place in traditional English departments. Systematic study of the history of Marxist thought is often undertaken by scholars in departments of sociology, philosophy, and political science, and less so in English departments. Moreover, in English departments, Marxist theory is often filtered through theories of literary interpretation, which places an emphasis on reading and analyzing literary texts, or through cultural studies with an emphasis on reading popular cultural texts. Rhetorical theories do not tend to emphasize Marxist categories or paradigms, or if they do, as in the case of Kenneth Burke, that affiliation is buried or mentioned only in passing. Moreover, introductory rhetoric and composition anthologies in master's level and doctoral level rhetoric and composition courses do not, for the most part, include sections on Marxist analysis, although issues of class and critical pedagogy may be raised without much acknowledgement of the Marxist frameworks that drive such theories.

These different layers of material life in English departments coupled with the turn away from Marxist thought in general in the American academy accounts for, in part, our field's partial and uneven engagement with Marxist ideas through critical pedagogy and cultural studies and our almost nonexistent engagement with materialist feminisms. As Kelsh points out, feminists in composition studies are missing a vital opportunity to link to global feminist movements via materialist feminisms. How, then, given the class contradictory relations of composition should feminists in composition studies go about engaging more systematically with materialist feminist ideas? What are sites of intervention for feminist materialist scholars in composition and rhetorical studies? How should feminist composition scholars take up what Kelsh, Ebert, and Hennessey and Ingraham refer to as a "global feminism"?

MATERIALIST FEMINISM AND
SITES OF LOCAL AND GLOBAL INTERVENTION

In *Ludic Feminism and After*, Theresa Ebert argues that feminist materialist critique "is one of the most effective means through which challenges to global capitalism can be carried out" (5). However, she argues that "critique in itself is not an end; it is simply a means for producing the historical knowledges of social totality that are necessary for any coherent praxis for a radical transformation of patriarchal capitalism" (5). While Ebert and Kelsh provide significant critiques of current feminist thinking, asserting materialist critique as a essential element in political struggles against capitalist exploitation, the question that haunts their analyses is the connection between their materialist analyses and the work of activists and activist scholars, both local and global, who work to effect the critical interventions hypothesized in their theories. I do not raise this point to imply a theory-practice split, suggesting that activists do the work and theorists merely hypothesize conceptual change, but to address the connections between a feminist materialist intellectual practice and a transformative feminist activist politics.

Materialist feminist ecological activist Gwyn Kirk provides us with a model of materialist feminist activist scholarship that documents how critical discourses work their way through social processes and networks of real people in complex rhetorical situations. Articulating an integrative materialist feminist approach to ecological issues that connects materialist critique and political activism, Kirk analyzes the intersections of critique and activism in the everyday lives of those organizing around ecological issues: environmental racism, deforestation and sustainable agriculture, militarization, reproductive rights, and labor exploitation. Kirk contends that "[i]f ecological feminism is to inform a vital ecological politics in the U.S., we need to emphasize the interconnections among oppressions, activists, and movements; to frame issues broadly to mobilize wide-ranging involvement and support, rather than emphasizing points of disagreement; and to show how the process of capital accumulation is reinforced by the ideological articulation of difference based on gender, ethnicity, and culture" (349). Kirk argues that materialist critique means "opening up a public debate that challenges and opposes the values and practices of this economic system—its hazardous production processes as well

as its consumerist ideology"—and promoting local economic projects, com-
munity-building, and education (361). In Kirk's case, the critique is always
tied to contextualized political work, and it is this connection between critique
and activism that offers feminists in composition studies a model for future
work, for activist scholarship.

There are many promising arenas for a materialist feminist-activist scholarship in our field, and one of the most promising is rhetorical analysis of how
international feminist social change movements enact rhetorical action. For
instance, many international and transnational feminists are currently engaged
in aspects of the antiglobalization movement, working on issues as diverse as
human rights, worker rights, environmentalism, antiracism, and feminism.
Feminist rhetors can analyze how these communities of activists maintain
coalitions and enact contextualized strategies and tactics for change. Moreover, this research can analyze critical rhetorical strategies in dynamic and
highly changeable contexts, thus providing a space for critical reflection and
assessment of our theories of rhetorical action, many of which are still rooted
in the classical era, a time when women's participation in the polis was slight
or nonexistent.

As scholars and practitioners of rhetoric, feminism, and literacy, we can
also broaden our focus from issues of English and writing in the American
and North American context to address issues of global or "World" English
(both written and spoken) and its material, economic, and raced, classed, and
gendered dimensions. A rich scholarship on comparative and contrastive
rhetorics and teaching English as a Second Language or Foreign Language
(TESOL/TFL) exists, but this work usually is not cited or engaged by scholars in composition studies. Our work in composition and literacy studies has
all too often been focused on language issues in the American or European
contexts, and we have virtually ignored other sites in the world where written
composition and spoken English are regularly taught and demanded as part
of a state-sanctioned system of schooling, often tied to corporate interests.
Moreover, indigenous language preservation and literacy as a tool of political
struggle for people of color (Lyons, Powell) are important issues to explore as
a counterpoint to the dominance of English as a "world language," the language of business and capital.

In addition, we can address how current struggles against labor exploitation in the American academy relate to the struggles of workers in other sectors of the "global economy," thus countering Hennessey and Ingraham's
charge that theory and practice have merely become a professionalized discourse instead of political praxis "aimed at redressing women's oppression and
exploitation worldwide" (2). In composition studies, we have often been
interested in the discursive representations of work and gendered narratives of
professionalization, as Kelsh notes, but less interested in the political processes
by which literacy workers come to consciousness and begin to change their

working conditions by participating in distinct political movements that relate to workers engaged in labor struggles in other sectors of the economy. We need a labor scholarship in our field that addresses how literacy workers seek to change their working conditions, one that analyzes the political frameworks and theories labor activists draw upon to ground their campaigns for labor justice. Increasingly, my work has been focused on chronicling the emergence of a national and international movement of contingent faculty who are organizing via unions and professional associations (see Schell). The rhetorics and activist strategies they draw upon are closely allied with that of antiglobalization activists who are directly battling corporate labor practices in areas as diverse as manufacturing (antisweat shop labor), agriculture (through the sustainable agriculture movement), the World Trade Organization, and the World Bank. This list of potential arenas for study and action is by no means exhaustive. It is often said that we are living in an "information age," but it is less often said that we are living in a time when the globalization of capital has brought widescale and often devastating changes to world economies, to labor situations, to the environment, and to peoples' lives across the globe. Our feminist theories of language and literacy work must account for the social and economic effects of these systems on people's lives and livelihoods and work to address and change them through pedagogical and rhetorical scholarship and activism. Clearly, there is much work to be done, and feminist materialist scholarship and pedagogy that is both activist *and* critical is a place to begin.

NOTE

1. I realize that globalization is an overused and hotly contested term; however, as Friedman argues in his popular book *The Lexus and the Olive Tree*, globalization "is the inexorable integration of markets, nation-states, and technologies to a degree never witnessed before—in a way that is enabling individuals, corporations and nation-states to reach around the world farther, faster, deeper, and cheaper than ever before" (9). However, globalization is not inherently liberating or democratic. On the contrary, it may have a brutalizing and exploitive effect, especially on the world's most vulnerable populations: women and children (see Mies, Sassen, Sandoval).

WORKS CITED

Bartholomae, David. "Inventing the University." *When a Writer Can't Write.* Ed. Mike Rose. New York: Guilford, 1985. 134–65.

Bizzell, Patricia. "Marxist Ideas in Composition Studies." In Harkin and Schilb, 52–68.

Brady, Laura. "The Reproduction of Othering." In Jarratt and Worsham, 21–44.

Crowley, Sharon. *Composition in the University: Historical and Polemical Essays.* Pittsburgh: University of Pittsburgh Press, 1998.

Downing, David, Claude Mark Hurlbert, and Paula A. Mathieu. "English Incorporated." *Beyond English, Inc.* Ed. David Downing, Claude Mark Hurlbert, and Paula Mathieu. Portsmouth: Heinemann, 2002. 1–21.

Ebert, Theresa. *Ludic Feminism and After: Postmodernism, Desire, and Labor in Late Capitalism.* Ann Arbor: University of Michigan Press, 1996.

Flynn, Elizabeth. "Review: Feminist Theories/Feminist Composition." *College English* 57 (1995): 201–12.

Friedman, Thomas. *The Lexus and the Olive Tree: Understanding Globalization.* New York: Anchor Books, 2000.

Harkin, Patricia, and John Schilb, eds. *Contending with Words: Composition and Rhetoric in a Postmodern Age.* New York: Modern Language Association, 1991.

Hartmann, Heidi. "The Unhappy Marriage of Marxism and Feminism: Toward a More Progressive Union." *Women and Revolution: A Discussion of the Unhappy Marriage of Marxism and Feminism.* Ed. Lydia Sargent. Boston: South End, 1981. 1–42.

Hennessey, Rosemary, and Chrys Ingraham, eds. "Introduction: Reclaiming Anticapitalist Feminism." In Hennessey and Ingraham, 1–14.

———. *Materialist Feminism: A Reader in Class, Difference, and Women's Lives.* New York: Routledge, 1997.

Jarratt, Susan, and Lynn Worsham, eds. *Feminism and Composition Studies: In Other Words.* New York: Modern Language Association, 1984.

Kelsh, Deb. "Critiquing the Culture of Feminism and Composition: Toward a Red Feminism." In Jarratt and Worsham, 100–07.

Kirk, Gwyn. "Standing on Solid Ground: A Materialist Ecological Feminism." In Hennessey and Ingraham, 345–63.

Laclau, Ernesto, and Chantal Mouffe. *Hegemony and Socialist Strategy: Towards a Radical Democratic Politics.* London: Verso, 1985.

Logan, Shirley Wilson. "'When and Where I Enter': Race, Gender, and Composition Studies." In Jarratt and Worsham, 45–57.

Lyons, Scott. "Rhetorical Sovereignty: What Do American Indians Want from Writing?" *College Composition and Communication* 51 (2000):447–68.

Mies, Maria. *Patriarchy and Accumulation on a World Scale: Women in the International Division of Labour.* Rev. ed. London and New York: Zed Books, 1998.

Powell, Malea. "Rhetorics of Survivance: How American Indians *Use* Writing." *College Composition and Communication* 53.3 (February 2000):396–434.

Reynolds, Nedra. "Interrupting Our Way to Agency: Feminist Cultural Studies and Composition." In Jarratt and Worsham, 58–73.

Sandoval, Chela. *Methodology of the Oppressed. Theory Out of Bounds,* Vol. 18. Minneapolis: University of Minnesota Press, 2000.

Sassen, Saskia. *Globalization and Its Discontents.* New York: The New Press, 1998.

Schell, Eileen E. "The Costs of Caring: 'Femininism' and Contingent Women Workers in Composition Studies." In Jarratt and Worsham, 74–93.

———. "Toward a New Labor Movement in Higher Education: Contingent Labor and Organizing for Change." *Workplace: The Journal for Academic* Labor. Special issue on Composition as Management Science. 4.1. http://www.louisville.edu/journal/workplace/issue7/issue7frontpage.html.

Trimbur, John. "The Problem of Post-Marxism: Radical Democracy and Class Struggle." *JAC: A Journal of Composition Theory* 19.2 (1999): 285–91.

Worsham, Lynn. "Writing against Writing: The Predicament of Ecriture Feminine." In Harkin and Schilb, 82–104.

Worsham, Lynn, and Gary Olson. "Hegemony and the Future of Democracy: Ernest Laclau's Political Philosophy." *JAC: A Journal of Composition Theory* 19.1 (1999): 1–34.

———. "Rethinking Political Community: Chantal Mouffe's Liberal Socialism." *JAC: A Journal of Composition Theory* 19.2 (1999): 163–99.

Chapter Two

WHEN OUR FEMINISM
IS NOT FEMINIST ENOUGH

JOANNE DETORE-NAKAMURA

"You're not what I expected," said the attractive blond woman in her forties, examining me from head to toe, on the first day of a women's literature class that I taught. I was dressed in my usual career garb—a short black skirt, a long red fitted blazer with black hose and matching pumps. In the words of Mary Daly, I looked like a "fembot,"[1] what she describes as "the archetypical role model forced upon women throughout fatherland" (198). In other words, I looked as if I belonged in the career section of the J.C. Penney catalog, not in a women's literature classroom. My experiences in this class would ultimately refine my ideas about teaching feminist theory, force me to acknowledge its fractures, sharpen my personal definition of feminism, and cement my conviction that the feminist academy, with its radical feminism, ultimately closed more doors than it opened to women of the working class and mainstream.

My argument begins with the schism between the theory and the practice of feminist pedagogy in the writing classroom. Feminist pedagogy is often defined as "student-centered, active, and collaborative classrooms; [with] students accountable for knowledge processes and contexts; a revised power differential between teachers and students; [and] a multiplicity of perspectives" (Fraiberg, screen 1). As an A.B.D. from Southern Illinois University at Carbondale with a major in American literature and a minor in women's studies, I came armed with this definition of feminist teaching and found myself without enough loaves and fishes to feed my hungry students and without any miracles.

For one thing, I had been encased in the Ivy Tower for almost five years pursuing my doctorate in a rather insulated college town in which the women's studies department was fairly radical. For another, I came face-to-face with an extremely oppressive administration, one so bad it became the subject of a controversial book, *Max and Me*, by former tenured sociology professor Marion Brady.

The oppressive structure had a trickle-down effect, and eventually it trickled into my composition classroom. I was told that a professor had no freedom to select textbooks at this college.[2] I was required to use the *Practical Writer*, a composition book that stresses the five-paragraph essay, for my composition classes. Newer composition strategies that stressed the process of writing such as freewriting, multiple drafts, peer review workshops, and the like were employed by few professors. One of the products of our oppressed status as faculty members was a certain amount of invisibility, so I used the book just enough to put it in my syllabus but relied mostly on my own materials. I also discovered that what I had thought was a liberal beach community was actually extremely conservative. My students were generally much different from the ones that I taught at my doctoral institution, a research I university. While we had an open door policy at Southern Illinois University, most of the students that I taught were well prepared and of traditional college age. The students whom I taught at the community college were generally older, about twenty-eight years old, and first-generation college attendees who often worked 40 hours per week while taking twelve credit hours (full time).

These students were overwhelmingly Republican, conservative Christians who held very traditional views concerning women. Shortly after coming back from maternity leave, I was told by several students that I needed to be home with my child, not "out teaching and neglecting" her. Another male student, from a fundamentalist Christian family, said that his father thought I was a "Jezebel," for working outside the home when I was a married mother. For many academics in prestigious universities, this type of patriarchal thinking is simply a matter of theory, not reality.

While life in America is certainly not like Taliban-controlled Afghanistan, the oppression endured by women of the lower classes and of some ethnic and racial groups is very real and occurs in varying degrees across the country. In my newly adopted southern city, I regularly opened the paper to read about the vandalizing of an African American–owned upholstery store, the defacing of a Jewish temple, and the desecration of a local mosque. Our community also forced out the one and only women's clinic that offered abortion.[3] This was the environment in which I hoped to begin teaching a women's literature course, hardly the liberal college town from which I had recently moved. Ever optimistic or naïve, I soldiered on.

"What do you mean? What did you expect?" I asked, all the while know-ing exactly what she had expected.

Nancy, the student in her forties, said rather sheepishly, "I sort of expected you to be wearing [pause] well, black pants, a T-shirt . . . that sort of thing." She continued, "I am really interested in reading women's literature, but I told my husband that I was a little worried, that well—?"

Nancy's was the type of interruption I had been encountering repeatedly in my education and in my teaching. I was the interruption,[4] a challenge to her idea of a feminist and to some feminists' ideas of the same. After all, I was a "traitor feminist" like Christina Hoff Sommers and Naomi Wolf. I was a third-wave feminist, who like Sommers and Wolf dared to question the absolutes of the feminist movement, namely that the movement bred victim-ization rather than victors and ostracized young women, young men, and het-erosexuals by emphasizing radical feminism as the norm. In my dissertation, I had written about the schism in feminism, what Steven Buechler terms the "gay/straight split" (117). Nancy was simply employing the definition of and iconography associated with radical feminism, which essentially made the words *feminist* and *lesbian* synonymous. My style of dress and my introduction as a feminist who planned to marry that summer took my students aback. I could not be a feminist *and* a heterosexual. I exemplified the oxymoron.

It is no wonder my students felt this way. Although those of us in the academy know that there are many types of feminist theory including liberal, essentialist, radical, psychoanalytic, and ecofeminist, the definition of *feminist* and *feminism* had not grown in the mainstream press. It becomes more titil-lating, a great ratings booster, to label all feminists as radical feminists. Acad-emics have somehow lost sight of the mainstream, and a separation between theory and practice has grown. According to Buechler, by the mid-1970s, les-bian feminists took radical feminism to its logical conclusions and pro-nounced that

> lesbian relations were the logical, desirable, and politically appropriate expression of feminist principles because only in such relations could the concept of 'woman-identified' women find full expression. The logic could not help but convey at least an implicit criticism of heterosexual women, whose sexual relations appeared at best to limit their commitment to femi-nism, and at worst to provide aid and comfort to the enemy. (117)

This idea was still pervasive in the 1990s and even into the twenty-first cen-tury. My students simply did not know that feminism could include feminine-looking women like me.

As an Italian/Sicilian-American woman from the working class, the feminist theory had always appealed to me because I had encountered oppression firsthand. It was not all academic to me; I saw life from the eyes of the underprivileged. Although my lighter skin afforded me the privileges of some of white culture,[5] I realized that class and ethnicity were often more important than color. Thus, I learned early on that I needed to be aggressive in the classroom when many of my white, Anglo teachers discouraged rather than encouraged me. Ever undaunted by competition in school or later on the job, I had to fight for every step I took into the middle class. I had long considered myself a feminist; however, after attending women's studies conferences and sessions on feminist theory in graduate school, I learned that, strangely enough, the feminist movement seemed to have little place for me.

Radical feminist rhetoric, which insisted that women should live separately from men, excluded heterosexual women, like the majority of my students, from the dialogue. What is more, I learned that feminist rhetoric, although often touted as open and inclusive, was in practice very restrictive and even prescriptive in promoting one viewpoint. Moreover, I found it ironic that most of the radical feminists who spoke of oppression came from the upper class, went to Ivy League colleges, and did not have to acquire student loans to pay for college. In short, it seemed that they had not experienced oppression themselves. Class can be an even larger barrier than race or ethnicity in some cases. How many professors working in prestigious universities actually began their education at a community college, not because they were not bright enough, but because they were not wealthy enough to gain entrance to a better institution? My guess is few. Yet their rhetorical tactics implicitly insisted that all "white" women, regardless of class or ethnicity, had the same experience. Furthermore, some radicals denounced heterosexuality, a product of the patriarchy not a natural choice.[6] For many mainstream, working-class women, the ideas of radical feminism do not coincide with their lives. Feminism instead fractures, leaving few possibilities for working-class women who do not identify as lesbian. In her article, "Rhetoric and Reality in Women's Studies," Daphne Patai writes about the prescriptive tendencies of women's studies departments to insist on one homogenized view of feminism—radical feminism.

"Yeah," said April. "I thought you'd be more [pause], well, you know."

"Masculine," Rachael quickly blurted out, contorting her body, afraid that she had gone too far.

Then I asked, "Please raise your hand if you identify yourself as a feminist."

I looked around at my new crop of students. Nancy, the older student, sat in the back and smiled an uncomfortable smile. In this class, most of the students were rather young for the community college[7] profile—most were in their late teens to early twenties—all were women except one young man, a tall, lanky kid with long, brown Jesus hair, hovering freely above his shoulders. Of the six or so students, only one, Rachel, raised her hand. All the women and the one man quickly added that they believed in "equal rights" but that they were not "that way" (gay). When I explained that there were many types of feminists (even men could be feminists) and gave them Sommers's definitions of "gender and equity" feminists, all the young women and the one young man recanted, saying, "I guess I would describe myself as an equity feminist." The inability to embrace the term *feminism* is not just a problem for young students. As Patai chronicles in her article, even celebrities who are willing to decry the virtues of the vagina and can take possession of the word, "cunt," are "unable to embrace or even claim the word" feminism": Glenn Close, for example, stated that she wanted no part of the 'clichéd image of what a feminist would be.' What perception of feminists did she mean? 'They don't like men—you know, kind of, um, butch'" (qtd. in Patai 22). I realized quickly that I could not come to class with the standard fare of feminist theorists. Instead, I would have to create a literature course that would appeal to this particular type of student, to make connections with these students and their lives. At the same time, I was wrestling with my dissertation and finding that many contemporary women writers rejected the feminist label as well. My hypothesis was that a revolution was afoot in the feminine plot structure of women's novels influenced by this very schism between the theory and practice of feminism in the lives of real women. Women writers had picked up on this before anyone else, and they realized that victim feminism was not the answer. More and more I found that women writers created female protagonists who were able to complete both a spiritual and a social quest, for the first time going beyond the boundaries of Carol Christ's and other's work. The friendship plot[8] was revolutionary, and I wanted to show my students that this new paradigm existed in contrast to the worn ideas of victim feminism.

I structured the course, Friendship and Community, around the theme of women's friendship and used some of the books that I discussed in my dissertation, namely Atwood's *The Robber's Bride,* Tan's *The Joy Luck Club,* Erdrich's *Love Medicine,* and Morrison's *Beloved.* In addition, I used film, including *The Group, The Joy Luck Club,* and *Waiting to Exhale.* The important foci that these books and readings offered was a new paradigm of feminism, one that allowed for relationships with the opposite sex and with a community of others while still finding one's identity as a woman, one that was apart from the traditional housewife of the 1950s. Female protagonists in these works did not commit suicide or alienate themselves by the novel's end. They fulfilled both a spiritual and a social quest for the first time and were welcomed back into the community of others, which also for the first time included men.

Although I had not thought about discussing the work of Sommers or of Wolf, as the class progressed, I felt it was the only way for my students to feel legitimized and, therefore, able to join the conversation. By reading the work of Sommers and Wolf, I was able to show my students that other young women felt locked out of feminism. Furthermore by understanding the controversy, they would be better able to unlock the door. That key was showing my students that there were debates within feminist theory. It was not monolithic at all. In fact Sommers, Wolf, Paglia, and others challenged the movement itself.

As Joy Ritchie writes in "Confronting the 'Essential' Problem," feminist teachers need not "keep these political and theoretical conflicts in the professional closet, separate from their students and classrooms" (256). Like the instructor whom Ritchie observed, I presented my students with as many different points of view as I could, given the confines of the class, and let them join in the discussion. This invitation to entertain a multiplicity of views was what feminist pedagogy was all about. However, this unveiling of conflicting views, the fractures of feminist theory and practice, seldom took place in the feminist classroom at the university level.

I began with Christina Hoff Sommers's assertion that the image of the radical feminist defines feminism for many mainstream women. Sommers notes that in a 1992 Time/CNN poll,

> although 57 percent of the women responding said they believed there was a need for a strong women's movement, 63 percent said they do not consider themselves feminists. Another poll conducted by R. H. Bruskin reported that only 16 percent of college women "definitely" considered themselves to be feminists. (18)

Although my students resisted the term *feminism* and with it feminist theory, I knew that they could become open to the theory if presented in a non-threatening way. My desire, like Shirley Wilson Logan's, was "to devise ways to speak the unspeakable, to talk about and have students write about issues surrounding race and gender, in composition classrooms and in all classrooms" (55). I knew that feminist rhetoric and theory could eventually set them free intellectually as it had done for me.

Prior to reading feminist theory, I had simply been frustrated with the oppression that I endured or witnessed as I was growing up. Reading feminist theory put a name to the imbalance of power that I witnessed daily in my Italian American, working-class culture, but my interest in feminist theory was not fed in a systematic way until I began my doctoral program.[9] Along the way, I realized that I identified less and less with victim feminism, with radical feminism, with the movement's pull toward the extreme Left. Yet, I still believed that feminist theory and pedagogy offered hope to students, who like me, were from the working class and needed language to describe their position in society if ever they were to rise above it.

As a new hire in 1995, I was eager to create courses that I thought were missing from our course catalog and were needed to empower my students. My department chair at that time was excited about the idea of a women's literature, so she wrote it in as a special topics course. Our campus provost told my chair, "Go ahead! No one will enroll anyhow." He allowed the course to be printed in the spring schedule, and six students registered for the course. A day before the class was scheduled to meet, my department chair called me into her office to tell me that our provost had canceled the class due to low enrollment. My chair suggested that I might have more success persuading the provost to reinstate the course and said that I should approach him calmly to plead my case. I did, but he wouldn't budge. He told me that it was his practice to cancel classes with enrollment in the single digits. While this was true, I knew that he had let classes run with fewer than ten students when the course was deemed important to the college. One of the Russian professors regularly taught fewer than twenty students for his total enrollment in five classes, so the rule did not hold true for everyone. I asked if he would reinstate the course as an independent study rather than as a regular class. I knew this meant that I would have to pick up another class for a total of six courses that semester and teach the course for $20 a student or $120 rather than for $1,250 as an overload course; however, I felt that the course was worth the extra work on my part. He agreed; the price was right.

The first task of the course, as I saw it, was to empower my students by giving them a voice in the course. However, I had to tell my students that they were now registered for an independent study, rather than for a regular class. Although most independent study courses met only once a week or every two weeks, we agreed to meet twice a week like a traditional class. I also told my students that this class would not be like any of the classes that they had taken before. They would be facilitators along with me. My idea of this feminist pedagogical theory does not presuppose that there is no hierarchy in the classroom. To suggest so would be disingenuous. As the instructor, I am still responsible for evaluating the quality of the students' work, and, therefore, I am in a position of power. However, we would share information regularly. Likewise, to suggest that reciprocal learning does not occur between the students and instructors implies that instructors simply fill the students' heads with information while the instructor gains nothing. This Freirian "banking theory" of education is antithetical to good teaching and to feminist pedagogy. However, the very idea that I would be a cofacilitator with my students in the class decentered my working-class students who were not used to the professor giving up power and giving it to her students. This teaching technique would enable "us to talk about ourselves as subjects not trapped in the subject/object dyad or that of authority vs. nonauthority or power vs. powerlessness" (Barlowe and Hottell 273). The transformation began with the physical setup of the room.

The classroom in which I taught was set up for a traditional lecture, with a podium up front for the professor and the student desks at a distance in neat rows. During that first class, I asked the students to use a circle formation like a seminar, and I took a different seat in the circle every class period, deliberately derailing the idea of leadership and an assigned position.[10] Again, I was still responsible for facilitating the discussion and bringing my scholarship to the classroom. I offered valuable scholarship and training to my students, but the learning process was reciprocal. Therefore, I did not consider my teaching style, "without a locus of authority" as Carmen Luke warns, which can be problematic for the student (qtd. in Ropers-Huilman, screen 3). I, like Barbara Applebaum, did not think that one needed to be nurturing or authoritative as a feminist teacher. To slip into binary oppositions is too easy a step. Instead, my approach is more akin to Applebaum's, which she terms "relational authority," in which the "nurturance-authority dichotomy dissolves" (Applebaum, screen 5) in lieu of creating a new paradigm based on trust. This technique often took my students off-guard. They would leave a chair vacant near the front portion of the class with their desks at a safe distance from mine and assume that was where I would sit. Instead, I would begin class by pulling up a desk and placing it right next to a different student each time, keeping a student's distance (which was closer) apart. After the first few meetings, students gave up on the idea of a leadership position and began to contribute freely as well. Thus, my class began to resemble the "collaborative feminist classroom . . . in which at least some power is shared," symbolized by the circle (Barlowe and Hottell 274).

For the course, I designed most of my assignments using what have often been termed "female rhetoric" or "feminist rhetoric" principles, which included using "open structure" assignments like journals, "valuing of personal experience" when relating to the novels, "writing [that] explores feelings, ideas or issues without . . . asserting a point" as in journal assignments or discussions, and taking an "intersubjective stance that sees connections between writer, subject and audience," which really was the thrust of my dissertation and of the course (Hayes 296). Here again, I would like to clarify that I view the term *female rhetoric* as a rather limiting one, which drawn to its reasonable conclusions presupposes that women are incapable of linear, "male" argumentation or at the very least are predisposed to nonlinear argumentation. As a teacher of composition, I contend that males and females who are new to argumentation practice nonlinear argument equally. For the purposes of this essay, I use these designations only to define differences between types of writing. Moreover, I did not use female rhetoric exclusively. Like many feminist teachers, I also required my students to create a research paper, which can be described as "writing [that] must make a point and offer generalizations" or part of the "male rhetorical tradition" (Hayes 296). To offer only female rhetoric or feminist rhetoric creates a disadvantage for the student who will find her/himself in a very competitive environment within the academy and outside of its ivory tower walls.

The next year that I taught the course, I added the film *The First Wives Club* to our list. Film was used as a respite in between novels to help the students keep up with readings, giving them enough time to finish the books. The seminar paper was the only assignment that used a traditional male rhetoric (essentially a literary analysis), although students could be very creative in the oral presentation portion of the assignment. The course assignments totaled one thousand points and consisted of the following:

- Attendance and Participation (250 points)
- Facilitation of a Class (100 points)
- Group Report (100 points)
- Response Journal (150 points)
- Seminar Report (100 points)
- Seminar Paper (300 points)

Along with the assignments, there were opportunities for additional reading and writing such as earning extra credit through the completion at least fifteen hours of service learning by volunteering at a women's center and then writing a two-page essay that related the student's experience to one of the books that we read. Students could also earn extra credit by watching a film that incorporated the theme of women's friendship—such as *Thelma and Louise* or *Fried Green Tomatoes*—and by writing a two-page review of it. Furthermore, students could earn points by critiquing other books that centered on women's issues or on women's friendship such as *The Feminine Mystique, The Second Sex, Loving Her,* or *Among Women.* In my syllabus, I had attached a short list of films, novels, and critical works that were related to the course. I have found that providing students with extra credit writing opportunities actually improves their writing skills by giving them another chance to write and/or to interact with their community through service learning.

In the case of service learning, my students were able to see the connections between life and theory after volunteering at a local residential facility for abused girls between the ages of six and 18. My student who had a self-described happy childhood in a nuclear family had had no reference point for the events in Atwood's book until she volunteered at the facility. Later, she wrote about how Atwood's book *The Robber Bride* came to life for her there and how important it was for young women to develop a healthy self-esteem and to heal any wounds inflicted by others.

Although the structure of the course appeared to set me up as "the expert," I made it clear that my research was a work in progress and that my ideas would be a starting point from which we could depart, not a finish line from which I would draw conclusions. I fully expected my students to become facilitators themselves, to argue with my ideas, to arrive at their own conclusions. To begin that process, I stated in the syllabus that the students would be "on call for five minutes or so" to give their own ideas about the book or anything else they wished to discuss. In fact, participation was a large percentage of their grade. I felt strongly that the success of the course depended upon the creation of a safe haven for truly free speech. Ironically, the safe haven in some women's studies classes can become oppressive, censorship-laden places that turn quickly into gripe sessions and male-bashing free-for-alls. When we segregate our classes based on gender or target a minority male, we engage in solipsism at the very least and oppression at the worst, which accomplishes little in the way of intellectual discussion. Although my students are free to find an entrance point through their own personal stories, my classes are not about airing their dirty laundry.

Paradoxically, I did not want to censor ideas. Judging from my students' palsied speech and contorted body language when they tried to discuss their ideas of feminism, they had been affected by the PC police, which silenced the only language with which they were familiar as inappropriate and gave them few substitutes or silence to replace it. To combat this, I told my students that they could ask me anything without fear of belittlement or censure.

The only ground rule was that their speech should not intend to cause harm. If it did inadvertently, we would say so calmly and explain why it was offensive to us. We would suggest other ways for the person to discuss the issue with less offensive terms. I gave the example that in a composition course that I taught, one of my students had used the term *colored people* to describe African Americans in response to a Brent Staples's essay "Walk on By." Using this technique, one of my African Americans students turned to the older woman and said, "I am uncomfortable when you use the term *colored people*. No one uses that any more. I would prefer *black* or *African American*." My older student thanked the younger one and then apologized, to which the younger one responded, "That's okay. You didn't know. Now you do." There was no Jerry Springer-style "debate," just an honest exchange, I told my students. I have had Springer-style disruptions before in other courses and had to stop the class, pointing out that that type of speech hurt and that I employed what Nancy Cornwell calls, borrowing from Gilligan, "an ethic of care" in the classroom: "Hate speech in the classroom may effectively be an expressive act that harms, intimidates, and silences students" (screen 3). Realizing that this approach could be considered contradictory, perhaps silencing students rather than freeing them, I can only say that the trust factor in the classroom allows my students to discuss their ideas freely, without censure but with explanation. That is what I wanted.

Another way that I reinforced the female and feminist rhetorical principle of valuing personal experience in which "the emphasis [is] on personal and multiple truths rather than on a single truth" is to require a reader-response journal. "Thus, autobiography and first-person narrative are appropriate discourse modes" (Hayes 296). In my syllabus, I noted that *we* would be disclosing "personal information about *ourselves* and *our* friendships." I deliberately included myself in the plural first-person pronoun because I intended to share personal information about myself as well. Not to do so would set up an imbalance of power, and I wanted to establish a sense of reciprocity. Moreover from my study of women's and men's friendships and disclosure in speech acts, I knew that to get a response, I must be prepared to give one first. I began the class with a short autobiography. I told my students that I had also graduated from a community college, that I was from the working class and a first-generation college graduate. I told them that I was finishing up my Ph.D. at Southern Illinois University and that I had moved to Florida from Illinois. I told them about my plans to marry that summer, about my experience with friendship, and about the process of writing my dissertation. I told them that I was a feminist, had minored in women's studies, and had a keen interest in empowering women. I asked them if they had any questions for me.

They did; most of them asked why I had come from Illinois to take a job at a community college rather than at a four-year college. I told them that I had graduated from a community college myself and had chosen the community college over a four-year college because the four-year college was in an overly racist town that I chose not to live in with my fiancé who was transracial. Others asked me if I was really a feminist and what my fiancé thought of that. I told them that I really was a feminist, an equity feminist, and that being a feminist did not diminish my fiancé's masculinity, if that is what they meant. He was raised by a liberal feminist himself and had no trouble with it. Others asked me about the course and its difficulty level. I answered all their questions and then had them pair up and interview each other. After about ten minutes, they introduced each other to the class. Some of my students said that they were taking the class because they were interested in women's literature but had never seen a class offered in it before. They thought it would be "fun." One student had taken a communications II course with me in the fall and had followed me to this course because she enjoyed my previous class and wanted to learn more about feminist theory since I had done a bit of it in my composition classes. My older student, Nancy, told us that she was auditing the course because she was now trying to do something for herself after being a stay-at-home mother and wife. She said that she had always wanted to take a women's literature course, but she had never been brave enough.

After our introductions, I had my students exchange names and phone numbers. Although I generally use peer groups of three or four, this group was so small that I decided to form one large group. I waited as the students greeted each other again, happily exchanging their personal information. After things quieted down, I established another norm for our class, which was confidentiality. I told them that the literature that we were reading and the journal questions that I planned to ask might elicit some painful and intimate events in our lives; therefore, we should agree not use personal information against one another. It did not mean that individually or collectively we could not become political if we chose to take our issues to the outside world. It simply meant we would respect each other's privacy.

On the second day or so, I introduced the idea of group presentations. This was another way through which I provided "opportunities to become so engaged that [the students] really teach themselves [and] they forget that they are learning and take an active role in their own learning" (Lundsford and Glenn 183), another principle of feminist pedagogy. The group presentation,

which would be a creative endeavor (i.e. a short skit, talk show, painting, musi-
cal score), was also an opportunity to gather scholarly information and to
engage in original inquiry into the work of the author and her cultural milieu.
This type of assignment created what Andrea Lunsford calls "the dynamic
interactions of the students, a demonstration of their abilities to discover and
create, construe and communicate their own knowledge" (Lunsford and
Glenn 183). In some sense, a male rhetorical tradition suggests that the only
type of valid assignment is a logical paper, and it does not validate most creative endeavors such as letters, quilts, or other nontraditional modes such as
skits. Therefore, in an effort to validate other modes of learning, I recognized
the importance of including this type of assignment as a feminist teacher.

Throughout the semester, I was always impressed by the creativity and
level of insight my students produced, often giving me what I call a "mojo
moment," a phrase I adopted in a nod to popular culture, which simply means
that I am able to sense my students' epiphanies of insight. Due to the small
number of students, the group presentations became informal, individual presentations. Nonetheless, they were outstanding. One of my students turned
out to be an expert in mah jong and demonstrated the game for us. Another
one had a knowledge of the paranormal, which rendered a fascinating look at
The Robber Bride. Throughout the two semesters that I taught the course, students offered presentations on the horrors of slavery with an original skit
pieced together with slave narratives; some psychoanalysis of mother/daugh-
ter relationships that culminated with the young woman discussing her own
uneasy relationship with her mother; a traditional analysis of the feather
imagery in *The Joy Luck Club;* and a retrospective of female images in advertising from the 1940s to the present, extrapolating how these images might
have influenced baby boomers like the heroines in the Atwood novel. Each
was fascinating and superb because the students had made a personal connection with the literature, some of them taking the project in their own direction rather than following any lead that I had suggested. Given that they were
only undergraduates, I thought this was a tremendous step.

As the class continued to meet, my students and I formed a deeper bond.
I tried to create a community in the classroom with the introduction of food
early on. I did not do this to cement any ideas of the feminist teacher as
mother/midwife.[12] My idea of offering food originates from my ethnic heritage as an Italian American in which offering food is the first step to forming a friendship. The second step is accepting the food. In Italian American
homes, both men and women offer food, so the introduction of food in the
classroom did not have any sexist connotations for me, and this is what I told
my students. Over food, one of our first assignments was to describe our
friendship history with women and/or with men. My students, women and
the one man, were never asked to bring anything; they simply showed up with
food class after class. One of my students made lasagna, another made fudge,

another brought cookies, a cake, popcorn, and pizza, and the list goes on. I even held class in a local Chinese restaurant when we were nearing the end of our discussion of Tan's *The Joy Luck Club*. As incredible as it seemed to me, three of my six students had never eaten Chinese food before. Although in my other composition courses I generally have more than a few students who are Asian, Hispanic, African-American or other races; however, this particular class was comprised of all white students from various European origins. Even so, I was rather surprised that this would be a first for most people. Having grown up in New York State, I had become accustomed to eating Polish, Irish, Chinese, Jewish, Greek, and many other types of foods as a regular course of weekly events. I encouraged everyone to order something different, and we all sampled each other's food. One of my students for whom this was a first remarked that she would never have come into a Chinese restaurant without this experience. "I would be too afraid . . . that I wouldn't know what to do, what to order," she remarked, which was echoed by my male student. The class gave my students confidence to try new things, to explore and to challenge long-held beliefs, and this confidence and willingness to experiment showed up in their writing and in their presentations.

One of those long-held beliefs was undoubtedly the definition of feminism. From that first day when my very presence seemed to challenge my students' view of feminism, I tried to impress upon my students that "feminism is not a single path, nor one belief; feminisms' so-called conflicts are instead dialogues between those who share some fundamental ideological principles, but who manifest them in radically different ways" (Barlowe and Hottell 269). I decided to trust my students with information that none of my colleagues thought they could handle—theory. Rather than stand at the podium for these informational dialogues that I felt were necessary to give my students the theory that they lacked, I would sit at the student desk and give handouts for those who might be visual learners. As a matter of course, I make it my practice to appeal to various learning styles by varying my presentation style. Through daily journal questions, I tried to get my students to see connections between the literature and theory that we read and the content of their own lives. For instance, in one journal question about *The Joy Luck Club*, I asked students about the novel and then asked them questions about their own lives:

> Lindo Jong says that she has two faces, a Chinese face and an American face. What does she mean? Does everyone have two faces or identities? Are you more likely to have them if you are from another culture? Atwood also uses the idea of the double. Is this the same thing? Why or why not? Do you have two different faces in your life? Explain.

Here I invited students to discuss the book first, then to form connections with a novelist that we studied previously. Last, I asked if this phenomenon had occurred in their lives.

One young woman, whose family were recent immigrants, explained that she often felt that she had to use two different faces—one for her family and one for her friends. I, too, had said that as a woman from an Italian American working-class background, I often felt like I wore two faces—one for my community and the other for colleagues. In my community, I felt free to use Italian American expressions such as "It's giving me agita" (sour stomach) or "Madonna mia!" (an expression of frustration), while at the same time, I felt uncomfortable throwing around some college-level words, which I knew would make my family uncomfortable. Largely due to that very discussion, I tried to fuse my own separate halves, creating a more fully realized person and embracing rather than hiding my own ethnic heritage, and so did my second-generation student.

My students were hungry for theory. I realized this when I began talking about the underpinnings of my dissertation during one lecturette. My students were quickly writing down names and asking me if I could give them some suggestions for further reading. This type of intellectual curiosity took me aback, as I had not witnessed it in any of my required composition classes until that point. This was the type of class for which I had hoped. Excitedly, I drew Showalter's diagram of the dominant/muted spheres on the board and discussed the "Wild Zone" (262). I saw the wheels turning, the light bulbs flickering on one after another. I had many "mojo moments" in which they suddenly understood the reason that their boyfriends did not understand them in the "wild zone" of constructed female communication patterns, for instance. My male student said he felt privileged to be a part of the wild zone discussion, which he said gave him unique insights.

I fed my students the basics of feminist theory first, giving them notes on Chodorow's theories of psychosexual development, which they said made more sense than Freud's ever did. I gave them large helpings of Gilligan's theory of morality, which is fraught with controversy but which I think illustrates central ideas of justice, which do not have to be defined as feminine or masculine.[13] I introduced them to Virginia Woolf, who discusses the need for financial freedom to pursue intellectual pursuits, a great starting point for students who were all conflicted with job and school obligations. We talked about Betty Friedan's *Feminine Mystique* and the advertising conspiracy she discusses that ushered women back into the home after World War II got them out into the workforce. My students, great connoisseurs of popular culture, began evaluating advertising in a new light and sparked one to research images of women in advertising for her final project. It was important to juxtapose Susan Faludi with Naomi Wolf, for instance, especially by looking at *Backlash* and *The Beauty Myth* against Wolf's next venture *Fire with Fire*, which was critical of the feminist movement. All movements have ebb and flow, a fringe continent and a mainstream. It was important for my students to see the many perspectives of the movement. It was important for them to see the conflict and argument within the feminist movement. By "bringing the debate to our students and allowing them to grapple with the gender issues associated with argumentative writing in the academy," I realized, like Alexis Easley in her article, "Toward a Feminist Theory of Teaching Argumentative Writing," that I could "help them to make better choices as writers and thinkers" (Easley, screen 3). Moreover, the chronicle of conflict and fractures within the feminist movement helped them to see the feminist movement as dynamic rather than something static and impenetrable. They were ravenous for the very information that they could not see as important to them just weeks before. I started seeing copies of books that I had casually mentioned in class stuffed into their backpacks such as Friedan's *Feminist Mystique,* Lerner's *Creation of Patriarchy,* or *A Room of One's Own* by Woolf. Others became Atwood fans, reading *Edible Woman* or *The Handmaid's Tale.* For students who had begun the class noting that they had never read an entire book from cover to cover, this transformation was amazing.

In addition to the literary strides we made in class, I began to hear about the ways in which my students integrated the new theories and the literature into their lives. They forged connections between theory and practice. One of my students decided to end a toxic relationship with a boyfriend after we finished Atwood's *Robber Bride.* Another student found a means to reconcile with her mother by watching the film version of *The Joy Luck Club* with her. She told me that they both cried and hugged afterward. My male student said he was able to open up more to his male and female friends about his feelings and to try new things. I had not counted on such profound changes occurring during the course of the semester.

I certainly had not counted on the class changing me, but it did. It was clear to me now that this class had to go on in some form and that I needed to reach more students. With some degree of resistance from the earlier administration, I began a women's history celebration on campus, which was eventually embraced by the new campus president. Moreover, I now include feminist theory and women's literature as a part of every one of my composition and literature courses, thereby reaching more students at a time. I also became a certified diversity trainer and through our Staff and Professional Development Office began teaching graduate courses for our faculty and staff ranging from Composition Studies to Gender and Communication to Diversity-Infusion Education, all of which are credited by a neighboring research I university.

Ironically the only place that I still feel like a lone voice in the wilderness is in the feminist movement. I feel like an exile really, especially at conferences for women's literature and feminist theory. I am in agreement with the observations of Nedra Reynolds who discusses how oppressive the feminist movement has become in terms of entertaining dissenting views:

Feminists daring to criticize other feminists have opened up spaces for analyzing difference; they interrupted the discourses of feminism in the singular to make possible feminism in the plural. When feminists dare to inter-
rupt one another in public places, the risks are very real. When their
interruption occurs in texts that are published and widely disseminated as
critique, the consequences deepen. (66)

That has happened all too often to feminist scholars such as Naomi Wolf,
Christina Hoff Sommers, and now Daphne Patia, whose new book, *Hetero-
phobia: Sexual Harassment and the Future of Feminism* also suggests that feminism has become more autocratic and exclusive in its agenda, barring heterosexual mainstream women from membership.

In many quarters, despite our best intentions, the feminist movement has
become what members hated to begin with—the establishment—that cen-
sored and silenced differing viewpoints. There must be room for debate within
feminism, or we will silence an entire generation of women, especially young
women. We will isolate them from the very thing that can give them a voice
to free them. In 1993 Naomi Wolf published the book *Fire with Fire: The New
Female Power and How It Will Change the Twenty-first Century,* which spelled
out the idea that feminist criticism and the feminist movement were squeez-
ing out or stamping out dissent. In the book, Wolf argues that the second
wave of feminism, which took hold in the sixties and seventies, is outmoded.
Wolf calls this type of feminism "victim feminism," which she says "casts
women as sexually pure and mystically nurturing, and stresses the evil done to
these 'good' women as a way to petition for their rights" (xvii). One of the
products of this brand of feminism is its insistence that dissent should not
exist. Wolf claims that among other tenets, victim feminists are "judgmental
of other women's sexuality and appearance," and their perspective "casts
women themselves as good and attacks men themselves as wrong" (137).
These codes are translated into a dress code, a sexuality code, and a thought
code. Instead, we learn that Big Sister is watching. Joan Mandle, the former
director of Colgate University's Women's Studies program and author of *Can
We Wear Our Pearls and Still Be Feminists? Memoirs of a Campus Struggle,*
blames her ousting after a successful six years as director on Colgate's fear that
she and, hence the program, was "not feminist enough" (qtd. in Patai, screen
45). If academics such as Mandle are pushed out because their views are not
radical enough, then what hope do mainstream women have of entering the
dialogue at all?

The silencing of mainstream women from the movement is dangerous
because we can inadvertently create a society in which a "Republic of Gilead"
could come into being.[14] The break between mainstream heterosexual women
and the movement has become pronounced enough to produce essays on the
topic such as the one by Celia Kitzinger and Sue Wilkinson entitled "The
Precariousness of Heterosexual Feminist Identities." In the essay, Kitzinger

and Wilkinson contend that "the qualifier 'heterosexual' is at best, an embarrassing adjunct to 'feminist'; at worst, it seems a contradiction in terms" (25). The essay details women who are afraid to admit their heterosexuality for fear of losing their jobs or their place within the movement. In short, Kitzinger and Wilkinson find that within the feminist movement there is a homo-matriarchal oppression that is just as restricting and policing as the former hetero-patriarchal oppression that women resisted.

As a professor of women's literature and feminist theory who teaches a majority of mainstream, heterosexual women, I have found the work of "traitors" such as Wolf and Sommers to be a bridge for my students, who need their views represented and validated before they are willing to cross over and make their way into the "wilderness of feminist criticism." Moreover, the women writers whom I teach such as Atwood, Erdrich, Tan, and Morrison resist the label "feminist" just like my students do. Like my students, authors such as Atwood, Erdrich, Tan and Morrison do not want to associate with a movement that pushes a separatist agenda in terms of genders. What I have found in my research on women writers and in the teaching of feminist theory is that writers such as Atwood, whose early work followed the lines of more radical feminism with female characters going it alone by the novel's end, have recently created novels whose quests are both spiritual and social and whose characters are welcomed by friendship and a community of both men and women, what I term the friendship plot.[15] In the third wave of feminism, empowerment feminism, women move from victim to victor, concentrating on the means of survival rather than on the process of victimization (Detore-Nakamura 26–32).

In my tenure at my conservative community college, I have moved from viewing myself as a victim of other people's views to a victor of my own empowerment, as an agent of change for my students and for the community as a whole. My efforts to bring diversity to our students were recognized when I received a merit pay award and then became a finalist for the Distinguished Educator for the 2001-Year. Now that I have left the community college for a tenured position at a four-year technical university, I am sure that I will face new challenges. However, I am grateful to my students at the community college who taught me the necessity of connecting feminist theory and practice in the classroom by illuminating all the warts and carbuncles of dissention and trusting them to create a clear visage with their own healing interpretations. In the final analysis, we come back to the purpose of using a feminist pedagogy in the writing classroom—to help our students become better critical thinkers and writers of the world around them. Give them contrasting voices, a tapestry of conflicting dialogues, and let them weave their own reality by pushing through the threads of thought, weaving through the various fractures, one by one, until they can see the old patterns and have the skills to create a new design upon the world.

NOTES

1. At a lecture at Daly's alma mater, The College of St. Rose in Albany, NY, Daly described the fembot as a woman who was dressed in a skirt, blouse, hose and matching colored-shoes and then added that these feminists were just pretenders. At the time, I was the only one in the audience of 700 who fit that description. I had been in charge of PR for the event designing the flyers, programs, and writing the press releases. At the end of the evening, I presented my book to Daly for her signature. She looked up at me and said in a wry tone, "What are *you* doing here?" I answered, "I'm the one in charge of PR. I got you an audience," where upon she shrugged her shoulders and signed the book, "For Joanne, Wishing you pure lust."

2. This policy has recently been changed with our new district president and we know have individual autonomy to select supplemental books for our general education courses.

3. To read about the struggle of abortion-provider and activist, Patricia Baird-Windle in this central Florida community, read her new book, *Targets of Hatred: Anti-Abortion Terrorism.*

4. See Nedra Reynold's definition of interruption in her article, "Interrupting Our Way to Agency: Feminist Cultural Studies and Composition," in which she defines it much like Deborah Tannen, as a positive, supportive overlap (60).

5. See Peggy MacIntosh's "Unpacking the Invisible Knapsack of White Privilege."

6. I consider homosexuality a natural choice as well, rather than to believe that it is learned. Although homosexuality and heterosexuality can be politicized, they should not be made to be a political choice. For me, the personal is not always political.

7. The average age of BCC's student is twenty-eight.

8. *Friendship plot* is a term coined and copyrighted in my dissertation, "From Victim to Victor: The Friendship Plot in Contemporary Women's Novels," Southern Illinois University at Carbondale, 1998.

9. Early on in my doctoral education, Dr. Ann-Janine Morey, Dr. Judy Little, Dr. Bruce Appleby, and Dr. Eugenie Gatens-Robinson fed my feminist interests. They provided me with courses and reading lists that helped to fill in the gaps that I had left in my self-directed search.

10. I actually gleaned this idea from something I had read in Elaine Pagel's books, *The Gnostic Gospels* and *Adam, Eve, and the Serpent,* which described the early Christian church's idea of drawing lots to select a different leader for each meeting, rather than ascribing authority to one person.

11. See Christopher Hayes's chart in which he compares and contrasts "male rhetoric" with "female rhetoric" in his article "Some Questions for Feminist Rhetoric."

12. See Susan Jarratt's "Feminism and Composition: The Case for Conflict" in *Contending with Words: Composition and Rhetoric in a Postmodern Age,* published by the MLA in 1991.

13. I found Gilligan's theories especially illuminating to discuss Faulkner's *Light in August* and had delivered a paper at the Twentieth Century Literature Conference in 1992 arguing that Faulkner advocated an ethnic of care in the novel. I have also found Gilligan's theories helpful in discussing Twain's sense of justice in *Huckleberry Finn.*

14. See Atwood's dystopian novel, *The Handmaid's Tale,* in which the conservative, Christian agenda and marketing executives collaborate to enslave women.

15. The term *friendship plot* and its definition is copyrighted by Joanne L. Detore-Nakamura in 1998 as written in the dissertation "From Victim to Victor: The Friendship Plot in Contemporary Women's Novels," published by Southern Illinois University at Carbondale.

WORKS CITED

Applebaum, Barbara. "On Good Authority or Is Feminist Authority an Oxymoron?" *Philosophy of Education* 1999. 25 June 2001 <*http://www.ed.uiuc.edu/EPS/PES-Yearbook/1999/applebaum_body.asp*>.

Barlowe, Jamie, and Ruth Hottell. "Feminist Theory and Practice and the Pedantic I/Eye." *Common Ground: Feminist Collaboration in the Academy.* Ed. Elizabeth G. Peck and Jo Anna Stephens Mink. Albany: State University of New York Press, 1998. 269–81.

Buechler, Steven M. *Women's Movements in the United States: Woman Suffrage, Equal Rights, and Beyond.* New Brunswick: Rutgers University Press, 1990.

Cornwell, Nancy c. "Rethinking Free Expression in the Feminist Classroom: The Problem of Hate Speech." *Feminist Teacher* 12.2 (1998) 107–18. FirstSearch. Brevard Community College Lib., Melbourne. 12 June 2001. <*http://newfirstsearch.oclc.org*>.

Daly, Mary. *Websters' First New Intergalactic Wickedary of the English Language.* Boston: Beacon, 1987.

Detore-Nakamura, Joanne L. *From Victim to Victor: The Friendship Plot in Contemporary Women's Novels.* Diss. Southern Illinois University at Carbondale, 1998.

Easley, Alexis. "Toward a Feminist Theory of Teaching Argumentative Writing." *Feminist Teacher* 11.1 (1997): 30–38. FirstSearch. Brevard Community College Lib., Melbourne. 2 February 2002. *http://newfirstsearch.oclc.org.*

Fraiberg, Allison. "Where Did the Feminist Teacher Go? Reconsidering Authority in the Multimedia Classroom." *Feminist Collections* 17.2 (1996): 1–3. FirstSearch. Brevard Community College Lib., Melbourne. 0=2 February 2002. *http://newfirstsearch.oclc.org.*

Gilligan, Carol. *In a Different Voice: Psychological Theory and Women's Development.* Cambridge: Harvard University Press, 1982.

Hayes, Christopher G. "Some Questions for Feminist Rhetoric." *Teaching English in the Two-Year College* 22.4 (December 1995): 295–302.

Kitzinger, Celia, and Sue Wilkinson. "The Precariousness of Heterosexual Feminist Identities." *Making Connections: Women's Studies, Women's Movements, Women's Lives.* Ed. Mary Kennedy, Cathy Lubelska, and Val Walsh. London: Taylor and Francis, 1993. 24–36.

Logan, Shirley Wilson. "'When and Where I Enter:' Race, Gender, and Composition Studies." *Feminism and Composition Studies.* 45–57.

Lunsford, Andrea A., and Cheryl Glenn. "Rhetorical Theory and the Teaching of Writing." *On Literacy and Its Teaching.* Ed. Gail E. Hawisher and Anna O. Soter. Albany: State University of New York Press, 1990. 174–89.

Mascia-Lees, Frances E., and Patricia Sharpe. *Taking a Stand in a Postfeminist World: Toward an Engaged Cultural Criticism.* Albany: State University of New York Press, 2000.

Patai, Daphne. "Rhetoric and Reality in Women's Studies." *Gender Issues* 19.2 (Spring 2001): 21–60. Online Version.

Reynolds, Nedra. "Interrupting Our Way to Agency: Feminist Cultural Studies and Composition." *Feminism and Composition Studies: In Other Words.* Ed. Susan C. Jarratt and Lynn Worsham. New York: MLA, 1998. 58–73.

Ritchie, Joy S. "Confronting the 'Essential' Problem: Reconnecting Feminist Theory and Pedagogy." *Journal of Advanced Composition* 10.2 (Fall 1990): 249–73.

Ropers-Huilman, Becky. "Scholarship on the Other Side: Power and Caring in Feminist Education." *NWSA Journal* 11.1 (1999): 131+. FirstSearch. Brevard Community College Lib., Melbourne. 12 June 2001. *http://newfirstsearch.oclc.org.*

Showalter, Elaine. "Feminist Criticism in the Wilderness." *The New Feminist Criticism: Essays on Women, Literature, and Theory.* Ed. Elaine Showalter. New York: Pantheon Books, 1985. 243–70.

Sommers, Christina Hoff. *Who Stole Feminism? How Women Have Betrayed Women.* New York: Simon and Schuster, 1994.

Wolf, Naomi. *Fire with Fire: The New Female Power and How It Will Change the Twenty-first Century.* New York: Random House, 1993.

Chapter Three

DIFFERENT ADMINISTRATIONS/
ADMINISTERING DIFFERENCE

A New Model for Feminist Administrative Practices in Rhetoric and Composition Studies

LAURA GRAY-ROSENDALE

FEMINISMS AND ADMINISTRATIONS

NITA, COCHAIR ONE: I think that our chief administrative role in CSW is to support women, plain and simple. It's not about feminism for me. Feminism has such negative connotations. It's not about women's studies. It's about equal treatment for everyone, that means women and men.

SALLY, COCHAIR TWO: Clearly we need to continue to revisit CSW's mission. I personally think it's a feminist mission—to value the differences of women, be they classification-based, racially or ethnically based, sexual preference-based, or something else. I disagree with you. Our connections to women's studies and feminist theory are essential to what we do. Without the connections to feminist theory and practice, CSW's mission has little intellectual direction.

MONIQUE, COCHAIR THREE: I guess I have to agree with you both a bit. I see CSW's mission as the common mission for

women. I guess I don't think men on this campus are really essential to this enterprise. It's about our treatment, our equality, and
our advancement. I feel we need more seminars that prepare
women for positions of leadership and success. If feminist theory
helps us to do that in certain situations, terrific. If not, maybe it
doesn't always have a place.

This exchange raises critical issues, though ones not easily settled: What constitute valid forms of feminist theory, practice, and administration? What ren-
ders administrative work necessarily feminist? What are the principles of such
approaches? In recent years rhetoric and composition has become increasingly
engrossed in the connections between feminist theory, feminist practice, and
our forms of administration and research. Some scholars have furnished note-
worthy tactics to investigate feminist scholarship's place within rhetoric and
composition (see Bishop; Davis; Jarratt and Worsham; Kirsch). Other
researchers have posed pointed questions about the history of women's roles
in the profession and the gendered nature of discourse about the discipline
(see Gilliam; Schell; Miller; Phelps and Emig; Enos; Gainen and Boice;
Geok-Lin Lim and Herrera-Sobek; Kramarae and Treichler; Peck and Mink;
Teske and Tetreault). Still other intellectuals have recommended additional
models for writing program administration that rely upon feminist, collaborative efforts (see Aronson and Hansen; Cambridge and McClelland; Dickson;
Gillam; Gunner; Harrington et al.; Keller et al.; Meeks; Miller). Finally, a
number of scholars functioning external to the discipline have explored new
leadership styles relevant to the work of rhetoric and composition studies that
integrate feminist principles (i.e., care and empowerment over command and
control methodologies; participatory or self-managing configurations such as
teams and task forces over traditionally structured, rigid, hierarchical frameworks) within the pragmatics of workplace situations (see Blackmore and
Kenway; Collins; Garvin and Reed; Smyth). Much of this research has significantly highlighted the troubling feminization of the discipline of rhetoric
and composition and the ways in which much of the labor, particularly at the
lower ends of the pay scale, is in fact shouldered by women. This scholarship
has profitably conversed about rhetoric and composition studies' historical
lack of institutional power and noted precisely how and why gender relationships have shaped these conditions.

    However, submitting cogent analyses concerning women's feelings of
stigma and alienation has also occasionally appeared to presuppose that the
meaning of the discipline's gendering is immutably fixed. And, while we have
oftentimes modified feminist theory to match the practices of our own discipline, we have not continuously done so in ways that also accept the crucial
challenges to feminist practice that might help inform our feminist theorizing
and our administrative labors. Likewise, in espousing particular predeter-
mined feminist stances, our conceptualization of our own victim status has at

times served to immobilize us, the feminists of our discipline, rather than to in fact call us to action (Lamb). Indeed, our rhetorical concentration on our marginalized standing may at times also effect to dispel discussions about the consequences of differences within the assorted feminist approaches we assume. As Phelps emphasizes, we must fight against this gendering and erasure of differences within feminisms. Rather than "tolerated and contained," the discipline's gendering and our roles as feminists must be "susceptible to transformation (though not a simple reversal) when its members, and particularly its women, begin to pursue their intellectual projects and enact their values with confidence and some measure of institutional support" (Phelps 290–291). Instead, we persist in needing innovative models for feminist administrative relations that do not merely acknowledge the rhetoric of feminization intrinsic to the discipline or of necessity suppose the importance of one feminist theoretical stance over another. Instead, we increasingly need methods and models that value potential plurality, differences, and divergences in their very tactics.

Likewise, rhetoric and composition specialists must travel beyond looking for those paradigms that depend on static conceptions of feminism as purity or unalloyed innocence, preferring not to lay pressure on feminisms' and feminist administrations' acceptance of consensus or enforcement of principles such as cooperation, dialogue, nonhierarchical structures, and nurturing caring. Similarly, we should defy conceptions of feminism and feminist administration that seek to excise difference at the same moments as it is advocated within our rhetoric. In point of fact, we need fresh models for feminist interactions in rhetoric and composition studies that make use of as well as deconstruct forms of hierarchical relations, division, and internal contradiction as part of their everyday, working efforts. We regularly discover that our administrative models that draw on feminist theories, despite providing the benefits of scaffolding and flattening hierarchies for power relations, still in their structures and practices uphold the dominance of certain advantaged voices over others and identifiable privileged models for writing pedagogy over others.

While many rhetoric and composition administrative standards may be at least partially intrinsically feminist, furthering possibilities of discursive power for women or utilizing feminist theory to influence how interactions within our administrations take place, we continue to have difficulties pinpointing models for feminist power relations that might aid our efforts. Despite our claims to the contrary, in their actual practices, very few models for feminist administration in rhetoric and composition are indeed predicated upon flux, instability, and difference as inherently valuable. Nor are many of these models in practice very vigilant about creating alternative structures that might eliminate the causal relationships often established between authority and hierarchical positions in favor of flexible, cooperative, self-managing work groups that still function within hierarchical structures. Instead, while we may employ a rhetoric of cooperation, supportiveness, and collaboration, finally our administrative efforts habitually rely principally upon top-down structures, sustaining one director of composition or writing program head, for instance, to whom all other members report.

This chapter expresses new conceptions for feminist practice, ones that time and again contest the very views of feminism itself. Drawing from my experiences over the years as the chair, cochair, and a member of the Commission on the Status of Women, I emphasize that this body's own contradictions around what constitutes beneficial agendas on behalf of women might function as a positive administrative model for rhetoric and composition studies. Rhetoric and composition studies administration could advantageously be redefined in ways that work against our attachments to precise theories or principles ascribed to by a particular group of people seeking very narrowly defined identities and roles. Instead, feminist praxis might newly be comprehended as possessing broader applications and functions, ones relevant to those who identify as feminists as well as those who do not, those who share and sustain mainstream ideologies about writing pedagogy that govern the discipline and those who would potentially present crucial obstacles for them.

CSW's efforts expose new feminist conceptions of power that are multifaceted and internally conflictual, relating more diverse understandings of difference than we often experience in rhetoric and composition circles (diverse allegiances across as well as within cultural, social, academic unit/institutional, racial, and ethnic boundaries). Though CSW's administrative efforts do sometimes also deploy a rhetoric of cooperation and collaboration, the precise practices of the commission, especially in its moments of fracture and conflict, more regularly than not truly bear this out and shore up these efforts. In rhetoric and composition administration we often rely upon somewhat limited, nonconflictual conceptions of feminist practice rather than encouraging their multiplicities. Likewise, while we have established the extent to which domination and empowerment are complexly intertwined with the inner workings of sexism, racism, heterosexism, and class oppression in rhetoric and composition studies, we have yet to tender substantial critiques concerning how sometimes limiting feminist conceptions of power can be themselves and how they can function in equally problematic as well as self-marginalizing ways. The commission affords new conceptions of feminist power of assistance to rhetoric and composition studies because they disrupt hegemonic ideologies while concurrently constantly calling attention to the construction of new ones.

HISTORICIZING THE COMMISSION

Their struggle for acceptance, opportunity, and success has been limited by a number of factors. Chief among these are the slow pace of society as a whole to recognize the merits of women in their new roles; the hostility of some people and their reluctance to open the doors any wider to women whom they may see as a threat to their dominance; the insidious effects of habit, attitude, and bias; and the difficulties of redefining the traditional roles of women and men within the family as they affect employment. ("Reaching the Vision: Women in Arizona's Universities in the Year 2000," 7)

In 1989 the three Arizona State universities formed the Commission on the Status of Women to make certain that "full participation of women is supported and contributions of women are valued." Mandated by the Arizona Board of Regents (ABOR), for over twelve years the commission has worked on matters of equity (gender equity, retention, salary equity, and recognition), career development (opportunities for professional development and advancement, evaluation of workloads, and issues of tenure and promotion across job classifications), and campus climate (family support, issues of diversity, and the creation of a safe working environment). CSW possesses one chair, a flexible group of between five and ten cochairs to whom the chair reports as well as who report to the chair, approximately forty or more commissioners who are accountable to these people and to whom these people account, and wide groups of campus advocates. The commissions have traditionally tackled issues of gender balance, endeavoring to counteract the problems of the glass ceiling, parental leave, lack of partner hiring, accommodating work schedules, promotion and tenure issues, and stopping of the tenure clock due to family and other life issues. CSW accomplishes this through the tireless efforts of smaller working groups, integrating women from all classifications across the university, dedicated to tackling these issues. In order to make this vision a reality, each campus has fashioned goals and working communities that would give support to the commission in reaching those ends.

Over the years the commission has been instrumental in women's accomplishments, generating a policy and implementation plan for partner accommodation; a safe working and learning environment statement (complete with codes concerning sexual harassment and assault); stress workshops for employees in all classifications, new diversity policies for the curriculum, students, and staff on campus; and affordable childcare and eldercare plans to reduce stress on female employees. This truly synergistic relationship between individuals, in spite of the external hierarchies and internal problems that constitute the group, is based on relatively horizontal methods for distributing information, group support of familial and other relationship concerns, and an interweaving of ideas as well as relationships to arrive at various products. For instance, over the past ten years we have worked together to produce these services for women in the campus community: twenty-four-hour access to protocols for reporting complaints of discrimination and violence, annual assessment of outdoor night safety, training for supervisors on prevention and resolution of repetitive strain complaints, flexible work and family leave policies for all full-time and part-time employees and students, strategies for hiring a diverse workforce, policies to bolster retention rates for all female employees, policies to sustain part-time employees, sexual assault protocols for the campus community, and many others. As Charles D. Garvin and Beth Glover Reed maintain in their essay "Feminist Administration: Style, Structure, Purpose," this kind of organization seeks to "create a climate in which differences can be expressed and lead to unity rather than separation" (81). As such, the bulk of the organization's authority rests with the collectivity, there is a fairly equitable division of labor, responsibilities are consistently shared and rotated, decision making is arrived at by all members, and the importance of specialized training and degrees is somewhat minimized (Kravetz and Jones).

FEMINISMS IN CONTESTATION: FOUNDATIONS FOR COLLECTIVE STRUGGLE

The Commission on the Status of Women is composed of women from across the university, including classified staff, administrators, service professionals, students, and faculty, all of whom have radically diverse daily experiences and work in a range of contexts. Much like our faculty, part-timers, and graduate students in rhetoric and composition who often transport contestatory beliefs, backgrounds, and ideologies to composition teaching, CSW members inhabit divergent spaces. While many administrative structures profess feminist interests, they may only pay lip service to incorporating differences and actually endeavor to marginalize conflict. However, CSW perceives internal contestations and differences to be decisive in accomplishing the goals of the larger administrative body. CSW members regularly debate the significance of childcare and eldercare, the consequence of the extension of medical benefits to partners, how a term such as *civility* can obscure the power of men over women, and even the commission's appropriate mission on the campus. Rhetoric and composition administrative structures can fall into the trap of sustaining difference at the level of language but renouncing it at the level of practice. We often rely on an enforced common curriculum, the perpetuation of ideological belief systems about writing that do little to question each other, and managerial structures designed to undermine and quell any semblances of conflict.

Unlike many rhetoric and composition administrative structures, members of CSW work primarily within and across differences. For instance, several years ago the Safe Working and Learning Environment policy was discussed by a group of twenty CSW members. Not only were there major differences aired about the items that appeared there, but also the actual words and phrasings were debated. What rhetorical choices should we make in order to address discrimination, harassment, sexual assault, and retaliation? Why? As Penny Weiss proposes in her book *Conversations with Feminism,* administrative inquiry on behalf of women's rights and roles can only occur productively within a context that permits such disagreements and where such contestations are made central to our exchanges. The application of feminist philosophy and theory utilizing the language of empowerment is simply not enough to make organizational structures truly empowering for those who partake in them. Our practices must also bear this out. Such administrative inquiry should likewise make room for interrogation of the hegemonic structures that our practices themselves initiate.

We see such differences in rhetoric and composition administration as well. For instance, we perceive divergences in graduate students', part-timers', and adjuncts' backgrounds who go through our teacher training programs. These differences may involve cultural, racial, ethnic, class, or gender backgrounds. Some people may arrive from upper-class backgrounds and may have more familiarity with how academic discourse might be taught. Other people may not. These comprise differences in interest and exposure to philosophies about writing. Likewise, matters of cultural background influence CSW's daily workings. Some women are also from traditionally privileged cultural groups. They are white, middle to upper class, or heterosexual, while other women are minorities, come from lower-class circumstances, or are self-identified lesbians. This can lead to critical deliberations about how identity and background mold how we do what we do. Furthermore, the women of CSW retain very different levels of interest in and exposure to feminism. Some women in the organization judge that the commission and its efforts are a feminist enterprise with political consequences. They study feminist theory and gender studies literature regularly and incorporate feminist perspectives into their teaching, research, service, and daily activities. Other women in the organization do not peruse feminist theory but are very thoughtful practitioners of feminist praxis for NOW, AAUW, or other organizations. As Elizabeth Grosz articulates, such feminist activists put significant pressure on feminist theorists to avoid playing "male power games" as well as "participating in and contributing to the very forms of dominance feminism should be trying to combat" (46). They can also act to dispute the structures of authorization in which theory is implicated, revealing the fact that difference does not exist as an "undifferentiated category." As Sara Ahmed affirms, such feminist activists also frequently propose that feminist practices are always already theoretical and therefore cannot be usefully separated since "feminism has always posed theoretical and critical challenges in *its very practicable demands*" (16). Still other members of the commission do not identify the projects of the commission with feminist theory or feminism in any way.

On the surface this last group in CSW seems not to be engaging the work of the larger organization. As Nita, the first cochair in the debate that opens this chapter conveys, feminism has a rhetorical valence that she supposes may destabilize the actual feminist agenda of CSW. Much like our graduate students from literary studies, anthropology, or history who may not distinguish the immediate value of rhetoric and composition studies and theoretical work, they seem not to be occupied in producing critical discourses for the discipline. In the case of both CSW and rhetoric and composition administration, however, these members serve to critically confront what Grosz recommends can be feminist theorists' and practitioners' potential "self-interest, of developing a 'biased' approach, in which pre-given commitments are simply confirmed rather than objectively demonstrated" (46). In the same way that those members of rhetoric and composition organizations who disagree with the tenets of our administrative structures put crucial pressure on us to scrutinize them more directly, such CSW members constantly help other members to reevaluate the methods of the group. Though these members do not depict themselves as feminists, in their practices they can perhaps be just as much if not more feminist than those who readily adopt the identity. They strive to meet one specific goal: the struggle for equality for all people. As a result, within one organization there are many identities taken up, ones that revere a feminism of difference (poststructuralist feminist approaches), ones that foreground a feminism of equality (liberal feminist approaches), ones that depend upon woman-centered agendas (radical and cultural feminist approaches) that subvert the conventions of feminist thinking but abide by some of its main tenets, and ones that deny feminism's role in their activities but still strive to meet many of its goals. The same is the case with graduate students in rhetoric and composition programs or faculty outside the discipline who may hold positions that appear to contradict the value of dominant ideologies in the discipline. These differences, be they in an organization such as CSW or a rhetoric and composition administrative organization, have the potential to make curricula and administrative structures themselves much stronger.

Community identity for women in CSW functions, much like Harriet Malinowitz advises, as a basis for community formation and liberatory social change. At the same time, such a community structure inevitably causes tensions, deconstructing itself from within as a "wistful fiction" (14). CSW's structure provides a valuable model for rhetoric and composition administration, challenging our attempts to rely on utopian conceptions of community while dismantling and erasing differences. Of course, if approaches become preset and prescriptive, these tensions might lead to bitter entrenchment, and dialogue would cease to be possible. We have seen this happen historically in many feminist circles from the most conservative to the most radical. CSW members, however, try to resist this, instead furnishing critical questions for their fellow members. Those who embrace a feminism of difference, a typically theoretically invested position, as well as those who take up a feminism of equality can at times feel that those who take up a prowomanist position depend upon concerns of biology too much, sustaining visions of women as nurturing, empathetic, supportive, and noncompetitive that have been oppressive to women historically. In their daily interactions they confront the prowomanists to consider how language constructs their identities and realities.

Though there are certainly contradictions within such groups, feminists of difference have contested both feminists of equality and prowomanists by advocating that we have to resist these universalizations about women's situations, look at the differences within individuals' plights, and reconfigure the concept of 'difference' in ways that are empowering for women who embody such differences. In all CSW meetings, matters of difference based on ethnicity, race, sexual preference, age, and class are raised on a regular basis and debated: How do each of these concerns get adequately addressed? How can we work together to achieve our objectives? This can sometimes lead to heated deliberations in which CSW members recommend the viability of one key term over another and then others dispute their single-focus allegiances. It is not unusual for members to come to a meeting initially with one perspective and have it altered by the meeting's end because of others' input. Likewise, we have viewed feminists of equality questioning the theory-heavy focus of the feminists of difference perspective over and against practice. They query, "How can this help us to adopt productive policies for women on campus?" At the same time they have contested the woman-centered perspective because it fails to adequately foreground women's *equal* intelligence, ability, and social value. They wonder, "What part can men play in CSW's efforts?" Finally, woman-centered feminists have disputed the positions held by feminists of difference for the same reasons as feminists of equality: Feminists of difference emerge as too theoretical and too combative in their tactics. Meanwhile, feminists of equality may be of the opinion that prowomanists too often claim to speak for all women, discounting the experiences of women who do not equate themselves with "feminists."

In rhetoric and composition administration, graduate students, part-timers, and faculty will also embrace radically different political positions and identities with regard to what constitutes valid writing theory as well as proper writing practices, such that bridging the gulf often hardly seems possible. Rhetoric and composition administrations are notorious for eruptions between Graduate Teaching Assistants (GTAs) and directors, part-timers and GTAs, as well as GTAs and GTAs. When difference is only perceived to be valuable *in theory* and not in practice, we witness inevitable clamp-downs in approach, silencing, and scapegoating. Productive dialogue ceases to be a viable avenue. In assuming feminist practice for rhetoric and composition administration, then, we might see the internal differences of CSW and the problems they pose as a constructive model.

While such stark contrasts in political perspectives, particularly with regard to feminism, differences in classification, and sociocultural groupings have and do lead to new hegemonic configurations being formed within the group in CSW, these develop into the foundation of projects and proposals on which CSW works as a community. For instance, when it became unmistakable that retaining female staff was a considerable problem on the campus, CSW members formed a group to recommend possibilities for partner accommodation. When it became clear that women in facilities' management were repeatedly besieged by instances of sexual harassment, CSW members strived for years to execute a policy for a safe working environment that was put into operation at a universitywide level. When it became transparent that a former president of our institution may not have apprehended the ways in which gender inequities still survived on campus, CSW members endeavored to educate him, raising their concerns and their voices.

However, new hegemonic structures in CSW can and do produce problems. At moments, for instance, caste systems in CSW certainly can get reinforced as faculty members inadvertently push to be heard over and against staff and service professionals. Such is frequently the case with rhetoric and composition administrations as well. The faculty members sometimes have greater influence than the part-timers or graduate students in certain contexts. However, since the women involved in CSW share a number of crucial traits, most critical among them a willingness to embrace such differences as inherent goods, new hegemonic structures that maneuver in feminist guises are regularly called into question and at times dissolved. For instance, when members of the diversity group recommended that diversity is comprised not only of racial and ethnic difference but class-based, sexual preference-based, and internationally based difference, critical debates ensued about what constitutes diversity. These traits have, for the most part, enabled a politics based upon working against joint oppression that permits solidarity to flourish rather than demanding a direct correspondence between identities or interests. Such might be the case with a rhetoric and composition administrative hierarchy that recognized both its institutional marginality and its centrality as a place from which to articulate radical change, acknowledging the very different interests of various players in the administration to be inherently valuable and incorporating such differences into the administrative structure itself.

Crucial common ground does subsist between CSW members, and in part because this ground is constantly reinforced, it is upon this surface and its fractures that collective struggle takes place. First, most of the commission members have families and/or partners. As a group, all commission members continue to be concerned about how their work lives and home lives can complement each other rather than inhibit each other. They are troubled about how their roles as women in the world constrain them to craft split identities between work selves and home selves, and they are troubled about this for all workers in the university environment. In recent years this shared set of goals has led members from many backgrounds, classifications, and political perspectives to join together to research the issues of child care and elder care in the university community and how these affect women, the complexities of diversity issues for women on campus, how matters of sexual harassment and assault impinge on female students as well as employees on campus, stress in the workplace for every job classification, and the like. Similarly, for rhetoric and composition studies administration, finding mutual points of interest among faculty, part-timers, and students becomes vital. How are their identities comparable? What split identities do they all occupy and how? How might these shared concerns enable them to work together on behalf of change?

Second, all of the women involved in the commission are female workers at Northern Arizona University, and they deal with many of the same administrative and institutional obstacles of working within this institution. Many of them endure demanding coworkers, long hours, belligerent or uncooperative bosses, lack of support in the workplace, failure of attention to diversity issues, and harassment in various forms. Members of the commission find common ground in conferring on such difficulties as well as working together to highlight and improve these problems for other administrative bodies like ABOR. Similarly, encouraging all members of the rhetoric and composition administrative body to get together on a regular basis to confer about common working conditions, in ways that underscore concerns of differential treatment and the intricacies of power relations, may lead to fundamental advances.

Third, all of the women on the commission deem that equity for women comes about in small steps, and while there may be momentary resolutions and moments of closure, the work is ongoing and recursive. All members impart a collective vision for women's betterment. Despite differences in philosophy, background, or approach, contributors trust that being involved in developing policy on behalf of women will help them to establish a university environment that will give important assistance to female workers. The willingness of rhetoric and composition administrators and participants to work gradually toward shifting approaches so as to appreciate difference more fully could be crucial as well. Such practices, based on the positive potentialities for and the differences within feminist practices, might lead to new management and administrative structures, new conceptions for erecting curricula, and critical innovations for teaching.

ALTERNATIVE FEMINIST CONCEPTIONS OF POWER: CSW'S WORKING GROUPS

In particular, the feminist conceptions of power utilized by the commission's working groups proffer new potentials for redefining feminist administration for rhetoric and composition studies. Such views of power are frequently complicated and confront conventional ideas about feminism and feminist relations of power that permeate rhetoric and composition's own discourses. They also put pressure on woman-centered arguments alone, opening up new possibilities for challenging the plights of feminization endemic to our discipline. Such viewpoints afford ways to formulate feminist administrations that appreciate women who self-identify as feminists and those who do not, encourage ones who perceive their roles as political activists and ones who see their roles as largely serving ABOR's dictates, precepts that happen to support women's rights. In doing so, these perspectives give rise to some key notions for feminist administrations in rhetoric and composition involving diverse administrative configurations that utilize feminist thinking while also being critical of its potential problems.

The Commission's efforts in working groups disclose that any feminist conception of power must be complex and internally conflictual, involving differences (dissimilar allegiances across cultural, social, academic unit/institutional, racial, and ethnic boundaries) as well as commonalties (shared general visions for directions and goals). As Louise Wetherbee Phelps advocates, such ideologies should never completely predate their own practices. Instead, they should be recognized as the "continually composed, collective product" of those involved (300). Rather than being negative attributes in CSW, internal conflicts and differences as well as constantly transforming frameworks, particularly those between feminist philosophies and agendas, have been essential to realizing the goals of the larger administrating body. Such collective organizing at the micro and macro levels can be decisively important to aiding rhetoric and composition administrative efforts. Despite differences, then, in fact *because of* differences, collective goals for curricula and programs can be accomplished.

For CSW what this has meant in practice could likely be threatening to some who hold feminist perspectives and who accomplish feminist administrative work in rhetoric and composition. In the commission's practices this may entail groups both working for women's issues and working against conventional feminist aphorisms about what equity means, groups both sympathetic to the critical nature of a "nurturing" leadership style and willing to critique them, and groups both conceptualizing the value of nonhierarchical or nonlinear thinking and championing the consequences of more traditional forms of argumentation within certain contexts. Feminist conceptions of power relations within CSW take into consideration the multiple functions of power. Within rhetoric and composition administrative efforts we have often seen power operating in relatively simplistic ways, as top-down, bottom-up, or synergisticly—as alternately productive or detrimental. CSW's structure imparts a model that perhaps widens our possibilities. The commission's members have worked to generate a context that distinguishes the multiple operations of power, sometimes in spite of themselves, perceiving that power is always partially coercive "whether it works overtly, through rules and rulers, hegemonically, through structures tacitly assimilated, or interactionally, through rhetorical forces" (Phelps 328).

The CSW working groups expose that power is continuously at work, and it is always operating in multiple ways, from multiple directions, and with multiple purposes and motivations. As Amy Allen indicates, power can perform as "power over" and can "constrain the choices available" to a person in a "nontrivial way" (123). It can also furnish "power to" or may evidence the "capacity of an agent to act in spite of or in response to the power wielded over her by others" (125). It can also encompass "power with," or the notion that power functions as a "collective ability that results from the receptivity and reciprocity that characterize the relations among individual members of a collectivity" (126). The commission members have been occupied with all three sorts of power relations. Rhetoric and composition administrative efforts can benefit a great deal from such a model in which power is not seen as necessarily an evil but that which is at all times already there and at work, conceding that hierarchies are to some degree inevitable. Instead, CSW unreservedly maintains that we should, where necessary, rework them and utilize them effectively to meet our goals.

Within the commission, much like administrative bodies in rhetoric and composition studies, occasionally internal silencing arises. This is an honest byproduct of distinctive personalities, desires, and even hierarchies within the group. Feeling the freedom to convey this, no matter how thorny, has fashioned a strong community. This has transpired between chairs and members, graduate students and cochairs, and members with other members. Cochairs have over time broached topics of racism and classism within CSW, and crucial debates have ensued. Classified staff members have repeatedly requested for faculty to set aside their issues for salary equity to labor on behalf of stress in the workplace issues that are impacting classified staff and service professionals. Student members have consistently petitioned for a greater voice in the commission and spread the news about the commission's efforts throughout the student population. Likewise, frequently members have assisted each other to gain agency and acted as advocates for other members who fear speaking. When members have acknowledged matters of discrimination, harassment, or civility that are negatively impacting other women on campus, they take part in small groups. Finally, at vital junctures members have stood together as an assembly, united around a policy decision linking women. Members have straightforwardly confronted the president and the Board of Regents in open fora when they have felt improperly treated, have not had their complaints satisfactorily understood, or have sensed that women on campus were not receiving sufficient support. In so doing, CSW demonstrates the force of a large body of members with a great deal of administrative power behind them. Such power is exercised self-reflectively, and people dispute each other where and when they feel it is not exercised equitably or efficiently. This view of feminist power relations has merit for rhetoric and composition studies: We have habitually resorted to models based on theories of bottom-up structures or flattened hierarchies that inevitably from time to time reproduce the very hierarchical relations they initially sought to avoid. Rather, we need to perceive hierarchy as operating in multiple sites and in multiple ways, while always open to disruption and debate.

Next, in their practices the CSW working groups disclose that any feminist conception of power must admit the extent to which domination and empowerment are complexly intertwined with the inner workings of sexism, racism, heterosexism, and class oppression and occur within feminist organizations as well. As bell hooks specifies, in working against dehumanization and alienation, we need to dispute how colonization operates at home. We can undertake this oftentimes through the development of a critical consciousness that enables otherwise colonized peoples to spread the "insurrection of subjugated knowledges" (8). At the large CSW meetings various members have drawn attention to heterosexism at work in how CSW conducts its goals and objectives, calling for lesbian voices to be heard and incorporated more fully. Members of color have recruited more women of color, and our diversity group has reached out to others on campus, incorporating issues of sexual preference and international identity more completely into its conceptions of difference. Feminist perceptions of power at work in the administrative efforts of rhetoric and composition must therefore be acquainted with multiple identities and selves as well as contradictions within selves across what Gloria Anzaldua refers to as mutually exclusive, sometimes discontinuous and inconsistent worlds. We should scrutinize those moments when our administrative efforts are not as successful as we might hope, seeking to open and expand differences of opinion rather than silencing them. In this vein, CSW's practices recommend that feminist structures and practices can have a wide range of outcomes, both positive and negative, and should always be open to reinterpretation.

Such understandings of power relations must also grant that marginality itself can be rhetorically authorized in troubling ways that recuperate its political potentials. In arguing on behalf of women's requests, CSW has sought to have a resounding voice in other areas across campus—including women's studies, business, human resources, and faculty senate. CSW works diligently to utilize language that does not construct the organization in terms of its ghettoized status but rather its very centrality to the administrative workings of the institution. All of the documents produced by CSW cautiously walk this line. In contrast, at such moments, clinging to our own "feminization" within administrative efforts in rhetoric and composition studies can be frought with problems, perhaps resulting in self-silencing and collusion with our own oppression. Likewise, we can problematically implement feminist theory as a method for our administrative work without letting our practices critically inform and reform this theory. Similarly, if we construct rhetoric and composition's disciplinary and administrative identity as one of marginality, we do not take advantage of the true complexity of our positions—our growing, powerful intellectual and disciplinary status and yet our often adjunct, practice-oriented history. Working-group members in the commission frequently try to fight against how administrations and institutions manage difference and force marginality, or as Trihn Minh-ha asserts, render it "supervised, hence recuperated, neutralized, and depoliticized" ("Acoustic Journey" 8).

While the commission holds the promise of operating as just one more space in which women's voices are sanctioned and then are subtly repressed or further marginalized, its members work hard against this. They often acknowledge their own differences within the group as well as the contradictions within their own positions, denying the easy containment of their voices. They make recurring presentations to ABOR and other university units about gender-based salary discrimination and the need for equity across the university's classifications, diversity issues, and childcare options. In foregrounding differences and conflicts as instances of learning and empowerment, CSW members propose the value of utilizing a feminist praxis that questions the very tenets of feminism itself for rhetoric and composition administration.

Additionally, feminist conceptions of power should be understood as rhetorical in nature: They must recognize the extent to which feminism can and does contest the linguistic systems, structures, and institutions that patriarchal discourse manufactures. In addition, feminist conceptions of power must account for the fact that feminist tactics can also participate within those structures in problematic, self-marginalizing ways. Just because CSW is a partially feminist organization, this does not mean that it does not work against its own objectives at moments. Women can treat each other in unsupportive ways, collude with male bosses to acquire what they want rather than supporting other women—all ostensibly in the name of feminist praxis. Thus CSW members tend to take nothing for granted, asking judiciously about the goals sought and rhetorical choices utilized to accomplish them.

Oftentimes administrative efforts in rhetoric and composition informed by feminist theory have failed to acknowledge this potentiality—how backlash does not always emerge from the enemy outside our walls, but from among ourselves. As the commission's own praxis seems to intimate, feminisms can never function as fixed states or entities. Instead they should be understood to behave as constant processes such that feminist practices themselves can and should challenge and confront terminologies and category systems, including those that have been historically their own.

The fact that many commission members are dubious about feminist theories, unless they have practical consequences, helps to make those members who name themselves "feminists" more thoughtful about their own applications of theory. All members come to comprehend the ways in which feminism can and has itself become a discourse that silences. For a discipline such as rhetoric and composition that has been so concerned about its own silencing and marginalization, such a recognition of the complexities of our rhetorical situations, how we participate in our own silencing, and the debilitating aspects that emanate from unproblematic and uncritical adoptions of feminist discourse is indeed critical.

Last, feminist conceptions of power then, as deployed by members of the commission, should be recognized as those that act to disrupt hegemonic ideologies and circumvent closure in favor of continuity. In a feminist conception of power relations, the praxis of the commission as a body reveals the need to distinguish how power relations operate among and between individuals, within particular contexts or situations, and in social relationships to one another. This can entail an examination of subject positions, cultural meanings, social practices, and structures. For rhetoric and composition studies this indicates that members of an administrative body need to have space for such transgressive efforts. An administration based on feminist practices is not something that is prefabricated and that members simply join. It is something that is assembled collectively by a group of people through conflict, struggle, debate, and contestation. As a result, these aspects are central to its survival and its ability to flourish.

Feminist conceptions of power, as exposed by CSW's daily operations, must invoke a dialogue in which people who retain different positions of power can talk through and across differences to understand each other. Feminist power structures must comprise a recognition of what Trihn terms the "other" in the "self" or that we can at times structure and reinforce our own oppression. How does CSW reveal this? The multiple identities represented by the CSW members divulge diversities in perspectives but also the notion that if we do not appreciate and prepare for the effects of these differences, we may weaken our abilities to reach our shared goals. For rhetoric and composition scholars this may mean assuming identities and positions that feel profoundly "unfeminist" or having difficult conversations with what we normally conceive of as our opposition or enemy. However, this should not be comprehended as something outside feminist administrative praxis but rather as that which is central to it. As Trihn establishes, difference should not be regarded as an "irreducible quality but as a drifting apart" that does not "nullify one's identity but is beyond and alongside identity" (*Woman, Native, Other* 104).

This indicates that if women in CSW only converse with each other, they cannot address the larger institutional forces responsible historically for their oppression. It also denotes that if rhetoric and composition administrators discern feminist praxis as merely necessary to their engagements with their own organizational members, this work will not be as groundbreaking as it could potentially be. Likewise, unless rhetoric and composition administrators solicit input from those not yet converted to the values of dominant writing pedagogies, our work will not be as productive as it could otherwise. Instead, members of the commission can and do interact with many larger institutional bodies and people in order to make their political needs known. They also seek to sometimes unhinge rhetorics of oppositionality that do not account for internal contradictions within positions. Members of the commission constantly put pressure upon each other to be responsible for their own assumptions and often disagree with each other about useful tactics and approaches. They also tend to act with each other so as to circumvent taking up positions of "victim" in rhetorically disabling ways. Again, given the history of what Susan Miller aptly terms the "women in the basement" within rhetoric and composition studies, we need models for feminist administration that work against such easily adopted rhetorical positions.

While the commission by no means perfectly manifests all of these tenets for a feminist praxis for power relations all of the time, it unquestionably functions to approximate them. This alone is unusual in administrative organizations, especially one that answers to a legislative body with a great deal of control over itself as well as the financial standing of the larger university institutions. In doing so, the commission remains a constructive model for women operating to help each other and themselves as well as for all rhetoric and composition's administrative efforts. Encouraging women's participation in their own lives and making their experiences more fulfilling and rewarding, in CSW they are able to engage fully in their own empowerment, giving them critical agency within an institutional body that otherwise may not present them a voice from which to critique that body. Women take part in critical studies, lively debate and disagreement, policy making, as well as restructuring how administration can work to help women and, as a result, all workers. This is the kind of web of power relations we should seek to cultivate in rhetoric and composition's administrative efforts as well.

In this sense, women in the commission can behave as what Trinh calls "displacers," or those who question "over and over again what is taken for granted as self-evident . . . disturbing thereby one's own thinking habits, dissipating what has become familiar and cliched, and participating in the changing of received values" (*Moon* 21). In such a context, feminist practices become organizational habits that truly destabilize closure, value the presentation of multiple views, and contest that any one set of theories can account for the multiple perspectives women bring to bear upon the issues discussed. As Trinh advocates, even feminism can function as an ideology, forcing rigid, categorical, and stabilizing influences (Foss, Foss, and Griffin 248). In her book *Constituting Feminist Subjects*, Kathi Weeks invites us to push beyond collectivities that result in little more than a "consensual aggregation of individuals" who simply embrace liberal individualism. Weeks affirms that instead we must find "possible ways of regarding collectivities not only as determined subject positions but also as active subjects . . . relatively autonomous agents capable of social change" (159).

In its very practices CSW has embraced this vision even if its practices are understandably now and then recuperated by larger social forces. We have witnessed this in recent ABOR decisions to elect not to include partners in same sex marriages as having the right to the same benefits as heterosexual partnerships, reversing a 1990 decision. We have observed this in our struggles to gain greater funding for our own efforts, despite more money allocated at the other two state institutions. We have viewed this in endeavors by the upper administration to direct our efforts in very specific, somewhat limiting ways toward the hot topics of the day such as diversity and civility. And these are the battles we will continue to fight. In so doing, the women of CSW aim to reformulate the strictures and constraints placed upon what feminism might mean, how it could work, and expand feminism's possibilities to comprise all women, not just an exclusive group of believers. To do so is to confront feminism's early historical propensity toward the construction of a unitary subject, its yearning for universality and homogeneity in favor of destabilizing what Trihn characterizes as the "established limits" of categorical thought (*Moon* 120). These women then espouse a framework that concedes the differences within the "self," crafting a community that depends upon and values their differences.

In doing so, the commission elaborates a useful model for administrative efforts in rhetoric and composition as well as a significant revision of the contemporary feminist thought that drives many of our disciplinary identities and scholarly efforts. While many rhetoric and composition programs have considered shifting the traditional administrative models driving them, sometimes creating joint appointments, team directorships, and more inclusive committee structures, if we look to CSW as a model, quite clearly we could do more. We need to explore the many possibilities that joint direction of rhetoric and composition programs affords. Rather than setting up one person as "in charge" of the efforts of the program, perhaps, as others have argued, a co-chairship with one person in charge of daily operations while many others co-direct is a more valuable, inclusive approach. This would shift the hierarchical relationships and reformulate how ideas are produced as well as how we talk about their production, the ways in which they come to dominate the landscape of rhetoric and composition studies, and how they are comprehended as knowledge. This might open our administrations to the practical merits of differences. If we take up such options, however, we should anticipate more debate, more openness and resistance to resolutions, and more questions about who does what and why.

While such debate may not please some administrators who are striving for neat, clean answers, our scholarship and practices may develop in crucial new ways yet unanticipated. Likewise, within rhetoric and composition pro-grams we need to persist in exploring the creation of smaller working groups to work collectively in ways that not only report to the chair and cochairs, but continually reform those positions and jobs as well. Conversations should not be simply occurring in a top-down structure such that syllabi, curricular deci-sions, and hiring choices are made by one or even a cochair group and fun-neled down to many. Instead, conversations should be stirring in multiple sites so as to both support and challenge the curricular structures set in place.

In doing so, perhaps we should not be so afraid to welcome those who do not share our perspectives into our discussions, ones we hold privately as well as publicly. This may mean engaging dialogue with faculty from traditional literature backgrounds, for example, who may frown upon contemporary rhetorical and composition theory. It may entail regularly inviting faculty from across disciplines who are dismayed at their students' writing skills and hold the rhetoric and composition administration responsible. We should also reg-ularly engage input on rhetoric and composition program issues from those outside English studies entirely. In their very different approaches, these "out-siders" force us to revisit our assumptions and presuppositions, often putting constructive pressure on matters we fail to question with any persistence. They also aid us in realizing our similar goals, to build bridges based on mutual interests as well as differences, the improvement of students' critical think-ing/writing skills.

Finally, we would do well to include more peer mentorship programs in rhetoric and composition programs at every level. In CSW peer mentorship has transpired with classified staff in a variety of ways, providing job advice, interview suggestions, and professional development seminars and job retrain-ing. CSW mentorship has also occurred with new faculty gaining support from veterans and service professionals gaining support from those in their units and outside, working across structural demarcations to find ways to manage difficult working situations. Students have located other students in CSW to furnish support but have also built mentorship networks with faculty, classified staff, and service professionals. While we often find more senior graduate students and faculty paired with newer faculty and graduate students in rhetoric and composition programs, peer mentorship that involves reci-procity and horizontal power relationships holds critical potentials as well. We should also seek out mentorship partnerships that expose the participants to a diverse range of ideas and possibilities rather than those who simply reaffirm our ideologies and belief systems.

When we begin to stretch our vision beyond our own models for femi-nist administrations in rhetoric and composition, we can start to pose crucial questions such as the following: Why do we structure our programs in the ways we do? What kinds of power relationships do we aim to set up with our faculty peers, including part-timers, adjuncts, and graduate students? Is our

assumption of only a few conceptions for feminist administration, ones relying on "correct" conceptions of what it means to be a feminist, indeed con-
straining our vision and the possibilities for feminism in our scholarly efforts
as well as our practices? Doing so can reposition us beyond a rhetoric of feminization, one that can be both empowering and debilitating, and towards a
rhetoric firmly based on the valuation of differences. Increasingly we need to
look to other administrative models, models that truly value difference, even
if they sometimes seem threatening to our own identities or to the identities
constructed for us within the discipline of rhetoric and composition studies.
As the three cochairs, Nita, Sally, and Monique exemplify, CSW proffers one
such possibility, one that may enable us to think outside the categories, even
the feminist categories that have traditionally constrained us.

WORKS CITED

Ahmed, Sara. *Differences That Matter: Feminist Theory and Postmodernism.* Cambridge:
Cambridge University Press,1998.

Allen, Amy. *The Power of Feminist Theory: Domination, Resistance, Solidarity.* Boulder:
Westview, 1999.

Anzaldua, Gloria. *Borderlands/LaFrontera: The New Mestiza.* San Francisco: Aunt
Lute, 1987.

Aronson, Anne, and Craig Hansen. "Doubling Our Chances: Co-Directing a Writing
Program." *WPA: Writing Program Administration* 21.2/3 (1998): 23–32.

Bishop, Wendy. *Teaching Lives: Essays and Stories.* Logan: Utah State University Press,
1997.

Blackmore, Jill, and Jane Kenway, eds. *Gender Matters in Educational Administration
and Policy: A Feminist Introduction.* London: Falmer, 1993.

Cambridge, Barbara, and Ben W. McClelland. "From Icon to Partner: Repositioning
the Writing Program Administrator." *Resituating Writing.* Ed. Joseph Jonangelo
and Kristine Hanson. Portsmouth: Boynton/Cook Heinemann, 1995. 151–60.

Collins, Patricia Hill. "Gender and Sexuality in Organizations." *Revisioning Gender.*
Ed. Myra Marx Feree, Judith Lorber, and Beth Hess. Thousand Oaks: Sage,
1999. 261–84.

Commission on the Status of Women Newsletter. April, 2001.

Dans, Debra Diane. *Breaking Up (at) Totality: A Rhetoric of Laughter.* Carbondale:
Southern Illinois University Press, 2000.

Dickson, Marcia. "Directing without Power: Adventures in Constructing a Model of
Feminist Writing Program Administration." *Writing Ourselves into the Story:
Unheard Voices from Composition Studies.* Ed. Sheryl Fontaine and Susan Hunter.
Carbondale: Southern Illinois University Press, 1993. 140–53.

Enos, Theresa. *Gender Roles and Faculty Lives in Rhetoric and Composition.* Carbondale: Southern Illinois University Press, 1996.

Foss, Karen A., Sonja K. Foss, and Karen L. Griffin. *Feminist Rhetorical Theories.* Thousand Oaks: Sage, 1999.

Gainen, Joanne, and Robert Boice, eds. *Building a Diverse Faculty.* San Francisco: Jossey-Bass, 1993.

Garvin, Charles D., and Beth Glover Reed. "Feminist Administration: Style, Structure, Purpose." *Feminist Practice in the Twenty-first Century.* Ed. Nan Van Den Bergh. Washington, D.C.: NASW Press, 1995. 70–88.

Geok-Lin Lim, Shirley, and Maria Herrera-Sobek, eds. *Power, Race, and Gender in Academe: Strangers in the Tower?* New York: Modern Language Association, 2000.

Gillam, Alice. "Taking It Personally: Redefining the Role and Work of the WPA." *Kitchen Cooks, Plate Twirlers and Troubadours: Writing Program Administrators Tell Their Stories.* Ed. Diana George. Portsmouth: Boynton/Cook Heinemann, 1999. 65–72.

Grosz, Elizabeth. *Space, Time, and Perversion: Essays on the Politics of Bodies.* New York: Routledge, 1995.

Gunner, Jeanne. "Decentering the WPA." *WPA: Writing Program Administration* 18.1/2 (1994): 8–15.

Harrington, Susanmarie, Steve Fox, and Tere Molinder-Hogue. "Power, Partnership, and Negotiations: The Limits of Collaboration." *WPA: The Journal of the Council of Writing Program Administrators* 21.2/3 (Spring 1998): 52–64.

hooks, bell. *Yearning: Race, Gender, and Cultural Politics.* Boston: South End, 1990.

Jarratt, Susan C., and Lynn Worsham, eds. *Feminism and Composition Studies: In Other Words.* New York: Modern Language Association, 1998.

Keller, Katerhine L., Jennie Lee, Ben W. McClelland, and Brenda Robertson. "Reconstituting Authority: Four Perspectives on a Team Approach to Writing Program Administration." *The Writing Program Administrator as Theorist.* Ed. Shirley K. Rose and Irwin Weiser. Forthcoming.

Kirsch, Gesa. *Ethical Dilemmas in Feminist Research: The Politics of Location, Interpretation, and Publication.* Albany: State University of New York Press, 1999.

———. *Women Writing the Academy: Audience, Authority, and Transformation.* Foreword by John Trimbur. Carbondale: Southern Illinois University Press, 1993.

Kramarae, Cheris, and Paula Treichler. "Power Relations in the Classroom." *Gender in the Classroom: Power and Pedagogy.* Ed. Susan L. Gabriel and Isaiah Smithson. Urbana: University of Illinois Press, 1990. 41–59.

Kravetz, Diane, and Linda E. Jones. "Supporting Practice in Feminist Service Agencies." *Feminist Social Work Practice in Clinical Settings.* Ed. Mary Bricker-Jenkins, Nancy R. Hooyman, and Naomi Gottlieb. Newbury Park: Sage, 1991. 233–49.

Lamb, Sharon, ed. *New Versions of Victims: Feminists Struggle with the Concept.* New York: New York University Press, 1999.

Malinowitz, Harriet. *Textual Orientations: Lesbian and Gay Students and the Making of Discourse Communities.* Portsmouth: Heinemann, 1995.

Meeks, Lynn, and Christine Hult. "A Co-Mentoring Model of Administration." *WPA: Writing Program Administration* 21.2/3 (1998):9–22.

Miller, Hildy. "Postmasculinist Directions in Writing Program Administration." *WPA: Writing Program Administration* 20.1/2 (1996):49–61.

Miller, Susan. *Textual Carnivals: The Politics of Composition.* Carbondale: Southern Illinois University Press, 1991.

Peck, Elizabeth, and JoAnna Stephens Mink, eds. *Common Ground: Feminist Collaboration in the Academy.* Albany: State University of New York Press, 1998.

Phelps, Louise Wetherbee. "Becoming a Warrior: Lessons of the Feminist Workplace." *Feminine Principles and Women's Experience in American Composition and Rhetoric.* Ed. Louise Phelps and Janet Emig. Pittsburgh: University of Pittsburgh, 1995. 289–340.

Phelps, Louise Wetherbee, and Janet Emig, eds. *Feminine Principles and Women's Experience in American Composition and Rhetoric.* Pittsburgh: University of Pittsburgh Press, 1995.

"Reaching the Vision: Women in Arizona's Universities in the Year 2000." Summary Report of the Board of Regents' Commission on the Status of Women.

Schell, Eileen. *Gypsy Academics and Mother-Teachers: Gender, Contingent Labor, and Writing Instruction.* Portsmouth: Boynton Cook, 1997.

Smyth, John ed. *Critical Perspectives on Educational Leadership.* London: Falmer, 1989.

Teske, Robin L., and Mary Ann Tetreault, eds. *Conscious Acts and the Politics of Social Change: Feminist Approaches to Social Movements, Community, and Power.* Columbia: University of South Carolina Press, 2000.

Trihn, T. Minh-ha. "An Acoustic Journey." *Rethinking Borders.* Ed. John C. Welchman. Minneapolis: University of Minnesota Press, 1996.

———. *When the Moon Waxes Red: Representation, Gender, and Cultural Politics.* New York: Routledge, 1991.

———. *Woman, Native, Other: Writing, Postcoloniality, and Feminism.* Bloomington: Indiana University Press, 1989.

Weeks, Kathi. *Constituting Feminist Subjects.* Ithaca: Cornell University Press, 1998.

Weiss, Penny. *Conversations with Feminism: Political Theory and Practice.* Lanham, Maryland: Rowman and Littlefield, 1998.

Part Two

Fractured Feminisms in Writing across the Curriculum and Writing in the Disciplines

---

Chapter Four

WRITING ACROSS THE
CURRICULUM WITH CARE

BRADLEY PETERS

FEMINIST TOPOI

Every semester *ex post facto*, I pick up the artifacts my students have composed and enter the valley of lingering doubts, wondering how much of the course issued from calculated accident rather than theoretical forethought. Lately, I have been wondering on a wider scale. I coordinate Writing across the Curriculum and have worked with our university's Writing across the Curriculum (WAC) Advisory Board to develop ENGL 250, Practical Writing, a prototype course that could bridge writing in the major and writing in professions. The course represents a modest but firm step toward the potential transformation of our general education curriculum.

Who enrolls in ENGL 250? Education majors do, whose advisors tell them to learn more about writing before they teach history, art, math, or science in the primary and secondary schools. A few business majors also wander onto the rosters. Junior-level transfers from two-year colleges enroll, thinking (or having been told) they have grown rusty or never learned to write in the first place. Students testing out of first-year composition enroll, because they want a course that sounds, well, more *practical* than composition. As a result, each semester opens with an interesting combination of resistance and anticipation. Mixed sentiments do not prevail among the students alone. The course raises questions for teachers. What does someone write in Practical

Writing? Why? When I came to the university, only TAs and untenured instructors taught ENGL 250. Most presumed that Practical Writing related to business communications. I had to see how the course might address a broader range of cross-disciplinary exigencies.

This chapter analyzes the feminisms I brought to ENGL 250. Why feminisms? In part, I heeded Harriett Malinowitz's challenge that WAC "does not generally present itself as a force that would help a student think like a feminist" (295). Malinowitz's definition of feminist thinking sounded as if it was what students *and I* needed to do in ENGL 250. Malinowitz says feminisms encourage learning that is active and integrated, not divided by "departments," but characterized by an ongoing exchange among students and faculty; feminisms help students rethink "the prevailing logic and politics of disciplinary order," enabling us all to imagine new ways of organizing knowledge, not as biologists, economists, or health professionals, but as comprehensively educated people vis-à-vis our own cultural backgrounds and life experiences (see 293–300). Malinowitz's feminized WAC does not assume a discipline shares its goals and beliefs unilaterally, collegially, without conflicts that often stem from the diversity of its members (see 305). She grows wary of WAC's support of students in "their quest for disciplinary legitimacy," if WAC endorses traditions that not only reproduce expected "discourses, practices, and conventions employed when writing and thinking in particular disciplines" but perpetuates disciplinary biases as well (294; 292). Malinowitz suspects that WAC often discourages critical perspectives, encourages intellectual passivity, and distorts or erases the conflicting knowledges of underrepresented groups (see 305).

I wanted ENGL 250 to address these problems. I envisioned three outcomes: (1) academic writing in the natural sciences, (2) academic writing in the students' own disciplines, and (3) professional writing. To have a source for more general disciplinary formats, conventions, and contexts, I chose *The Harcourt Brace Guide to Writing across the Curriculum* (Jones, Bizzaro, and Selfe). But noting Malinowitz's warning that texts often "trivialize or obfuscate the real struggles" that characterize disciplinary discursive practices and "inherited disciplinary rituals," I also chose Michael Hawkins's *Hunting Down the Universe*. Hawkins touts a theory that much of the matter in the universe is comprised of primordial black holes. In Malinowitz's words, he critiques the "inherited disciplinary rituals" of science writing that often constrain researchers to build on traditional theories rather than seek new knowledge— a problem that made him go public with his theories. He provides a rhetorical discussion of scientific writing that challenges tradition, encouraging readers to "assess how forms of knowledge and method are hierarchically structured in disciplines so that some achieve canonical or hegemonic status whereas others are effectively fenced out" (293). To accompany this reading, the students would interview professors in our natural science departments, doing a project that compared different ways of teaching scientific writing on campus and squaring their findings with Hawkins's critique.

I felt the science-writing project would prepare students to examine their own disciplines more closely. They would look at textbooks for basic concepts, biases, controversies, and possible ellipses. They would interview professors and analyze assignments that routinely "encultured" them in disciplinary conventions. They would obtain samples of other students' writing and describe its features. They would look in course catalogs, assess syllabus websites, and compare their programs of study to programs at other institutions. As a new WAC coordinator, I had two objectives: I wanted students *and me* to have a clearer contextual understanding of *how* to write and *what* to write in their disciplines, based on what "various forms of local knowledge" the different professors at our university valued (see Malinowitz 300–01). Where would we find evidence of "dissonant voices" or "competing interests" that might show how local knowledge and writing practices were *not* unitary (305)? And how might these findings help the students?

After this project, the students would turn to the ways that disciplinary knowledges get translated into professional writing tasks and information distributed to the public. Following Malinowitz's example of how the medical community rarely includes women in disease research or health writing, I chose Beth Howard's *Mind Your Body: A Sexual Health and Wellness Guide for Women,* a readable text by a columnist and magazine editor who consulted women physicians (see Malinowitz 296). With Howard modeling health writing, the students would interview professionals in careers they anticipated entering. They would gather samples of worksite writing, analyzing both the features and the situational contexts where the samples were composed. They had to try to find out about issues of professional ethics, legal implications, employee relations, gender and ethnic inequities, public image, or other influences that might impinge on the writing tasks—in keeping with what Malinowitz says about the "serious ideological acrimony" and marginalization of groups that often shake apart workplace collegiality (300). Then students would assemble a portfolio of original writing based on the formats and contextual situations that their research identified.

Although much of the writing in ENGL 250 would be exploratory and subjective, falling under the rubric of "writing to learn," the course would lend equal mind to "writing in the disciplines" (learning the disciplinary conventions and practicing the writing structures). Malinowitz asserts that students should exercise strategic choices in such matters, "to play by the established rules or to challenge them" (309). This assertion parallels Louise Wetherbee Phelps's interpretation of an ethic of caring in writing instruction, where

the teacher is placed in the role of "one-caring" to particular, concrete students as "one-cared for." Caring is not simply a feeling, although it is affective in nature: it involves a "motivational shift" that redirects [the teacher's] motive energy (e.g., my drive to improve society, to effect reform, to reproduce myself and my own values) toward the student and invests it in his or her projects or, more precisely, in enhancing the student's ability to choose projects wisely and pursue them effectively. (49)

However, Phelps's interpretation of an ethic of caring also warned me to expect "fractured moments" when my most appropriate response to the students—or their most appropriate responses to me—might diverge from Malinowitz's ethics (to which I felt very committed). For instance, the students might want to resist cross-disciplinary projects that had "gender and class and race and other constraints to them," or they might accept those constraints, or uncritically ignore them (see Hirsch and Olson, "Marginalized Lives" 34). We might discuss strategies to contest "self-admiring, self-stimulating, self-congratulatory" individuals who would penalize students for unconventional thinking in the academy or the workplace, or we might end up discussing how to accommodate such authority (see Cixous 283). We might talk about how to blur genres in different disciplines productively, deconstructing the politics that rewarded certain forms of writing over others, or we might study how to replicate them precisely (see Malinowitz 304). The important point was to focus on how feminisms could inform the course so that we would not retreat to less fluid, less interactive, or less caring approaches.

Still, I worried about the impossibility of synthesis or even coherence as I ruminated on *topoi* I had gathered from Malinowitz and other feminisms. The assignments would translate these *topoi* into acts of feminist invention—avoiding essentialisms, recognizing situational context, caring, resisting phallocentrism, honoring truths rather than Truth, blurring genres, uncovering alternatives, experimenting. But to what extent would I explain, rather than remain silent about "the imperfect processes of [my own] thinking," to let the students glimpse my intent (see Belenky et al. 215)? How valid were my reasons for even thinking that feminisms could shape the course, given Stephen Heath's claim that men who do feminism resort to "a strategy of female impersonation"? (see Fuss 35). And what about the students? What unpredictable positions would they assume, if they trusted me and got a grip on what we were really up to? What variations on the projects would they expect me to validate or support?

The following discussion will examine where I revised the first written project, as the ethics of caring fractured the ethics of critique. Then I will assess what students gained from the two other written projects. Harding's notion of "strong objectivity" will help me evaluate how feminisms fractured when students had contradictory perspectives, felt disconnections, or doubted practical applications of the knowledge we acquired. Then I will speculate on how a course of fractured feminisms repositions students, teachers, and WAC in a large, research-oriented university.

STRATEGIC RESISTANCE

The first major assignment in ENGL 250 required the students to engage in activities that David Russell advocates most—"discourse analysis, rhetorical analysis, ethnographic accounts, cultural criticism"—and I explained in detail how these activities would help us gain "insight into the ways discourses interact to create academic knowledges" (74). The students did not object at the beginning. They saw the sense in discerning biases or conflict in something so apparently objective as scientific writing. They were open to finding relevance between science and them.

In interviewing professors of science—concurrent with our reading of Hawkins—students were surprised to discover a full range of attitudes that resonated with Hawkins's critique of traditional scientific thought. Some professors did not assign writing to undergraduates until their junior or senior years, because they felt undergraduate education was a ritual, not an enterprise in acquiring real scientific literacy. Other professors assigned writing only to test what students had learned and could recite. More fortunately, one student interviewed a professor who talked about scientific writing as an exercise in passion, an opportunity to explore, a way to learn how to care about the discipline. But that professor was a notable exception.

Although the interviews yielded many interesting and useful discoveries, the course text did not. By our fourth week in the semester, almost all the students seemed to have reached a point where they felt our work with Hawkins was a reenactment of what made them avoid the sciences in the first place. They could not penetrate the highly specialized language and abstract aims. They could not find connections between the study of the universe and their lives. Jacob, a philosophy major, articulated his classmates' discontent in his weekly email journal. He described his own struggle, compared it to classmates' complaints, conceded that he still was learning something about coping with science classes, but asked why we could not work instead with texts in a course where each student currently wanted some help.

Jacob showed me the higher ground to which I could rally the rest of us. After I read his well-reasoned, well-written protest to the class, I told the students that Jacob's suggestion coincided with a feminist thinker who advocated "the skill to reflect on ourselves as we read, and to be aware of deep-seated emotions and responses" (Nye 450). We had read Hawkins that way, I said, so now it seemed sensible to do what Jacob proposed and apply what we had learned to a text that each student felt was more immediately useful and relevant.

The students all looked slightly nonplussed. Was a professor *allowed* to throw out a course text he had chosen in favor of one that students might choose? How on earth would that work? I told them we would continue interpreting, sharing our interpretations, and articulating what authors were trying to get us to understand. Then we would critique the ways the authors went about it, just as we had critiqued Hawkins. Chantal, an African American student who was rapidly becoming the class skeptic, asked unexpectedly, "What if some of us still want to keep reading Hawkins? I've just started to understand what he's saying, and I've worked too hard to stop now." I told the class we would vote on it. Most immediately opted to work with another choice of texts. But four wanted to stay with Hawkins. One was Chantal, and one, surprisingly, was Jacob.

I told the students it made little difference if some of them stayed with Hawkins while the majority scurried elsewhere. The course had to serve their needs. So I said I was arguing from two positions, *dissoi logoi*, in support of continuing with Hawkins and in support of departing from him (the kind of sophistic pedagogy Susan Jarratt advocates as complicit with feminisms). But, I added, they must argue from two positions, too. During the next class, they would write about what they had learned from Hawkins. They would defend staying with the text as well as abandoning it. Then they would write what they personally had decided to do. They would identify the other disciplinary text with which they were going to work, if they chose that direction. They would elaborate on what they found most difficult about the text and how they figured the author was trying to influence their knowledge. They would indicate how the text fit into the course where it was assigned, they would describe some of the text's formal features, and they would define key concepts upon which the text seemed to operate. They would speculate on what the text taught them about the discipline's writing conventions. Or they would do the same with Hawkins.

The students prepared well for the in-class exercise, and I decided to make their drafted responses fit in with our first major written project. Then we continued to do more work with the texts they chose. The students mined the texts for important passages, found online and library sources that supplemented the texts, and began drafting their projects.

When a fracturing moment makes its impact on a feminist-oriented course in such a way, Elizabeth Flynn calls it an act of strategic resistance against some condition that seems unfair or unjust—"The strategic resister identifies a problem and takes action to mitigate or eliminate the problem" (22). I certainly did not expect to subject the students in ENGL 250 to such a problem, but I thought all of us might learn more if I applied the ethical test that Louise Phelps advocates. She says our decisions should be *for the sake of our students* and not for the sake of our own agenda—political or otherwise— or for the sake of a program requirement, a skill, a faculty consensus, a tradition, a text, *or even a compromise* (see 49–50).

But had I too readily let students derail my adaptation of Malinowitz's approach? No and yes. One student reported that she earned an *A* on a botany test. Her work on that course's text helped her understand the reading assignments for the first time. Others verified that the switch had gone well for them, too. Yet they gave limited evidence of carrying their critique of scientific writing over to other disciplines. Some found biases in history, but not math, educational theory, art criticism, or business. I suspected that too many students were struggling with reading comprehension to grapple with conflicting disciplinary stances as well. Just so, one student tried to demonstrate that scientific discourse was far more slanted than journalism, yet by comparing Hawkins, her interview in physics, and her journalism textbook on news writing, the student did not make an entirely improbable case.

A FEMINIST METHODOLOGICAL SCHEMA

Malinowitz and other scholars (e.g., Walvoord, Anson) say WAC is a movement, not merely a method, and Sandra Harding's science-oriented schema of feminist methodological principles might be one of the best ways to keep the movement moving in classroom life. Harding's principles assert: (1) students must conduct open discussions of their relationships to written projects; (2) students must know that the purposes of their writing projects are grounded in disciplinary principles that relate to them; (3) students must clearly discover their own agenda for doing such projects (see Kirsch 256; Harding, "Feminist Method"). Patricia Sullivan would add that students must develop an understanding of the gendered nature of most human activity (49). And Malinowitz might observe that Harding favors "identification and alliance with marginal identities and perspectives" (309).

Applying Harding's methodology helped students maintain a "strong objectivity" that characterized their more substantial learning in the other two major assignments in ENGL 250. They forged powerful links among (1) knowledge based on conflict as well as consensus, (2) knowledge based on their gendered experiences, and (3) knowledge supportive of their own priorities. WAC needs evidence of such feminist applications. Thus, I will momentarily delay discussion of the "fracturing moments" in feminism that also occurred.

HUONG'S DISCIPLINARY CRITIQUE

Huong, a sophomore, had missed his primary education while living in a refugee camp in Thailand. When he joined his family in America, he went into a high school ESL program and entered university four years later, wanting to teach ESL. He had been advised into ENGL 250. In composing his disciplinary critique, Huong mentioned the kinds of disciplinary writing outlined in *Writing across the Disciplines*, wondering how many forms he would have to teach. He found that courses in his major did not address disciplinary

writing needs or ESL adequately. He wondered if some of the ESL inade-
quacies correlated to program cutbacks in local schools and the gathering
force of the English-only movement. He found more favorable attitudes and
well-developed ESL training at other universities. A male professor also puzzled Huong, implying that he did not highly regard teaching ESL as a profession for men. Huong began questioning the wisdom of specializing in ESL.
He analyzed many writing-in-math exercises and felt this kind of writing
might benefit ESL students because of the simple, direct language combined
with formulae, graphs, or other visual aids. Once he left ENGL 250, however,
he went on to major in English, taking as many undergraduate courses in linguistics and writing as the department offered. His investigations led him to
see how he could cobble together his own program in a curriculum that denied
the needs of a growing regional population of ESL students.

SERENA'S DISCIPLINARY CRITIQUE

Serena, a junior, came to the university through a special-admissions program
for inner-city students who showed potential for performing well but lacked
supporting scores on college admissions exams. She had enrolled in ENGL
250 without being prompted by an advisor. Serena wrote her disciplinary critique as a speech to freshmen in the same program. She praised how favorably
the university's elementary education curriculum compared to other universities, emphasizing the practical aspects of writing assignments in different
courses—that is, the lesson plans, syllabi, classroom observations, summaries
in educational theories, and reflective journals on class management. She
noted her discipline's emphasis on two state competency exams in writing:
(1) to get admitted into the program and (2) to get certified. Serena strongly
felt elementary teachers should teach writing, based on her own experience of
winning several writing contests as a child. But she did not understand why
teaching writing at the elementary level was not emphasized more in her curriculum. She also questioned why neither her interviewees nor her coursework
addressed the concerns of student teachers who intended to return to inner-
city Chicago schools such as the one she had attended. Moreover, she felt her
discipline should make more of an effort to recruit African American men as
elementary teachers. "Why should only women be teaching our African
American kids?" she asked, in a conference with me. "This situation sends the
message that it is okay for boys to drop out."

MELINDA'S PROFESSIONAL WRITING PORTFOLIO

Melinda, a junior, was the first to attend college in her family, and she had
brought along a strong working-class ethic, sometimes putting in as many as
fifty hours a week as a restaurant hostess, to earn her way through school. She
agreed with her advisor that she needed ENGL 250. She wanted to teach his-

tory, as her high school role model had. Although Melinda did no more than the necessary minimum during her first two-thirds of the semester, she responded enthusiastically to assembling a professional writing portfolio. She had expected to deal with nothing more than lesson plans, tests, and notes home to parents, but when she discovered that her history teacher also wrote key documents for textbook, curriculum, and assessment committees; that she wrote grants for school equipment; and that she consistently wrote evaluations of other teachers as well as letters of recommendation for students, Melinda commented in conference that she never knew her teacher's writing tasks involved so much responsibility, or so much power. Her teacher also volunteered time as a counselor at a women's center and told Melinda that she must learn to balance her economic needs, her desire to get an education, and her health issues. While reading Howard's *Mind Your Body,* Melinda discovered she had symptoms of endometriosis. Consequently, Melinda's portfolio analysis stated that a woman could overextend herself by working *for* others, or she could empower herself by doing writing that actually got things done or even *changed* things.

HAL'S PROFESSIONAL WRITING PORTFOLIO

During his university career, Hal, a senior, had come to terms with his sexuality and got very involved in the leadership of the campus support group for lesbian and gay students. He considered several majors before he settled on art, because he wanted a profession that would not create tensions between who he was and what work he did. Hal enrolled in ENGL 250 because he was deaf and felt his written work contained many problems common to American Sign Language speakers. When the assignment for the professional writing portfolio came up, he mentioned he was student curator at the university art museum and had to put together materials for the upcoming summer show schedule. Hal designed a glossy four-color promotional brochure. He did a graphically enhanced version of minutes for the campus activities board for visual arts, on which he served, and in which he announced his project for bringing several gay artists' works to the museum. He had secured funds from the university's Presidential Commission on Lesbian and Gay Concerns (he included a draft of the funding proposal, as well). He also did a press release about the shows, identifying the artists, describing one well-known work, and promoting a contributing faculty artist. In his portfolio analysis, he discussed what he had learned about grant writing when he interviewed an art professor. Hal commented that the assignment enabled him to incorporate a lot of techniques he had been exploring with computer graphics, an important component of writing for hard-of-hearing people. He also noted it was the first course assignment where he had focused so much on gay and lesbian contributions instead of their struggles.

FRACTURES AND THEIR JUSTIFICATIONS

The foregoing accounts tend to affirm Malinowitz's predictions that when students take up feminist aims, they are likely to dissociate themselves with "the landlords of knowledge domains" and "align themselves with the disenfranchised," above all, "when students have a tremendous personal or ideological investment in a piece of reality" that a curriculum has deferred or slighted (Malinowitz 310). Yet I also see why such an approach would risk repercussions for students and teachers alike, if in fact more than one section of ENGL 250 brought pressure to bear on those who make decisions about and maintain curricula for reasons mostly having to do with who influences "the politics of outside funding and the control of disciplinary resources" (309). I shy away from risking such repercussions, and I suspect that WAC can engage with disciplines in a more negotiating fashion. However, before I elaborate on those negotiations, and the institutional conditions surrounding them, I should mention a few more incidents where a feminist approach to WAC fractured in ENGL 250.

Such an approach invoked the kind of resistance I expected—for example, when one male student criticized reading Howard's *Mind Your Body,* he asserted that the course should not deal with public writing about feminine sexuality and health. Even though the text addressed men's sexual health as well, he said, "Guys should find out about these things themselves, not in a college classroom where neither women or men should get preferential treatment." I wondered if he had experienced classes where he had been taught that "feminism is about women" only (see Baym, "Feminist Teacher" 75). Still he admitted, as did other men in class, that his girlfriend became interested in the use of Howard in our class, read the book, and initiated more than one conversation with him about sexual concerns. Would he have conceded this point as readily had a woman taught the course, or had he resisted in the first place, because I had used a feminist rationale for discontinuing our work with Hawkins's text? Either way, I resorted to the strategic use of feminist silence rather than engaging in the counterresponse of dialogical teaching that Malinowitz and others advocate (see Glenn 177; Flynn 25).

More disturbing was another male student whose written work, when he turned it in, was stunningly original, beautifully written, and full of quirks of reasoning that, had he fully developed them, would have been brilliant. I told him as much and also said that he had the potential to become not only the best writer in class but also one of the best writers with whom I had ever worked. In the only email journal entry he sent to me that semester, the student mentioned a philosophy professor who had invited him into his office near the end of the previous year, to give him a similar message, and to say that he would be getting an *A* that he really had not earned, because his final paper had proved so superior to any other student's. Although I continually urged the student to turn in at least the minimum needed to pass the course—which he barely did—I did not follow my colleague's example. I failed him. Even if a student's resistance exposes how questionably a discipline may reward a gifted intellect, an ethic of caring must ultimately exercise tough love when a student acts unwisely or self-destructively.

Most disturbing was Chantal, who decided that semester to become an English major rather than pursue premed in biology. When Chantal stayed with Hawkins's book, she focused upon deciphering content, but she could not grasp Hawkins's criticism of science. When she moved on to her disciplinary critique, she struggled just as mightily to define literary studies, not seeing the difference between summarizing literature and analyzing it. She paid several visits to my office, and as I tried to help her identify characteristics of disciplinary writing in literary studies, we talked about a course she was taking that included authors from thirteen different cultures. How did she use her own language to describe those stories? How did her own language compare with the language her professor used? Chantal's efforts underscored students' struggles to acquire the cross-cultural, cross-disciplinary literacy practices that professors too often expect them to patch together unhelped (see hooks 112). Her experience represented what Malinowitz calls "feminism's discontinuities and internal disruptions" (308). She eventually discovered some ways to code switch between the rhetoric of African American vernacular English and academic rhetoric in literary studies, but we had to set aside disciplinary critique to concentrate on this more immediate need. A feminist approach that focuses on a critical agenda but does not explicitly address the complicated challenges that bidialectical students face must necessarily fracture like so, or it will cease to be feminist.

My next comments digress from an analysis of how feminisms fractured in the specific classroom experience that I have been analyzing, but I think this discussion has to reflect, howbeit briefly, upon what a course such as ENGL 250 means, if, as Malinowitz says, it adopts a pedagogy of feminisms that seek to disrupt "inherited disciplinary frameworks and their requirements for specialized knowledge" (308). Even modest attempts at such an approach cannot have a salutary impact on writing instruction, if WAC reifies the labor conditions of first-year composition. The faculty who teach ENGL 250 must have the kind of professional security that will place them at the core rather than at the margins of effective, cross-curricular writing instruction. So the WAC program at our university, with the help of supportive university administrators, has requested and is establishing at least a few positions of regular continuing employment for those (besides me) who will continue to teach ENGL 250. We have located these positions in the Writing Center's budget. We also seek to change the classification of ENGL 250 to an interdisciplinary course in our catalog, one that will fulfill general education requirements. The story of how this situation came about cannot be told here, but if all goes well,

we will be able to develop a small team of WAC professionals who can negotiate with cross-curricular faculty to integrate and improve some of the
approaches that seemed to work best in the experiment I have described.
Accordingly, ENGL 250 could become a site for cross-curricular faculty discussions about what writing in the disciplines means, in terms of students'
needs, disciplinary conventions, and critical disciplinary inquiry. This move, I
hope, will also signal a call for change to our university's departments and colleges in resonance with Theresa Enos's advice for equitable reform for writing
faculty (see 133–34). In turn, this move has helped me realize that feminist
thinking has (dare I say it?) an *essentially* fracturing tendency that not only
chips away at institutional hierarchies and inequities but at itself as well, as it
must do.

In ending my discussion of the first section that I taught of ENGL 250,
I conclude that the experiment seems at once less desultory and more fractured than I had realized. Malinowitz herself offers an explanation, saying that
"feminisms, lacking in coherence even individually, may be variously seen as
complementary or incommensurable" (308). This, perhaps, constitutes the
very strength of what we have come to call "fractured feminist thinking." Just
so, feminisms in their various applications to WAC strike me as more worthwhile by far to pursue than to abandon, and I venture a guess that the students
who joined me in this experiment would probably agree.

WORKS CITED

Anson, Chris. "Writing across the Curriculum." *Encyclopedia of Rhetoric and Composition: Communication from Ancient Times to the Information Age*. Ed. Theresa Enos.
New York: Garland, 1996. 773–74.

Baym, Nina. "The Feminist Teacher of Literature: Feminist or Teacher?" *Gender in the
Classroom: Power and Pedagogy*. Ed. Susan Gabriel and Isaiah Smithson. Urbana:
University of Illinois Press, 1990. 60–77.

———. "The Madwoman and Her Languages: Why I Don't Do Feminist Literary
Theory." *Feminisms: An Anthology of Literary Theory and Criticism*. Ed. Robyn
Warhol and Diane Herndl. New Brunswick: Rutgers University Press, 1997.
279–92.

Belenky, Mary, Blythe Clinchy, Nancy Goldberger, and Jill Tarule. *Women's Ways of
Knowing: The Development of Self, Voice, and Mind*. New York: Basic Books, 1986.

Cixous, Hélène. "The Laugh of the Medusa." *The Signs Reader: Women, Gender, and
Scholarship*. Ed. Elizabeth and Emily Abel. Chicago: University of Chicago Press,
1983. 279–97.

Enos, Theresa. *Gender Roles and Faculty Lives in Rhetoric and Composition*. Carbondale:
Southern Illinois University Press, 1996.

Flynn, Elizabeth. "Strategic, Counter-Strategic, and Reactive Resistence in the Feminist Classroom." *Insurrections: Approaches to Resistance in Composition Studies.* Ed. Andrea Green Baum. Albany: State University of New York Press, 2001. 17–34.

Fuss, Diana. *Essentially Speaking: Feminism, Nature, and Difference.* New York: Routledge, 1989.

Glenn, Cheryl. *Rhetoric Retold: Regendering the Tradition from Antiquity through the Renaissance.* Carbondale: Southern Illinois University Press, 1997.

Harding, Sandra. "Introduction: Is There a Feminist Method?" *Feminism and Methodology: Social Sciences Issues.* Ed. Sandra Harding. Bloomington, Ind.: Indiana University Press, 1987. 1–14.

———. *Whose Science? Whose Knowledge? Thinking from Women's Lives.* Ithaca: Cornell University Press, 1991.

Hawkins, Michael. *Hunting Down the Universe: The Missing Mass, Primordial Black Holes, and Other Dark Matters.* Reading, Mass.: Helix Books, 1997.

Hirsch, Elizabeth, and Gary Olson. "Starting from Marginalized Lives: A Conversation with Sandra Harding." *Women Writing Culture.* Ed. Gary Olson and Elizabeth Hirsh. Albany: State University of New York Press, 1995. 3–42.

hooks, bell. *Teaching to Transgress: Education as the Practice of Freedom.* New York: Routledge, 1994.

Howard, Beth. *Mind Your Body: A Sexual Health and Wellness Guide for Women.* New York: St. Martin's Griffin, 1998.

Jarratt, Susan. "Feminism and Composition: The Case for Conflict." *Contending with Words: Composition and Rhetoric in a Postmodern Age.* Ed. Patricia Harkin and John Schilb. New York: Modern Language Association, 1991. 105–23.

Jones, Robert, Patrick Bizzaro, and Cynthia Selfe. *The Harcourt Brace Guide to Writing across the Curriculum.* Fort Worth: Harcourt Brace College Publishers, 1997.

Kirsch, Gesa. "Methodological Pluralism: Epistemological Issues." *Methods and Methodology in Composition Research.* Ed. Gesa Kirsch and Patricia Sullivan. Carbondale: Southern Illinois University Press, 1992. 247–69.

Malinowitz, Harriet. "A Feminist Critique of Writing in the Disciplines." *Feminism and Composition Studies: In Other Words.* Ed. Susan Jarratt and Lynn Worsham. New York: Modern Language Association, 1998. 291–312.

Nye, Andrea. "Words of Power and the Power of Words." *Rhetoric: Concepts, Definitions, Boundaries.* Ed. William Covino and David Jolliffe. Boston: Allyn and Bacon, 1995. 441–51.

Phelps, Louise Wetherbee. "A Constrained Vision of the Writing Classroom." *Profession* (1993): 46–54.

Russell, David. "Activity Theory and Its Implications for Writing Pedagogy." *Reconceiving Writing, Rethinking Writing Instruction.* Ed. Joseph Petraglia. Mahwah, NJ: Lawrence Erlbaum, 1995. 51–77.

Sullivan, Patricia. "Feminism and Methodology in Composition Studies." *Methods and Methodology in Composition Research.* Ed. Gesa Kirsch and Patricia Sullivan. Carbondale: Southern Illinois University Press, 1992. 37–61.

Walvoord, Barbara. "The Future of WAC." *College English* 58 (January 1996): 58–79.

Chapter Five

WOMEN'S WAYS ADAPTED, ADJUSTED, LOST

Feminist Theory Meets the Practices of Engineering Education

LINDA S. BERGMANN

In scientific and technical writing, it is a commonplace that one admits only those data that are impersonal, that are not affected by the person or location of the experiment or observation. Literary theory too is usually written as though it exists apart from the locations in which it is written and abstracted from the working conditions of those who write it—a situation that leads, as James Sosnoski has observed, to the marginalization of most of the professorate, or at least all of us who do not teach in the elite institutions that serve as the default standard academic location. Compositionists, however, tend to recognize the effects of local conditions and to mediate between the universal and the local. The work of composition fosters an understanding of the importance of situation, and this is an understanding that can enrich feminist theory and pedagogies. My focus in this chapter is on how being faculty members at a particular kind of location, that is, at technological universities or engineering schools, affects women's thinking and practices as feminists, teachers, and scholars. Working in locations where first-generation feminist battles are still being fought (Just before I started writing this piece, I was asked "Are you lady teachers called 'professor'?"), I am very aware of the institution-specific practices and beliefs that shape the experience of this corner of academia. I have shared ten years of my professional life with women at two different universities whose main focus was engineering, women who tended to function in a "survival mode" and to band together for companionship and power in the face of even major theoretical differences. These necessary adjustments and compromises, and the fractures of theory they caused, shaped at least my own pedagogies and practices in ways that need to be examined and constitute an experience that should not be effaced in generalizations about the academy or academic women.

In her essay in *Feminism and Composition Studies: In Other Words*, Nedra Reynolds takes James Berlin to task for ignoring the centrality of *location* to cultural interpretation. She asserts the importance of who is doing what to whom in what situation by enacting a strategic interruption to an ongoing compositionist conversation:

> We must also analyze the point of consumption: the site where negotiation and resistance are most likely to take place. In his own cultural studies approach, however, Berlin does little more than include a gender unit in his suggested syllabus, and he misses an obvious question about his pedagogical practice: How does the syllabus position women students, especially on a male dominated, engineering campus like Purdue, when it asks them to read an article about cowboys? (67)

As I wrote the first draft of this chapter, I was preparing to move to Purdue, having spent the previous ten years at smaller technological universities that are even more "male dominated, engineering campuses" than Reynolds envisions Purdue to be, and having made something of a specialty out of teaching students at these schools to write. At the technological universities I know best, women students are indeed positioned by a range of conditions, including the expectation that male-dominated texts are the norm. Here women teachers and scholars fighting first-generation battles over, for example, gender-inclusive pronouns and professional titles, find themselves far removed from the second- and third-generation theoretical issues that are raised and worked through by many current, cutting-edge feminist theorists.

This is a risky piece to write in many ways. It would be easy to misconstrue what I am writing as being in opposition to feminist pedagogies and their theoretical underpinnings or as being dismissive of them, and that is not at all what I mean to do, because feminism has been and remains at the heart of my intellectual life. Moreover, the hostile environment that I am going to describe is subtly constructed, and the problems I can put my finger on seem petty when committed to type. And while complaint is a major form of the oral discourse of the academy, it seldom finds its way into print; it can easily sound like whining and overreacting. Even more troubling is the fact that, having built my career in engineering schools, I am loath to seem ungrateful to these institutions that have nourished my work life in many ways. There are men and women at these schools—faculty colleagues, administrators, and students—who have enriched my thinking and my scholarship in more ways than I can remember and for whose friendship and guidance I will always be grateful. These reservations notwithstanding, I feel that I must write about women's positions in technological institutions, because feminists need to be reminded that second- and third-generation theorists may be living not far down the road from "the land that time forgot" and because we all need to be wary about assuming that "earlier" battles have been won once and for all and that now we can forget the more basic issues of gender equality.

Let me start with a few examples of what academic life is like for women faculty in engineering schools. The second-class condition of women faculty in science and engineering has been well documented by the 1999 "Study on the Status of Women Faculty in Science at MIT." One key point disclosed by interviews with women faculty is that

> the difference in the perception of junior and senior women faculty about the impact of gender on their careers is a difference that repeats itself over generations. Each generation of young women, including those who are currently senior faculty, began by believing that gender discrimination was "solved" in the previous generation and would not touch them. Gradually however, their eyes were opened to the realization that the playing field is not level after all, and that they had paid a high price both personally and professionally as a result.

This report reverberated throughout technological universities, with impact beyond science and engineering departments. A follow-up report at MIT in the Spring of 2002 shows that women there still see that university as a "man's world" in which they are marginalized (Smallwood A9). At my previous university, dominated by engineering, the issue of retention of women faculty has become an open concern since the initial report was published. According to a recent institutional fact book, in 2000–2001 there were 27 female tenured and tenure-track faculty members and 224 males. A study done in the fall of 2000 tracking the progress of women faculty hired since 1985 showed that of 31 female tenure track hires in fifteen years, 11 had left or were in the process of leaving, a number that rose to 14 (including me) by the end of the 2000–2001 academic year. There is considerable, and I believe genuine, administrative concern about the problem of attracting and retaining the critical mass of female faculty necessary to stop this drain of talent. There is a widespread feeling among the female faculty that this is a difficult environment for women, and a feeling by at least some of the women that it is hostile. Part of the hostility perceived by women at engineering schools may be discipline related, since these schools tend to hire more women faculty in the humanities and social sciences than in the science and engineering departments that dominate the schools intellectually and financially. Female faculty in the traditional liberal arts fields often feel even more marginalized than our friends in science and engineering departments, because we teach primarily "service" courses in support of technological majors, we conduct research that may have no immediate applications, and we seldom bring major funding to academic programs or departments. Used to seeing women in support roles throughout the university—as secretaries, student services staff, admissions officers, and so on—students and colleagues tend to see women faculty in English or history or economics as similarly supportive "service providers," to treat us as such, and to feel angry when we resist this characterization. Few students or faculty in the engineering departments have a very clear idea who we are in our professions—or even that we have any professional life at all—and the process of educating people who we think should know better to the fact that we too are professionals—who conduct research, publish peer-reviewed papers, and work as consultants—can be disheartening. Furthermore, even male members of traditional liberal arts departments at engineering universities tend to feel beleaguered and disrespected, resulting in a wagon-circling mentality that even further marginalizes these faculty members from the university's mission and that may exacerbate the isolation of women faculty from the university mainstream.

The day-to-day lives of women faculty at engineering universities are full of petty humiliations that we seldom talk about because they seem so small; but writing about them can suggest the attitudinal structure that can dominate the academic environment in these locations. The questions of what to do with us and how to "treat" us, questions that I hope have long since been resolved at more comprehensive institutions with larger percentages of female faculty, still loom large at engineering schools. The engineering schools I have taught at are still so male dominated that many male faculty members, no matter what their politics, have little experience in dealing with women as equals, as individuals, and as colleagues; there are few women engineering faculty, and the male faculty seem to be particularly traditional in attitudes and lifestyles. Women faculty, then, always seem to be identified by our gender first, and we are seldom allowed to forget it. For example, as a new faculty member at one institution, I was invited to join the faculty wives' club, as though I had the time or inclination for the multitude of daytime activities it offers, or as though I had a resident spouse to bring to the primarily couples-oriented events on evenings and weekends. I was never, however, eased into the informal coffee and lunch groups—composed almost entirely of men—that serve as the communication links across campus. When I summoned the initiative to join these coffee or lunch tables, the men welcomed me of course (they are, after all, "gentlemen"), but they usually called attention to my gender. They issued subtle and irritating hints that I had stepped out of my "appropriate sphere" in assuming a faculty position, often in the form of jokes about their submission to nagging or dominating wives at home, the implication being that women's exertions of power are more acceptable in the house than on the job. Social relations in such a location can be tricky, and the "rules" are strange. I could make an appointment to meet with a male colleague in his office or mine, but lunch could be tricky and was best avoided. Only in the English department did I sometimes escape from these constant reminders of my gender—but a Writing across the Curriculum director cannot stay ensconced in the English department and hope to generate a successful program.

The students at the engineering schools at which I have worked have had little experience dealing with professional women and next to none with women professors; they show even less understanding of women's disciplinary expertise or standing than the faculty display. Female faculty across the disciplines have trouble gaining acknowledgement of their position from students; particularly rankling to women faculty is that while students almost always address male faculty as "Dr." or "Professor," too many of them address female faculty as "Mrs." or "Miss," even in the face of direct requests for a specific mode of address. I have watched students become angry when female faculty are not available in their offices at all times; last year, a student went so far as to open the closed door to my office when I failed to respond to his knock, telling me, "I knew you were in here." Female faculty are expected to be motherly and nurturing and not very demanding; we are not expected to carry much authority or to display much expertise. The typical student—or maybe just the most irritating student—sees no reason why my opinion about an issue in my field of expertise should carry more weight than his. Traditional gender expectations meld with the widespread idea that English is the birthright of all who speak it—not a real discipline like the ones engineering students are learning—to deny professional authority to the female English teacher.

In addition to perpetuating this subtle—or not-so-subtle—hostility toward women, students at engineering schools tend to be very conservative socially, religiously, and politically. They see faculty who espouse progressive ideas as wanting to deprive them of the fruits of success to which they feel fully entitled. Many engineering students expect (accurately) to make higher starting salaries right out of college than professors with Ph.D.s in the humanities and social sciences earn, and do not hesitate to tell us so. Believing that money talks and success counts, they meet overt feminism with overt hostility and with negative course evaluations, which can have dire consequences for junior faculty and significant ones even for senior faculty women.

In addition to specific sexist acts, often minor, by individuals, there is a kind of ethos in engineering schools that exacerbates these antifemale and antifeminist strains, an ethos comprised of tradition, personality types, and the current corporate model of the university. The tradition of engineering education, as I have written with my colleagues in an earlier article, is a "weed-out pedagogy" (Meinholdt, Murray, and Bergmann). An engineering colleague at one school described the old days—which he did not see as the "good old days"—in which freshmen were told, "Look to your left, look to your right: only one of you will graduate from here." Faculty still tend to pride themselves on the toughness of their courses, and students, on their ability to surmount that toughness in any way possible. This tradition of mutual hostility or mock-hostility between students and faculty has fallen away in an age in which retention of students is an administrative priority, but its flavor persists in the ethos of these institutions. The engineering school environment validates quantitative educational practices: strict grading systems based on earned points, "plug and chug" exercises in using formulas, and a heavy reliance on grade point averages as indicators of student success and on numerical teaching evaluations to measure faculty effectiveness. Central to engineering education are "the files" of old exams and papers, compiled by fraternities (and now, in an attempt at democratization, by Student Services), for students to consult and use as models and sources for their own work. Creativity is encouraged in design projects, not in written or oral communication, which tend to be highly formulaic.

Even engineering faculty working for change can find the expectations and assumptions of composition pedagogy difficult to understand and implement, and feminist pedagogies may seem even more foreign and inapplicable to their discourse and their classrooms. Engineers think in terms of products designed to meet definite and articulated "specs" (specifications) of clients, they think of writing as "writing it up," and they think of teaching writing as delivering their specs to the students and ensuring that they are followed. They do think rhetorically, with a high awareness of audience, in particular. And they do think creatively, although creativity comes in the design of products and processes, not in the act of writing. Risking gross oversimplification of the large body of research has been done on the composing practices of different professional fields, I am going to assert that engineers write different kinds of documents, using different writing processes than we commonly teach in composition courses. Writing in specific professions, David R. Russell argues, is deeply rooted in activity systems of which English faculty are not a part and which we rarely understand, unless we make a conscious effort to learn them and adapt our teaching and our expectations for student writing accordingly.

Although it may seem that engineers are more rule-driven than compositionists, this is probably because they write more documents for which there are clear formal criteria and established generic expectations and models (Winsor 27–29). Writing, then, seldom seems like a creative act for engineers, engineering faculty, or engineering students. The forms in which they are expected to write are pretty much set, and so is the content, which is usually derived from observation and experimentation. As Charles Bazerman observes of scientific writing: "The object is taken as given, independent of perception and knowing; all the human action is only in the process of coming to know the object—that is, in constructing, criticizing, and manipulating claims" (166). Once the object is known, the human activity is expected to be for the most part effaced. There is a rhetorical stance in this kind of discourse, but in contrast to much of the discourse of English studies, it describes activity that has already taken place—including intellectual activity—rather than showing the making of knowledge in progress. "Writing to learn" is a foreign concept to engineering faculty and one to which they are not very receptive, perhaps because they use it less than English faculty do. Very often engineers will sketch out ideas or graph and chart them rather than writing them out in words, and teams of researchers often reach conclusions through oral discussions that are later summarized in writing. The language they consider appropriate for most written documents in science and engineering is therefore highly transparent as well as impersonal, given as much as possible to the transmission of information rather than the making of meaning.

The stories engineering students tell about learning to communicate—both to speak and to write—tend to emphasize pain, embarrassment, and learning from mistakes, not the nurturing environment that feminist writing pedagogies embrace. Engineering students have told me that they learn little about writing from English classes of any sort, be they writing or literature-based courses. They recall English classes as involving personal writing—a kind of self-expression that in their minds should not be graded and cannot be evaluated fairly. According to student lore, they learn to write because a tough teacher in a field such as history or metallurgy laid down specific rules about form, content, and grammar; sometimes they recall learning to write by following the rules, sometimes by breaking them. Or they learn to write on the job, when a corporate executive for whom they were interning tore apart a paper they wrote and showed them how to reconstruct it.[1] The few engineering teachers who spend class time on communication tend to conceive of speaking as monologue, not as dialogue; and of writing as the clear transmission of information, not the generation of meaning. Or, since they are used to relying on consultants, they bring in an outside expert (like me) to lay down the rules. Students who have trouble speaking are encouraged to join Toastmasters, which is attractive to engineers because it emphasizes adherence to clearly articulated standards and formulae.

Engineering students tend to have personalities that respond well to this kind of pedagogical tradition and the discourse it expects. The counseling staff at one engineering school where I was employed does considerable work with Myers-Briggs Type Indicators, in the effort to help faculty, students, and administrators understand each other and head off personality clashes. In general, engineering students at this institution tend toward introversion over extroversion, sensing over intuition, thinking over feeling, and judging over perceiving—preferences that give them fundamentally different and potentially clashing learning and working styles from faculty in the humanities and social sciences, and particularly from female faculty. These students are often impatient with what they see as the fuzzy thinking of personality types in which intuition and feeling are more dominant, and these perceptions can intensify their identification with the "tough-minded" traditional culture of engineering education and its survivalist ethos. Furthermore, because undergraduates are seldom allowed access to the making of knowledge in engineering courses, they seldom see the "messiness" of actual research, and thus they perceive science and engineering as highly precise disciplines. They carry an ideal of the precision of science that is not yet tarnished by much direct experience of the hit and miss aspects of the experimental process, an ideal that is exacerbated by how much the relatively neat and straightforward scientific practice of "writing up" finished intellectual work seems to contrast with the free-flowing invention, the encouragement of creativity, and the expression of individuality that composition faculty seem to encourage. Because these students are caught up in the process of being socialized as engineering professionals and defensive about their place in this world, they are prone to display scorn for unquantifiable kinds of knowledge and inexact styles of learning, which they think of as typical in the humanities—styles that are often culturally identified with women. Feminist writing pedagogies, particularly those that foster self-discovery and expression, seem foreign and even antithetical to the aims of engineering education.

In addition to the traditional assumptions and practices of engineering education, also contributing to the uncomfortable ethos for feminist theory at engineering universities is the growing dominance over the past few years of corporate thinking and modeling in academic institutions, a kind of thinking that eschews theory, focuses on quantifiable products, and rewards entrepreneurship. As Bill Readings notes in *The University in Ruins,* the incursion of corporate thinking into university life occurs at comprehensive institutions as well as engineering schools. But the humanities and social sciences departments that can provide some counterbalance to the corporate influence at less applications-oriented institutions are smaller and weaker at engineering schools; and the recent trend toward earmarked legislative allocations given to applied research at selected universities has fed this corporate mentality. Engineering by its nature is geared toward applications—practice trumps theory any day. But in the current educational and research climate—in which the language of teacher and student is being replaced by the language of consumer, client, and service provider—the faculty and students who survive and prosper at engineering schools are increasingly those who share or come to share a corporate language and style and who assert entrepreneurial qualities that push them to the top of the academic heap.

What I am describing here is a hard environment for women, an even harder one for feminism, and dry ground indeed for feminist theory and pedagogy. In such an environment, we direct our energies toward creating a manageable space, rather than toward refining our positions; we look for points of connection with each other, rather than points of difference. Such compromises do not lead to the refinement of theory. Some female faculty and administrators at these schools work together because they need each other as collaborators and friends, avoiding the edgy theoretical, political, and even personal controversies that might drive them apart in more hospitable locations; others are driven apart by their frustration with the circumstances of their professional lives and lose the leaven of collaboration with other women that can help theory develop.

What, then, is the value of feminist theory in such an environment—and what kind of space can be made for feminist pedagogy in it? It is tempting to simply abandon efforts to develop and maintain feminist pedagogy in such an inhospitable environment, but I am convinced that students, faculty, and administrators at engineering schools need deep and repeated exposure to an articulated feminist position even more than those at more comprehensive universities, even though this puts a heavy burden on the women who teach these future engineers. We must continually negotiate our positions, determining whether we best serve our values by maintaining a dissenting but ignored presence on the margins of the institutions, or whether we should adapt and adjust to this hostile institutional culture, a move that may leave us so compromised that we lose all efficacy for bringing about significant change. My own approach—the result of considerable trial and error—has been to adapt and adjust, maintaining a high academic profile and a modulated feminist tone. I am well aware, however, of the possibility of losing my feminist identification in this process and of losing my theoretical edge.

The most obvious adjustments—fractures, perhaps—come with devising a viable classroom presence and pedagogy. Feminist approaches to learning, which rely more heavily than traditional pedagogies on collaboration, the dissolution of hierarchies, and the encouragement of personal learning, defy both the institutional traditions of engineering schools and the personal inclinations of the students and teachers who dominate them. The kinds of collaboration described by Mary Belenky and colleagues in *Women's Ways of Knowing* involve the creation of emotionally rich classroom communities in which knowledge is shared and skills are developed. Engineering education, however, focuses on teamwork, which, as I have argued elsewhere, embodies a substantially different set of practices and expectations (Bergmann 9–10). Collaborators share knowledge and create understanding together, whereas team members are selected for their distinct specialized knowledge and share in the production of a specified "deliverable." I have not had much success with head-on defiance of teamwork assumptions in engineering institutions. In order to make collaborative projects work for these students, I have had to make the processes goal or product driven, since engineering students tend to sabotage group work that does not seem well defined. However, I try to infuse the inevitable teamwork with at least some collaborative practices whenever I design group projects for students or help engineering faculty design writing projects or programs. For example, students in my research writing course are required to create a sizable working bibliography for their research groups. While they habitually parcel out the pieces of the work, they can be pushed to collaborate on formatting, evaluating, and using the product they have created, and they usually find it easier to master the conventions of citation when they work together and share knowledge. Because engineering students are oriented toward direct problem solving, they are apt to merely assign the "best" practitioner on a team to do the bit he or she already does best; thus, it is necessary to direct them explicitly to consider the extent to which ensuring that every group member actually learns the processes of research, design, and professional communication should take precedence over merely producing the most successful design or report. Although I feel obligated to leave groups sufficient working room to determine the extent of their product orientation and to develop their own approach, I encourage them to reflect on their development of interpersonal skills and personal expertise as part of the production process. And I will ruthlessly intervene when I see women students assigned to secretarial roles or deprived of the "bench experience" they need for effective professional development.

In addition to being highly goal oriented, engineering schools are hierarchical, like the corporations for which they educate workers. Women who do not assert their place in this hierarchy are denied respect, hence the concern with faculty titles, which was foreign to my experience at more comprehensive universities and liberal arts colleges. It is one thing for everyone to be on a first-name basis, but another for students to refer to male faculty as "Dr." or "Professor" (whether or not they have a Ph.D.) and to female faculty as "Mrs.," "Miss," or by their first names. It is insulting to attend faculty meetings where administrators introduce female faculty by their first names and male faculty as "Dr." In such a location, it is a necessary feminist practice (and an effective one) to point out these lapses to the people who are responsible for them and to make manners of reference matters of public discussion.

But despite this necessary concern for the outward trappings of professional status, women at engineering schools have an unusual opportunity to make strategic moves that subvert conventional academic hierarchies. Like other feminists, we recognize the hierarchical structures of our institutions as created rather than "natural," and even as we insist that we "lady teachers" should get our share of the trappings of professorship, a good many of us openly recognize the artifice of the academic structure, and even, heresy of heresies, admit this artifice outside the closed circle of the professorate. This breaking of ranks allows us to form alliances with other women that cut across traditional academic status boundaries so that we can collaborate on mutual goals such as providing professional development opportunities for women students, faculty, and staff. One of the side benefits of having so few women at a university is that barriers of discipline and status seem less compelling, and women faculty at the engineering schools at which I have taught interact with each other across boundaries more often and more easily than faculty I have known in other locations. For example, I have co-authored a paper and grant proposals with friends in psychology, engineering management, and various fields of engineering; and a full professor in my former department is collaborating with a part-time lecturer on an article. We also form alliances with professional staff women that I have not seen at institutions with a higher proportion of female faculty, and many of us work to plug into clerical and student information networks as well. Because we form friendships and mentoring relationships across ranks and disciplines, we are able at least occasionally to free ourselves from the blinders of departmental politics and from that belief in the intellectual superiority of our own discipline to which English faculty in particular are too often prone.

The trappings of hierarchy are considerably more entrenched in the classroom, however, and women faculty in engineering schools may need to assume a more formal relationship with students than feminist pedagogical theories advocate. Because engineering students' expectations for teaching and learning are so highly imbued with the idea of hierarchy, the assumption that answers are either right or wrong, and the concern with proving mastery of bodies of knowledge, it is difficult to get them to accept and respect a non-authoritarian pedagogy. Women faculty who fail to assert their authority may be treated with considerable disrespect and even contempt. Moreover, women faculty at engineering schools need considerable authority to initiate and maintain even the most basic first-generation feminist positions. For example, I have been drawn into arguments with students about whether they should be required to use gender-inclusive language and whether writers such as Toni Morrison and Maxine Hong Kingston are "important" enough to require male students to read them in a contemporary literature course. These issues may have been settled long ago in other locations, but they were not settled at that school, and I am simply not willing to relinquish authority over the terms of this kind of discussion or to lose this kind of argument. Women students in engineering schools often encounter situations in which the male experience is considered paradigmatic, and in many classes I have had to draw on all of the authority I could muster to provoke students to question that paradigm. The question of how to decentralize the teacher's presence and create a problem-posing atmosphere in the classroom without letting it come under the domination of the fraternity boys snickering in the back row is one to which my friends and I have repeatedly returned, with no really satisfying resolution. It is a dilemma that makes for a very difficult transition into the profession for junior faculty women, many of whom come from graduate departments that have large proportions of women, that tolerate or even privilege feminist points of view, and that simply cannot prepare them for the kind of indifference or hostility to women faculty that they face. Teaching skills acquired in comprehensive and cosmopolitan research institutions do not immediately transfer to an English class at an engineering school, and junior faculty women are particularly vulnerable to poor teaching evaluations when they do not meet students' expectations for an authoritarian classroom.

It is difficult to bring personal knowledge into teaching and learning in an environment in which respect for personal knowledge is not widely fostered. Personal knowledge and personal narrative can easily be dismissed as "soft," which is a derogatory term in this kind of institutional setting. I have had far more success teaching writing courses that focus on teaching engineering students "academic writing" (despite my suspicions that there is no such genre), if success is indicated by students' evaluations and my own judgments of the quality of their papers, than I have with teaching more personal, expressive writing. Nonetheless, because I believe that personal knowledge is a necessary adjunct to scholarship as well as a central feminist move, I incorporate personal genres into writing courses at all levels: in first-year composition, a paper in which personal learning experience is examined from a Freirian perspective; in research writing, a paper describing the process of the research and its progress in the mind of the researcher; in an advanced course in the theory of writing, a literacy autobiography. And I overtly and explicitly raise as a topic for serious discussion the relationships between personal and professional knowledge and between private and public discourse. Only by recognizing and addressing students' resistance to the personal can I devise processes for overcoming it.

Women in composition are in a good position to articulate the effects of location, because the widespread first-year composition requirement locates us in institutions of all sorts. And as rhetoricians we understand, I hope, that pedagogy is rhetorical and that teachers and students function in a dynamic relationship that holds out the possibility of change by the students, by the institution, and in ourselves. We dim our understanding, I believe, when we ignore the realities of place and try to efface the specifics of the particular social milieu in which we live in order to imagine ourselves as belonging to a larger academic community that exists in the imagination and outside of our experience. We limit our effectiveness as teachers and as colleagues when we act and write as though we cannot acknowledge the actual circumstances in which we live and work, and we have a difficult task countering the resistance to our ideas and even to our presence if we do not bring it out into the open.

Despite students' resistance—or perhaps because of it—women faculty at engineering schools need to press students, both men and women, to rethink their basic conceptions about and responses to gender, because there is little else in this environment to induce them to move beyond conventional stereotypes. Feminist theory raises issues such as who women really are or whether we "really are" anything in particular, how much we fashion ourselves and how much we are the products of socially constructed roles and behaviors, and whether there is the potential for us or for others to "really be" at all. These are issues that students need to think about and grapple with, at engineering schools even more than at more comprehensive universities. Engineering students may find few other opportunities in their curriculum to question the status quo or to seriously consider what constitute "natural" qualities or behaviors because engineering education focuses more on applying received knowledge than on questioning it. If we want the situation of women in our country and the world at large to improve, we cannot continue to graduate class after class of students who are primed for technological careers and have the potential for significant authority and influence but who have had no positive contact with feminist theory and practice. We cannot forgo the opportunity to assert the presence of women in this location, even if we would ourselves flourish more in a more nurturing environment.

NOTE

1. A detailed account of how students characterize their experiences learning to write, based on a series of focus groups with students at the University of Missouri-Rolla, is in the process of being written by Janet Zepernick and Linda Bergmann.

WORKS CITED

Bazerman, Charles. "What Written Knowledge Does: Three Examples of Academic Discourse." *Philosophy of the Social Sciences* 11 (1981): 361–87. Rpt. in *Landmark Essays on Writing across the Curriculum*. Ed. Charles Bazerman and David R. Russell. Davis, Calif.: Hermagoras, 1994. 159–88.

Belenky, Mary, Blythe Clinchy, Nancy Goldberger, and Jill Tarule. *Women's Ways of Knowing: The Development of Self, Voice, and Mind*. New York: Basic Books, 1986.

Bergmann, Linda. "WAC Meets the Ethos of Engineering: Process, Collaboration, and Disciplinary Practices." *Language and Learning across the Disciplines* 4.1 (2000): 4–15.

Fact Book 2000–2001. The University of Missouri-Rolla Office of Institutional Research and Budget Planning.

Meinholdt, Connie, Susan Murray, and Linda Bergmann. "Addressing Gender Issues in the Engineering Classroom." *Feminist Teacher* 12 (1999): 169–83.

Readings, Bill. *The University in Ruins*. Cambridge, Mass.: Harvard University Press, 1996.

Reynolds, Nedra. "Interrupting Our Way to Agency: Feminist Cultural Studies and Composition." *Feminism and Composition Studies: In Other Words*. Ed. Susan C. Jarrett and Lynn Worsham. New York: MLA, 1998.

Russell, David R. "Rethinking Genre in School and Society: An Activity Theory Analysis." *Written Communication* 14 (1997): 504–54.

Smallwood, Scott. "Women Still Feel Marginalized at MIT, Study Finds." *The Chronicle of Higher Education* 5 April 2002: A10.

Sosnoski, James J. *Token Professionals and Master Critics: A Critique of Orthodoxy in Literary Studies*. Albany: State University of New York Press, 1994.

"A Study on the Status of Women Faculty in Science at MIT: How a Committee on Women Faculty came to be Established by the Dean of the School of Science, What the Committee and the Dean Learned and Accomplished, and Recommendations for the future." *The MIT Faculty Newsletter* 11.4 (March 1999). *http://web.mit.edu/fnl/women/women.html#The Study*.

Winsor, Dorothy A. *Writing Like an Engineer: A Rhetorical Education*. Mahwah, N.J.: Erlbaum, 1996.

Chapter Six

THE OVERLY MANAGED STUDENT

Gender and Pedagogy in the Science School

ROSE KAMEL

My pedagogy is rooted in a fractured feminist theory that eschews the essentialism and dualism grounded in sociobiology, for a pluralistic theory inclusive of race, class, and ethnicity. The acknowledgement of the value of both biological and sociocultural elements challenges much about various feminist theories' attempts to separate the two. Instead, I share current theorists' views that though sex defines a woman as a biological organism and gender is socially constructed, these definitions have to be constantly mediated. In fact, as Nelly Oudshoorn observes, "no unmediated *natural* truth of the body can be said to exist [my emphasis]." Instead, it makes sense to contend that

> [o]ur perceptions and interpretations of the body are mediated through language, and in our society, the biomedical sciences function as a major provider of this language. . . . If understanding the body is mediated by language, scientists are bound by language as well. Consequently, the assumption that the biomedical sciences are the providers of objective knowledge about the "true nature" of the body could be rejected. (Oudshoorn 201)

In a more diversified milieu the language of biomedical knowledge and that of the humanities could bridge the hurdles disparate disciplines set in their path. However, at our science-oriented school, University of the Sciences

117

in Philadelphia, undergraduate preprofessionals majoring in science, pharmacy, physical therapy, and occupational therapy, the language of humanities does not fare too well. Therefore, the long-term purpose of Literature and Medicine, the course I have designed and implemented for the past four years, is to help students mediate between the quantifiable language of data absorbed in large lecture halls and the ambiguities of literary texts and films focusing mostly on doctors and patients. In the short run of a spring semester elective, they must learn to grapple with the philosophical concept stated in the syllabus that patients are more than the sum of their body parts and therefore must be defined as the subject, rather than the object, of their illnesses. In term projects and take-home essay exams, therefore, their writing should demonstrate that overmanagement notwithstanding, they can assume agency as subjects of their discourse—easier said than done.

Beyond the obligatory Freshman College Composition and Introduction to Literature, a core-curriculum component obliges sophomores to take Intellectual Heritage (intellectual history generated by celebrated West European white men) and thereafter an elective in history or literature beginning in their third year. Nevertheless, given the large number of women students (about 60 percent and of these, 40 percent Asian), the problematics of gender and race invariably permeate classroom discussions and crop up in their writing. My hope, then, is that both men and women will discover in the process of close reading and thoughtful writing a way to interrogate their ideas about gender and, therefore, write more authoritatively on the vexed issue of sexism embedded in the assigned texts and films.

Navigating my way around the shoals of a rigorous curriculum in their major fields, culminating in many in-class exams consisting of computer-graded true-false or multiple-choice questions, I am nevertheless stymied. Though many of my colleagues teaching pharmacy and science courses would like to encourage more critical thinking, the pedagogical model of learning in a corporate school hierarchically administered undermines their intention. Consequently, science faculty members continue to perceive their students as passive beings, a perception students learn to share and one that reenforces the historical stereotype of women. It is not simple to apply feminist theory in a class of upwardly mobile students concerned with getting corporate jobs in an uncertain global economy. Half the students "electing" this course are men who more than their women counterparts feel uncomfortable with the ambiguity in which the course material is historically framed and philosophically centered. Furthermore, my knowing less science than they and asking for help in filling the gaps tends to discomfit them, I suppose, because instructors in their major fields adhere to a masculinized preconception that they are supposed to be knowledgeable and prescriptive in all matters. Furthermore, in a university geared to get students lucrative jobs dominated directly or indirectly by giant pharmaceutical corporations reinforcing competition, encouraging

their "team players" to overlook conflicts of gender, class, and race, it is difficult for students to avoid the kind of stereotyping that reinforces bipolar
assumptions, that is, rational men and emotional women, aggressive men and
nurturing women.

For me the challenge lies in encouraging agency in student response as
readers and writers to a historical overview of genres from Jean Baptise
Moliére's *The Imaginary Invalid,* Daniel Defoe's *Journal of a Plague Year,* to
Charlotte Perkins Gilman's *The Yellow Wallpaper,* and Ken Kesey's *One Flew
over the Cuckoo's Nest.* Last, we discuss articles on AIDS culled from Britain's
Guardian and the *New York Times* exposing U.S. pharmaceutical companies'
policy of refusing to allow the patenting and sale of antiretrovirals that could
prolong the lives of AIDS victims in Africa and South America.

The problem I am faced with is how to encourage my students to "own"
their ideas and validate that ownership through the writing process. To foster student agency, I encourage journal writing and narrative cross-over (a
point I will develop later), allowing for a first-person person perspective at
variance with the written requirements in their major fields where term
papers omit personal views and are therefore presumed to be objective. We
begin by reading a given text or viewing a film analytically with the tacit
assumption that we learn to recognize its ideological underpinning as such
and respond to it before asserting our own viewpoints. I use *we* and *our* advis-
edly, aware that the dialectical contradictions in my working-class background and current middle-class status as a tenured woman professor do not
necessarily correspond to the particularity of the contradictions my middle-
class students experience, all of which complicates matters if I begin in the
"lecture mode" by defining *ideology.*

I have learned, instead, to revert to the reader response theory with
which they are familiar in other humanities courses, stipulating that we bring
to a text or film our life experience, including that which identifies us as gendered beings, socially constructed. For example, reading William Carlos
Williams's "The Use of Force" aloud, they become aware of the doctor narrator contemptuously dismissive of the sick child's working-class parents and
growing more irrational, combative, in fact, brutal, prying the four-year-old
girl's mouth open to examine her throat for symptoms of diphtheria. "After
all I had fallen in love with the savage brat," he concludes, exposing the class
and gender bias underlying his symbolic rape of the child. "But the worst of
it was that I too had got beyond reason. I could have torn the child apart in
my own fury and enjoyed it. It was a pleasure to attack her. My face was
burning with it" (58–59).

In class discussion both men and women ignored the class and gender
assumptions embedded in the text and almost unanimously agreed that the doctor did what he had to do to save the life of a four-year-old throwing a tantrum.
Only one man, a science premed, demurred, saying a good pediatrician would

take the time to make the battle a game: "I see it all the time with my little sister. The pediatrician shows her how a tongue depressor works and lets her try it
first on dolls and then on him." My attempt to explain the story in its historical
context (early twentieth century) foundered; nor did they consider the factor of
class conflict that seemed obvious to me, having grown up with it, not to mention having taught the story for years.

Nor did the students question ideological assumptions either in discussion or in their take-home exam to the sexism Jack Nicholson conveyed in
One Flew over the Cuckoo's Nest. Again and again, men and women asserted
that since Nurse Ratched was "a control freak," the protagonist was right to
choke "that bitch." Two women demurred—one because as a "devout Christian" she objected to the "four-letter words," the other because as a "feminist"
she objected to the film and the novel's categorizing women either as "ball-
clippers" like Rachel or "ball enablers" like Candy, the hooker. The last comment got the expected laugh and ended the discussion. Gone was my historical introduction anchoring the novel in Orwell's warning about totalitarian
stifling of political dissent, personified by Chief Broom Bromden's indictment
of the mental hospital as a symbol of corporate assault on Native Americans,
untrammeled land, and political dissent. Likewise dismissed was the socio-
logical perspective in Philip Wylie's *Generation of Vipers,* which blamed white,
middle-class "moms" of the 1950s for robbing men of their manhood. My
hope is that since these political and cultural tensions are far from over, they
will give students food for thought in the future.

In *Literature and Medicine*'s special issue on writing and healing, Charles
Anderson observes that "the ambient nature of healing that arises from writing is what makes it so difficult for biomedical science to measure, test, and
certify. But this does not invalidate its effects or diminish its importance.
Instead, it asks us to break the rules, to probe with different instruments, to
look with different eyes" (xi). I discovered that one way for students to "probe
with different instruments" was to assign a written project where they
responded to gendered language by narrative cross-overs, that is, imagine
themselves an antagonist such as the doctor-husband in *The Yellow Wallpaper.*
I respond to their essays in writing, sometimes underlining its ideological
underpinning, sometimes raising questions on aspects of the topic that the
student overlooks. In one particular assignment both men and women identify with John, rather than with the first-person narrator suffering from post-
partum depression.

> John [the husband and her doctor] is practical in the extreme. He has no
> patience with faith, and intense horror of superstition, and he scoffs openly
> at any talk of things not felt and seen or put down in figures. John is a physi-
> cian, and perhaps—I would not say it to a living soul, of course, but this is
> dead paper perhaps that is the reason I do not get well faster. . . . So I take

phosphates or phosphites—whichever it is, and Tonics, and journeys, and air and exercise, and am absolutely forbidden to "work" until I am well again. Personally I disagree with their ideas. Personally, I believe that congenial work, with excitement and change, would do me good. But what is one to do? I did write for a while in spite of them: but it does exhaust me a good deal—having to be so sly about it or meet with heavy opposition. (801)

Having read the story and reviewed *Masterpiece Theatre*'s production of *The Yellow Wallpaper*, students inhabiting John's consciousness pretended to discover the entries above after the wife succumbed to the experience and became insane. Their gendered responses differed subtly but significantly. The men had "John" record his guilt for leaving his wife to give a talk to medical colleagues before returning to see the wallpaper torn bare and his wife creeping away into lifelong madness. Typical examples from men's entries are as follows:

1. She should have had more work to do around the house. Then I could do my research and know she was getting better. Maybe she had too much time on her hands. [Response: What work other than housework the servants took care of could she have done?]

2. Charlotte was sicker than anyone suspected, and I'm sorry my work caused me to overlook symptoms of schizophrenia. [Response: What symptoms?]

3. I should have let her have more company than just my family. Women are *naturally* more sociable [my emphasis]. [Response: What do you consider natural? What do you consider socially imposed?]

Typically the women's responses differed:

1. I should not have yelled at her for discovering the library and reading too much. After all, being in the nursery with windows barred would make anyone go crazy. [Response: Why?]

2. If I had let her write more she might have become a poet or even been a scientist. I'll never really know. [Response: At that time period, 1892, would you consider a potential woman scientist an asset or a threat in the lab?]

3. Instead of treating Charlotte like a child I should have listened to her the way I expected her to listen to me. Women should express their feelings. If she was too sensitive, it was probably my fault.[1] [Response: Why?]

In viewing the film none of the students commented on John's privileged status as a middle-class physician with money and position enough to seclude Charlotte in a large country house where cooks, nannies, and chambermaids make embroidery the only work she can do.[2] Because they did not believe that the film exposed the class system, they did not notice the scene (added on to the story) where the visiting psychiatrist tells John of a mental hospital where he supervises poor women for whom, he claims, an appeal to their feminine vanity speeds recovery. Since my response would have to be the same for thirty essays, I commented in class on the differences and tensions between social class at the end of the nineteenth century: doctors, doctor's wives, mothers, and sisters versus servants and mental hospital patients. As happened in "The Use of Force," the contradictions inherent in class conflict escaped them, so I put all further discussion "on hold."

The clearest response to the nuances of gender happened after we read Margaret Edson's play *W;t* (semicolon in the title, Edson's) and reviewed the remarkable video-taped performance of Emma Thompson as the university professor, Vivian Bearing, renowned for her interpretation of John Donne's Holy Sonnets, which as her graduate mentor points out, purposefully ignored the semi-colon and used a comma in the last line of "Death Be Not Proud"—"And Death shall be no more, Death thou shalt die,"—to signify "Nothing but a breath—a comma—separated life from life everlasting" (14). Twenty-eight years later the professor is afflicted with stage-four ovarian cancer.

In writing the screenplay Mike Nichols and Emma Thompson took the audience beyond the screen barrier, as it were, to witness the anomie of the hospital and hear the militaristic language oncologists use in testing the "toughness" of the patient in order to withstand eight cycles of "aggressive chemotherapy, Hexamethophosphacil and Vinplatin to potentiate" (36) at full dose with lethal side effects equal to the spread of her tumor. The overview of the hospital corridor studded with high-tech equipment was juxtaposed with closeups of the oncologist, Kelekian, and his resident, Jason Posner, who had been Bearing's student as an undergraduate. Like Kelekian and Posner, Bearing has been locked into literary precision insulating her from personal contact with students and colleagues. Her suffering while she desperately attempts to maintain her dignity is harrowing in depicting a virtually masculinized universe wherein "the clinical," that is, personal interaction with patients means the formulaic "how are you feeling today?" to a vomiting, writhing woman without the inquirer looking up from the data on her chart long enough to make eye contact.

Nearly every student had lost someone to cancer, and even those who had not had enough field experience working in clinical pharmacies to recognize the impersonal way that most hospitals deal with patients suffering terminal illness. My objective, arguably that of the playwright and the actors, was to have the students experience the dichotomy between the masculinized jargon both of the doctor and the patient, as opposed to Bearing's gradual apprehension that she needed the compassion of her nurse, Susie Monahan, to frame her suffering in plain English (often punctuated by agonized moans).

On the final take-home exam, consisting of three questions, the only obligatory question was a written response to *W;t*, worded as follows:

JASON TO SUSIE: What do they *teach* you in nursing school (78)?

Both Vivian Bearing and the doctors who treat her cancer aggressively, fail to comprehend how their uses of *language* (Bearing's strict textual analysis of Donne's *Holy Sonnets;* Kelakian/Jason's rigid use of medical terminology to diagnose and treat a tumor) objectify and dehumanize the body and soul. Only Susie who lacks the physicians' formal training in oncology responds to Vivian with the language of touch and the voice of empathy. Why do you think she can do so? Respond, using either the oncologist's (Kelekian's) voice or Susie's to structure your narrative.

In class discussion, a surprising number of men went beyond the boundaries of the question to voice their resentment of Vivian's uncompromising pedagogy. They cited Vivian's flashback to the way she dealt with the student who wanted an extension on turning in his paper.

STUDENT 1: I need to ask for an extension. . . . I'm really sorry and I know your policy, but see _____

VIVIAN: Don't tell me. Your grandmother died?

STUDENT 1: You knew.

VIVIAN: It was a guess.

STUDENT 1: I have to go home.

VIVIAN: Do what you will but the paper is due when it is due. (63)

The student leaves; the camera focuses on Vivian, whose suffering has taught her to regret her inflexibility.

As I have said earlier, nearly all the men have had relatives or friends who died of cancer. And yet they found it difficult to empathize with an English professor proud of her accomplishments in a discipline as strange to them as theirs is to me. About half cited the flashback above to conclude that she was "too opinionated"—hence if not responsible for her illness, then deserving of it. None considered the central issue: specialists' use of language to distance themselves from their patients/students. In contrast, all of the women saw her as a suffering human being who used textual analysis to shield herself from human contact. Some cried openly at the end of the film.

Their written response to the take-home essay indicated in these excerpts reveals gender-specific tensions between male doctors and the female nurse and patient. In the hope that the writing process would clarify power struggles they have experienced as overmanaged preprofessionals, I did not respond in writing.

March 3. Problems with pain management, so I prescribed morphine. When conscious patient talks about her work. Delirious, either due to infection or effect of morphine. Didn't understand a word. Asked Jason who was her student before he came on board to join the team. Jason distracted by project. Understandable. Didn't pursue it.

March 7. Nothing more to be done. Hex and plat destroyed her immune. Why the hell didn't she come in for annual checkup? Might have bought some more time, but we'd have to find another subject. If this hadn't worked it would have been back to the rats.

March 10. Communication failure. Jason screwed up on the no code, ordered full and the nurse went ballistic. Still, a good experiment. Worth another try if we can get a subject like Bearing. Asked Jason to work out a grant proposal from NIH.

For the female students, particularly some of the Asians who use Susie's voice to mirror their cultural identity (Susie is played by an African American), their writing clearly demonstrates less reification of the patient, more personal involvement.

Thursday, March 1. How could Jason leave Vivian alone with her feet in the stirrups while he ran around looking for me because he had to have a "girl" in the room to do a pelvic? Telling her to relax doesn't help because anyone can see how nervous he is when he has to let go of his chart (Caucasian).

Sunday, March 4. It's sad that no one comes to visit her. She says she likes it that way but in Madras where my parents came from even if the parents were dead, some family member would come and bring her bland ice or other food she could digest without throwing up. When my grandmother was in HUP [Hospital of University of Pennsylvania] with colon cancer the family came over in shifts and kept telling her all the old family stories and they brought pictures of relatives in India. In American hospitals patients die alone. It's scary.

March 8. She had four treatments of hex and vin at full dose. Lost all her hair and barfs non-stop. Tonight at home she had a high fever and had to take a cab to ER. Lucky I was on night shift and got her a bed. Jason smirked and said she was going through "shake and bake," like she was some kind of pancake (Caucasian).

March 10. Looks like she's dehydrating even though Jason keeps telling her to push the fluids. I know she doesn't talk much but my Aunt Seema broke her arm and complains day and night. The family visits her anyway.

The last entries are all from the same student, a Korean woman.

March 12. I told Vivian about the codes if her heart stops. At four A.M. she rang for me and looked awful, like a bald mannequin you see in the shopping mall. I asked would she like popsickles and [she] asked me to have one too, just to keep her company. Then I say there's something we must talk about and she looks me right in the eye and says the treatment isn't working. I say the tumor definatly *[sic]* shrank but other tumors spread. If her heart stops beating she can have full code where they resusitate *[sic]* or no code where they'll let her pass away in peace. I think she should choose no code, but she's a tough lady and may want to go on anyway. She asked if I would still be her nurse and I said of course, sweetheart.

March 13. The pain got so bad I wanted Kelekian to give her a Patient-Controlled Analgesic where she could push a little button on a pump and control the amount of medication she needed. But all he could say was Dr. Bearing are you in pain? And give her morphine. I told him the analgesic would keep her alert, he wouldn't listen and the morphine put her in a coma.

March 14. Tonight Jason told me what a tough course he had with Doctor Bearing on John Dun *[sic]*. He said the paper was about survival anxiety, I ask him whether the poet survived and he laughs and says, what did they teach you in nursing school. So we have to use a catheter to draw the urine, I tell her it won't hurt and Jason says with his sarcastic smirk "like she can hear you." I know she can't but it's nice to talk as if she could hear and I even put lotion on her hands.

March 16. I'm still mad at Jason he didn't pay attention to the DNR [do not resuscitate]. He called in a Code Blue when he saw the flat line on her monitor. I yelled she's DNR and he yelled she's RESEARCH. I threw him off of the bed and only after the team got there he remembered Kelekian signed for No Code. I just pushed him away and straitened *[sic]* the sheets. In Korea they show respect for the dead. After I covered her I patted her arm and said a prayer.

The use of the comma splice by this third-year pharmacy student inhabiting Susie's consciousness does homage to Vivian's final interpretation of "Death Be Not Proud," "The comma, a small breath separates life, death and the afterlife?" (as cited earlier, p. 8). (In returning her exam, I congratulated the student on her format—a tribute to Susie, Vivian, and John Donne; I also informed her that what worked in a humanities take-home exam might not elsewhere if she wanted to pass the College Proficiency Exam and graduate. She laughed and said that in fact she had passed that exam the day before.)

My purpose—to see patients as subjects of their illness by using first-person narratives as an act of agency—apparently succeeded with this student. I am mindful, nonetheless, that students' imaginary immersion in narrative crossover can only go so far. If the dominant hierarchy Kelakian personifies has engendered strong enough resistance for the student to assume a writer's agency to fight an oncologist's depersonalization of a dying patient, how many more men and women will see Kelekian and the ambitious Jason as intruders on a woman's body and obstructionists on her right to have some control in the way she dies.

A few of the men and women I teach are, in fact, premed, and like *W;t*'s Jason Posner they're taking this humanities course and others because "it will look good on our transcripts when we apply [to medical school]." Nevertheless, no matter what branch of medicine they choose, their careers will allow them little time for integrating the ideas of writerly agency they were exposed to in a humanities elective. Indeed it is likely that by the time they practice, years of being managed (even more rigorously in graduate school) will provide few opportunities for them to challenge hierarchical concepts of gender, which, in fact, they probably have internalized in order to survive professionally. Furthermore, if they are idealistic enough to attempt to subvert an essentially corporate system of medical care that is competitive, profit oriented, and ultimately depersonalizing, they cannot do so without forming networks with like-minded peers or the rare mentor who empowers them to integrate professional judgment with a patient's needs.

Has the limited success I have experienced during the four years I have taught Literature and Medicine influenced the feminist theory underscoring my pedagogy? Only in the sense that any theory has to be continually renegotiated in order to meld with practice, that all theories are themselves necessarily fractured by practices. In helping overly managed students become agents of their discourse with peers, patients, and supervisors, I do not expect an interdisciplinary course to enable them to sift through information overload enough to identify the ideological premises that reward professional detachment from emotion rather than integrate it with critical thinking and writing. Nonetheless, I know from my own experience grounded in years of interrogating essentialist theory that the process of covering a blank legal pad or computer screen with something thought about and felt is generative and ultimately transforming. Doing so can potentially transform the very theories we teachers bring to bear in order to understand our students' work and lives.

NOTES

1. To maintain student-teacher confidentiality, all direct quotations from students and summaries of their ideas remain anonymous.

2. For an excellent study on medical control of both middle- and working-class women, see Barbara Ehrenreich and Deirdre English, *For Her Own Good: 150 Years of the Experts' Advice to Women.*

WORKS CITED

Anderson, Charles A., ed. *Literature and Medicine,* 10.1 (Spring, 2000): ix–2.

Edson, Magaret. *W;t.* New York: Faber and Faber, 1999; *W;t,* Screenplay, Mike Nichols, HBO April 2001.

Ehrenriech, Barbara, and Deirdre English. *For Her Own Good: 150 Years of the Experts' Advice to Women.* New York: Doubleday Anchor Books, 1978.

Gilman, Charlotte Perkins. "The Yellow Wallpaper." *The Heath Anthology of American Literature,* vol. 2. Ed. Paul Lauter. Lexington, Mass.: D. A. Heath, 2000. 800–12.

Oudshoorn, Nelly. "On Bodies, Technologies, and Feminisms." *Feminism in Twentieth-Century Science, Technology, and Medicine.* Ed. Angela N. H. Creager, Elizabeth Lunbeck, and Londa Schiebinger. Forward Catherine S. Stimpson. Chicago: University of Chicago Press, 2000, 199–213.

Williams, William Carlos. "The Use of Force." *The Doctor Stories.* Compiled Robert Coles. New York: New Direction, 1984. 56–60.

Part *Three*

FRACTURED FEMINISMS IN THE CLASSROOM

Chapter Seven

The Challenges of Establishing a Feminist Ethos in the Composition Classroom

Stories from Large Research Universities

SHELLY WHITFIELD, VERONICA PANTOJA, AND DUANE ROEN

Drawing on our experiences in composition classrooms and programs at large research universities, we describe some of the challenges facing a teacher striving to establish a feminist ethos in a composition classroom. Part of the struggle can be internal to the individual teacher—one in which conflicting Bakhtinian voices compete with one another. An internalized *svoj* ("one's own word, one's own world view"—*Dialogic Imagination* 427) dialogues with an internalized *cuzoj* ("the word or world view of another"). To exemplify such struggles, we offer the narrative of a teacher whose feminist academic work contrasts with the subject positions of some of her students. We examine some of the fractures that emerge as a result. However, such struggles are as varied as the individuals and sites in which they are enacted. Frequently, the struggle between *svoj* and *cuzoj* is more public, and here we reflect on the narratives of some young, usually female teachers who enter the classroom to find voices that are skeptical of or openly hostile to a feminist ethos. Negotiating these hostilities is neither simple nor easy, even for the most experienced teachers. Although we draw on a range of sources and our own professional experiences, we weave these voices and events within a case study.

ETHOS IN OUR NEW MILLENNIUM

When Aristotle pondered the concept of 'ethos' (character) as he presents it in *The Rhetoric,* he probably could not have imagined the social complexities of an early-twenty-first-century composition classroom. In Aristotle's words,

> Persuasion is achieved by the speaker's personal character when the speech is so spoken as to make us think him credible. We believe good men more fully and more readily than others: this is true generally whatever the question is, and absolutely true where exact certainty is impossible and opinions are divided. This kind of persuasion, like the others, should be achieved by what the speaker says, not by what people think of his character before he begins to speak. It is not true, as some writers assume in their treatises on rhetoric, that the personal goodness revealed by the speaker contributes nothing to his power of persuasion; on the contrary, his character may almost be called the most effective means of persuasion he possesses. (25)

With the exception of the obvious masculine pronouns that reflect the relative status of men and women in Aristotle's world, including the academic realm of that world, other features of Aristotle's concept of ethos motivate us to contemplate issues of ethos often found in university composition classrooms at the dawn of the third millennium. Among other things, these contemplations led the three of us to develop the following case study, a composite of experiences that we have witnessed in university composition classrooms in recent years. By exploring this case study, we aim to analyze not just our own personal narratives but also the experiences shared by other teachers. In essence, the primary players in our case study—Holly, Mark, and Alex—are constructed through several identities, and the episode that follows is tailored from multiple experiences.

Feminist and other critical theories influence Holly's pedagogy, but she— at this stage in her teaching career—has not yet clearly articulated them as direct influences on her teaching methodologies. She knows what she believes: teaching is a political act and "experience is understood to be socially, materially, and ideologically produced" (Lee 58). She wants her students to be critical consumers and producers of texts by studying what Bruce McComiskey describes in *Teaching Composition as a Social Process* as the three levels of composing: textual, rhetorical, and discursive (6). By negotiating and composing through these three levels, students can learn about the "linguistic characteristics of writing" at the textual level; they can grasp the "generative and restrictive" elements such as audience and purpose at the rhetorical level; and, most valued by Holly, they can uncover the "institutional forces that condition [their] very identities as writers" (6–7). Therefore, to Holly, each reading selection, each writing assignment, and each class activity is an opportunity for her to enact some of her beliefs. But even with her clear vision of how composition should be taught, Holly is not entirely prepared for a student such as Mark—a student who feels threatened by Holly's pedagogical beliefs and actions. Considering this, we recount the events, activities, and conversations that took place in Holly's classroom in the initial four weeks of her first semester teaching first-year composition.

CONFLICTS 101: HOLLY'S NARRATIVE, OUR NARRATIVE

Holly, a young, enthusiastic graduate student in the English department at a large state university, thought she was fully prepared to teach first-year composition courses. Four weeks into the semester, however, she was becoming more and more frustrated with student resistance to her feminist/critical pedagogy and carefully planned writing activities, which she considered to be just as valuable to her male students as to her female students. From the first day of the semester, Holly explained to her students that she saw the composition classroom as an arena for them to become more effective writers and critical thinkers. She believed that, as Amy Lee argues in *Composing Critical Pedagogies,* "writing about one's history is thus a means to understanding how we have come to be positioned and composed in the here-and-now, to recognize that experience itself is inscribed by systematic social and material conditions" (58).

Many of Holly's students appeared to be fully engaged with the class, identifying with her youthful energy and responding positively to active-learning strategies that compelled students to explain their various perspectives on course issues. Yet a handful of students—enough to make the classroom environment uncomfortable at times—struggled against her reading and writing assignments. Sometimes their mutiny was subtle. When Holly introduced a writing assignment, for example, some grumbled complaints under their breath. At other times, when Holly was placing them into peer review groups or facilitating discussion circles, these same students whispered, "This is stupid" or "Who cares?" Holly believed this defiant group of students—consisting of one woman and two men—had a leader, Mark, a bright and opinionated student, who often questioned Holly's teaching methodologies and expertise. And Mark's mutiny was not all that subtle.

By the end of the first week of the semester, in whole-class discussions about the reading, Mark dominated the conversations, asserting that the readings held hidden agendas, and some of which, in his opinion, had nothing to do with the purpose of his first-year composition course. Mark claimed these agendas tended to have the sole purpose of making men—usually Euro-American men—feel guilty about the injustice their actions had caused in the world. During the second week of the semester, he especially struggled against an activity Holly led, in which the class generated a list of fairy tales that the students remembered enjoying as children. She then asked her students to respond in their journals about why they enjoyed these particular stories and what they learned from them. When students were asked to share their responses, most students commented that the fairy tales taught life lessons about such values as "never give up," "listen to your elders," and "good things happen to those who wait." Many students enjoyed the fantasy and magic in the stories, while other students remembered finding pleasure in the animated Disney movies portraying some of the listed fairy tales. After students shared their initial responses, Holly asked her students to find alternative readings of the fairy tales through guided small-group discussions. She posed the following primary question to her class: "What else do we learn from fairy tales?" By answering this question and the questions that followed, students were encouraged to locate and then interrogate the stereotypes and assumptions found in many fairy tales. Mark's immediate vocal response as he trudged over to his group was, "Here we go again. Now fairy tales are evil. We will discover that the prince is not Prince Charming, but Prince Harming. Right, Holly?"

Holly explained to Mark again, after she had just offered this explanation to the whole class, that the purpose of this activity was to encourage them to think critically about ordinary texts. By envisioning themselves as critical writers and readers, they could begin to "recognize and question the different constructions of 'authority,' textual logic, and structure that are normative in specific contexts" (Lee 2). From this standpoint, they might identify conventions that define certain forms and rhetorical uses of writing and learn how to accommodate these forms and uses within their own writing.

Yet Mark's aggressive and sometimes rude behavior was reserved not only for Holly. Sometimes Mark even interrupted his classmates in the middle of their responses, and Holly would have to mildly reprimand him by saying, "Mark, one moment please. Let Carmen finish and then we will listen to your response." Mark, wearing an all-knowing smile, then claimed he had nothing to say when Holly turned the class's attention to what he wanted to share about the readings.

Having recently read John Bean's *Engaging Ideas,* Holly was attempting to re-invent journal writing as much for herself as for her students, because much of her primary and secondary education had used journals through expressionistic approaches. Many of her English teachers shared the "conviction that reality is a personal and private construct," and truth is discovered through individual expression (Berlin 145). Thus, Holly's educational journal writing was not usually shared with or read by any audience other than herself, and the ideas presented within were never critiqued or questioned. But it was in Holly's undergraduate education at a small liberal arts college that journal writing was used as a tool to make "sense of 'reality' by a process of linguistic invention and documentation" (Berthoff 638). By reflecting and responding in an academic journal, or what her professors called a "scholar's log," Holly discovered her "sense of reality" was socially constructed, and she also learned how to merge her private and public voices into effective writing—writing that accomplished the goals that she had established. By thinking of the contents of her scholar's log as public discourse, Holly moved her writing beyond a solitary act and private vision into a world of complex social interpretations and processes. Therefore, through her own classroom-assigned journal responses Holly hoped to effectively carry out one of her pedagogical principles that everyone's voice in the class needs to be articulated, acknowledged, and examined. Mark's refusal to be acknowledged—and most important, *examined*—when it was his turn to speak tended to be a deliberate sabotage of Holly's goal.

At the beginning of the third week, in one of the class discussions in which the students were sharing at least one paragraph from their "remembering event" paper, Celeste had just begun reading her writing when Mark interrupted her. He complained that all the "girls" in the class were writing emotional narratives, and frankly, he was tired of hearing stories about being dumped on prom night and struggling with being a single mom. Before Holly could respond—or even react—many of the women in the class were expressing their anger at Mark's comments. A couple of the men in the class—Mark's usual support group—laughed at Mark's interruption and the women's responses to his remarks. The class consisted of fourteen women and six men. Holly realized that ignoring such discourse in the classroom would discourage many of the students—especially female students—from taking risks and sharing their writing. She also knew, as evidenced by her own immediate anger, that Mark's behavior was inappropriate and intolerable. After class, Holly scheduled a conference with Mark for that same afternoon.

Holly had three or four conferences with Mark in the first four weeks of the semester, more than double the number of times she met with any of her other students. Holly initiated the first conference so that she could discuss his whole-class and small-group discussion behavior, hoping to find a way not to censor his comments, but instead to offer strategies on how he could be an effective discussion participant. She also wanted to discuss Mark's writing and carefully review the comments she had written on his first paper. Mark requested the other conferences—two by the end of the fourth week—so that he could debate the resubmission grade he had been given on the first paper and voice his criticism that he did not like working in peer review groups.

In both of these meetings, Mark directly challenged Holly's expertise as an English instructor. He claimed that her suggestions on his paper were vague, and he believed that she used peer review groups so that she could shirk her responsibility to provide immediate feedback to students' writing. Mark stated several times in these conferences that "telling a student to think more is just a cop out. It usually just means I don't think like you or you don't know what you want me to think. Why should I be penalized if you don't know how to help me fix my writing?" Of course, Holly knew this was an excuse on Mark's part and that he had an underlying motive in expressing this criticism because he had only made editing changes and no substantial revisions for his resubmission. But Holly did question whether she took as many pains with Mark's writing as with the other students' because he refused to put his writing, his thinking, his beliefs, and himself through revision processes. She also could not help reflecting on her inexperience as an instructor, which was obvious by her age, and whether she was effectively implementing the pedagogical principles that she embraced. Setting aside her lack of experience, however, Holly also felt that she was a competent, innovative English instructor and that Mark was just an exceptionally challenging student who was purposefully trying to undermine her classroom credibility, her ethos.

The predicament for Holly was trying to discern why Mark wanted to undermine her credibility as a teacher. She began to reflect on the obvious. Mark was an eighteen-year-old male who possibly had difficulties being taught by a twenty-two-year-old woman who expected students to be held accountable for their ideas and beliefs. Holly may have unsettled Mark's expectations of what a college teacher should be and how such a teacher should teach. He also attended a large research university with more than forty-five thousand undergraduates that attracted many students who did not know why they were going to college, except that all their friends were taking that next step. Many of the incoming first-year students, drawn to the university from around the United States and the local metropolitan area, are enticed by the resort appearance of the campus: palm tree-lined walkways, bright-hued flowers thriving year around, and weather throughout the academic year that most vacationers dream about. Most important, the student body typically wears clothes to match resort weather by dressing in sandals, shorts, tank tops, and T-shirts. The casual appearance of the students that is accepted and sometimes nurtured by the campus is independent from the design of the more than one hundred rigorous academic and research programs offered by the university. For Mark, appearances might be the primary force that establishes boundaries and codes of behavior. If his expectations are unsettled by appearances, then he will need help seeing his teacher and his university as complex entities. Mark needs to understand that Holly is an intelligent teacher with good intentions about his progress in reading, writing, and thinking critically and that she is not a woman "out to get him." Likewise, Mark may also need to realize that while he attends a university with an informal campus life and appearance, this does not mean he is enrolled in a program that boasts that same informality.

Mark was not satisfied with her explanation that when she used the word *think* contextualized in her statements that she was asking him to explain and elaborate on the significance of the event written about in his paper. He also did not accept that peer reviewing would increase the effec-

tiveness of his own writing as he learned to read and comment on other people's papers, an invaluable part of becoming a critical consumer and producer
of texts. Most frustrating was Mark's unwillingness to listen to Holly when
she explained why his response to Celeste's essay was inappropriate. When
she talked about mutual respect, Mark called it a "mother's nagging." When
Holly talked about intellectual growth, Mark scoffed. She explained that
Celeste was taking the personal experience of being a single mom and scru-
tinizing its social and public representations, some of which are hostile representations as seen by Mark's classroom behavior. Holly knew Mark would
be back for another round of debates, attempting to pull her into a power
struggle. Thus, even though she wanted to be as independent as possible, she
decided to seek advice from her director.

Because Holly leapt immediately into graduate school after she had completed her undergraduate degree, she was relieved to discover that her university offered a three-week orientation preparing graduate students for the role
of first-year composition teaching assistants. Yet now she wished she had dedicated as much attention to the Intergroup Relations Center's workshop, Fostering Constructive Dialogue in the Classroom, or the center's online document, "Guidelines for Constructive Dialogue in the Classroom," available to
all faculty and teaching assistants on campus, as she did to the syllabus-and-
course-design workshops. Alex, the composition director and primary facilitator of the orientation, listened carefully to Holly as she explained the interactions in her classroom and her one-to-one conferences with Mark. He was
especially concerned and disturbed about Mark's hostile comments that he felt
degraded women, especially the berating of Celeste's essay and commentary
about being a single mother. After discussing some proactive strategies Holly
could implement in her classroom to inhibit Mark's aggressive behavior, Holly
asked Alex to visit her classroom in the near future, specifically requesting a
"surprise" visit. She did not want Alex's visit to observe only Mark's behavior,
but also her teaching approaches.

Holly's students were doing an in-class writing activity when Alex
entered the room and quietly sat down. Alex noticed that Holly was writing
with her students, obviously caught in the thoughts of her own composing
processes. The room was silent, except for the tapping of computer keys.
Occasionally, however, Alex heard some whispering and smothered laughter
in the corner of the room. He quickly eyed two young men leaning over one
terminal screen, and from his view, it looked as if they were surfing the Internet rather than participating in the writing activity. A few more minutes
passed as the noise level increased from the corner of the room. Holly stood
up from her computer and asked her students to print out what they had written, so it could be placed in their folders and used for a later activity.

After the class was settled, Holly transitioned the students into their
peer-response groups, in which they would be responding to each other's

drafts on their "remembered person" essay, guided by focused questions and statements. Once the students were busy in their groups, Holly walked around the class, sometimes joining a group as an active listener. As Holly got up to leave one group, a student asked about the stranger sitting in the classroom. Holly explained that the composition director had stopped in for an informal observation. As Holly completed those words, Mark's head popped up as he swung around in his seat to look at Alex. Within seconds he had gathered his papers and graded homework assignments and was headed toward Alex. Holly asked Mark to return to his group to finish the peer-response session, but Mark angrily replied that the "silly girls" in his group were no help, and he was not going to miss the opportunity to finally talk with someone who could help. Alex was not surprised to see that Mark was one of the young men giggling in the corner earlier in the class period. As Mark placed his papers on Alex's desk, Alex strongly recommended that Mark return to his group to finish class for the day. He assured Mark that he would schedule an appointment to speak with him at a later time. The rest of the class stared at Holly.

RESOLUTIONS 101: BALANCING THEORY AND PRACTICE

We have described the initial teaching experiences and reflections of Holly so that we might offer some analysis of the pedagogical theories that inform her teaching practices. Through our interpretation of her experiences, we hope to provide solutions that may bridge the gap between theory and practitioner, which has been illuminated by Holly's narrative. Holly's composition pedagogy exhibits some features of feminist pedagogies, as described by Susan Jarratt: "[T]he decentering or sharing of authority, the recognition of students as sources of knowledge, a focus on processes (of writing and teaching) over products" ("Feminist" 115). A potential difficulty with the values implicit in the approaches that Jarratt lists, though, is that students do not always share them because they sometimes have expectations that the teacher should be the source of authority and knowledge and that products are what count. An alternative explanation of the mismatch is that Mark's desire for certainty leaves him with little patience for the probabilistic nature of rhetoric that Aristotle describes in *Rhetoric*.

To bridge this gap in values and expectations, teachers such as Holly—actually all teachers—need to facilitate conversations with students, beginning with goals for a first-year composition course. To establish her ethos within the profession, Holly might use the Council of Writing Program Administrators' (WPA) *(http://www.wpacouncil.org/)* "Outcomes Statement" *(http://www.mwsc.edu/~outcomes/)* as a source of authority. The "WPA Outcomes Statement," the product of years of conversations and numerous revisions, covers a full range of goals for first-year courses—rhetorical considerations, general reading and thinking skills, composing processes, and surface-feature conventions. To demonstrate the value of shared authority and knowledge during the first week of the course, Holly might pose the following question to students to initiate discussion: "Why do you think the national organization has endorsed these particular goals for first-year writing courses?"

The strengths of such an initial question are many: (1) students see the goals as national and professional, not just the teacher's idiosyncratic quirks; (2) when students explain the rationale for the "Outcomes Statement" they are also endorsing them (that is, becoming invested stakeholders); (3) the question encourages students to be engaged with learning/composing in the ways that bell hooks suggests: "I encourage students to work at coming to voice in an atmosphere where they may be afraid or see themselves at risk" (*Talking Back* 53). Anyone who has worked with students in first-year writing courses has seen signs of their feeling at risk, even when they mask those signs with bravado.

Following this conversation about the "WPA Outcomes Statement," Holly might modify Karen Hayes's activity (Eichhorn et al.) to pose the following question: "Given the goals of the 'WPA Outcomes Statement,' how can a teacher work with you to reach these goals?" By asking students to write individually in response to this question, Holly can find out what each student may need to reach the goals. By subsequently facilitating small-group discussions and then a full-class discussion with diverse written responses, Holly can encourage students to understand the range of learning styles and needs in the classroom. Such conversations may also help students understand that they need to help one another achieve their goals. Instead of the teacher—in this case, a female teacher—assuming the role of lone nurturer (a role with risks for the teacher), everyone in the classroom, both males and females, can share the responsibilities. (See discussions of nurturing roles by Susan Miller; Ellen Holbrook; and Phyllis Mentzell Ryder, Valentina Abordonado, Barbara Heifferon, and Duane Roen.)

Given Mark's comments about women, Holly probably needs to talk with Alex, her supervisor and, we hope, her mentor. Mark has certainly contributed to the kind of "chilly classroom climate" that Bernice Sandler has studied. He may also have violated his university's sexual harassment policies, not the quid-pro-quo clause but the hostile-learning-environment clause. In such cases, teachers need to report incidents to their administrative supervisors, who in turn should consult with campus offices of student life, equal opportunity, and general counsel. In this particular context, Alex has worked with these three offices for several years. As a result, they record his reports in case a student exhibits a pattern of harassment, but they have given Alex the green light to have "fireside chats" with mild offenders such as Mark because they recognize, as Susan Jarratt does, that Alex, by virtue of his gender, has an ethos that Holly may find more difficult to achieve with students such as Mark. That is, Mark will not see Alex as having "an agenda." The university has guidelines for these fireside chats, but Alex has found the following question to be highly salient in helping students such as Mark understand the effects of hostile words: "How would you feel if another man said that about your mother/sister/grandmother/daughter/partner/spouse?" The question rarely fails to facilitate a frank, fruitful discussion about the potentially destructive power of language, one of the very conversations that Holly is trying to facilitate in her classroom through her reading and writing assignments.

As Alex works with first-year TAs throughout the year, he needs to equip not only Holly but also other new teachers with time-tested strategies for facilitating the kinds of active and interactive pedagogy that the program promotes. One way of doing that is to introduce TAs to principles of cooperative-collaborative learning, principles that provide structure for group work and that attend group dynamics. Specifically, as Johnson and colleagues and Kegan note, effective cooperative-collaborative learning is marked by individual accountability, equal participation, positive interdependence, simultaneity, team-building activities, and a teacher's role of "guide on the side" rather than "sage on the stage." Holly has some vague sense of this kind of pedagogy because it parallels her feminist pedagogy, but she needs to gain a greater understanding of the specifics of cooperative-collaborative approaches. Further, by fostering this kind of pedagogy, students can more clearly understand the social-epistemic nature of composing.

Our experience and feminist theory make clear that effective teaching consists of far more than nurturing. As Jarratt argues, we often need to put a student writer's thinking in conversation with other ideas—a Hegelian dialectical journey from thesis and antithesis to synthesis or a Bakhtinian exchange between *svoj* and *cuzoj*—to help give voice to those ideas (*Rereading* 112–16) and to help establish a writer's ethos. Likewise, in *Talking Back*, bell hooks reflects on the role that oppositional thinking played in her own coming to voice. In *Teaching to Transgress*, hooks observes that teachers who best help students come to voice are "on a mission" to engage learners in a Freireian liberatory pedagogy (2). In such a pedagogy, participants in the classroom must have "interest in one another, in hearing one another's voices, in recognizing one another's presence" (8). hooks goes on to explain that showing students how to listen to everyone in the class "doesn't mean that we listen uncritically or that classrooms can be so open that anything someone says is taken as true," but instead we listen to individuals seriously before responding, possibly interrogating their ideas (150). Because Mark equates being able to express one's ideas in class as being able to espouse Truth, he struggles to ensure his "Truth" is heard even if it means silencing others. Yet establishing the kind of classroom forum that hooks describes encourages students to heed one another's voices and not just the teacher's authority. If Holly silences Mark before the class can respond to and significantly challenge Mark's particular position, then Holly's intervention may be interpreted as an act equally as counterproductive as Mark's.

Even though Paula Treichler wonders whether anyone should label a set of pedagogical practices as "feminist," we suggest that narratives like the one included in this chapter provide opportunities to ask questions such as the following: What are "feminist" pedagogies? What is critical thinking? What kinds of pedagogies encourage the range of thinking that Holly values in classroom discussions and in students' writing? What kind(s) of teacherly ethos help to encourage the kinds of learning that Holly values? By considering these and other related questions, we can begin to understand the fractures or fissures that occurred in Holly's classroom.

CODA

We assume that Holly's case strikes some familiar chords for readers of this chapter, and we hope that our commentary also resonates with the expertise that readers bring to bear on the case. Although we have offered one configuration of critical lenses for analyzing Holly's situation, we readily acknowledge that many other configurations are available. As we finish writing this chapter, we have the hope that colleagues in the field will offer their insights. We hope that the chapter serves to spark more conversations about how mentors in the field can best prepare and support teachers like Holly as they work with students like Mark.

WORKS CITED

Aristotle. *Rhetoric and Poetics of Aristotle*. Ed. Friedrich Solmsen. Trans. W. Rhys Roberts. New York: Modern Library, 1954.

Bakhtin, Mikhail. *The Dialogic Imagination: Four Essays by M. M. Bakhtin*. Ed. Michael Holquist. Trans. Caryl Emerson and Michael Holquist. Austin: University of Texas Press, 1981.

Bean, John C. *Engaging Ideas: The Professor's Guide to Integrating Writing, Critical Thinking, and Active Learning in the Classroom*. San Francisco: Jossey-Bass, 1996.

Berlin, James A. *Rhetoric and Reality: Writing Instruction in American Colleges, 1900–1985*. Carbondale: Southern Illinois University Press, 1987.

Berthoff, Ann E. "From Problem-Solving to a Theory of Imagination." *College English* 33 (1972): 636–49.

Council of Writing Program Administrators Outcomes Statement. *http://www.mwsc. edu/~outcomes/*.

Eichhorn, Jill, Sara Farris, Karen Hayes, Adriana Hernandez, Susan C. Jarratt, and Karen Powers-Stubbs. "A Symposium on Feminist Experiences in the Composition Classroom." *College Composition and Communication* 43 (1992): 297–322.

Holbrook, Sue Ellen. "Women's Work: The Feminizing of Composition." *Rhetoric Review* 9 (1991): 201–29.

hooks, bell. *Talking Back: Thinking Feminist, Thinking Black.* Boston: South End, 1989.

———. *Teaching to Transgress: Education as the Practice of Freedom.* New York: Routledge, 1994.

Intergroup Relations Center. "Guidelines for Constructive Dialogue in the Classroom." Tempe: Arizona State University. *http://www.asu.edu/provost/intergroup/resources/classguidelines.html.*

Jarratt, Susan C. "Feminist Pedagogy." *A Guide to Composition Pedagogies.* Ed. Gary Tate, Amy Rupiper, and Kurt Schick. New York: Oxford University Press, 2001. 113–31.

———. *Rereading the Sophists: Classical Rhetoric Refigured.* Carbondale: Southern Illinois University Press, 1991.

Johnson, David W., Roger T. Johnson, and Karl A. Smith, *Active Learning: Cooperation in the College Classroom.* Edina, Minn.: Interaction Book Company,1991.

———. *Cooperative Learning: Increasing College Faculty Instructional Productivity.* Washington, D.C.: ASHE/ERIC Higher Education, 1991.

Kagan, Spencer. *Cooperative Learning.* San Juan Capistrano, Calif.: Kagan Cooperative Learning, 1992.

Lee, Amy. *Composing Critical Pedagogies: Teaching Writing as Revision.* Urbana: National Council of Teachers of English, 2000.

McComiskey, Bruce. *Teaching Composition as a Social Process.* Logan: Utah State University Press, 2000.

Miller, Susan. "The Feminization of Composition." *The Politics of Writing Instruction: Postsecondary.* Ed. Richard Bullock and John Trimbur. Portsmouth, N.H.: Heinemann-Boynton/Cook, 1991. 39–53.

Ryder, Phyllis Mentzell, Valentina Abordonado, Barbara Heifferon, and Duane Roen. "Multivocal Midwife: The Writing Teacher as Rhetor." *Alternative Rhetorics: Challenges to the Rhetorical Tradition.* Ed. Laura Gray-Rosendale and Sibylle Gruber. Albany: State University of New York Press, 2001. 33–51.

Sandler, Bernice Resnick, Lisa A. Silverberg, and Roberta M. Hall. *The Chilly Classroom Climate: A Guide to Improve the Education of Women.* Washington, D.C.: National Association for Women in Education, 1996.

Treichler, Paula A. "A Room of Whose Own? Lessons from Feminist Classroom Narratives." *Changing Classroom Practices: Resources for Literary and Cultural Studies.* Ed. David B. Downing. Urbana: NCTE, 1994. 75–103.

Chapter Eight

RIDING OUR HOBBYHORSE

Ethics, Ethnography, and an
Argument for the Teacher-Researcher

GIL HAROOTUNIAN

In this chapter I argue that ethical teaching comes from a harmony of theory and practice, a state that mandates encouraging the identity of teacher-researchers in the field of composition. I support this by examining the upside-down results that occurred when the ethnography, an assignment designed to enable students to interrogate the macrocategories of gender, race, and class in their cultures, was introduced into certain writing studios at Syracuse University (SU). This assignment, crafted to guide students to critique their cultures, its biases, and its silences, became instead an assignment through which students trumpeted those prejudices. I analyze why this happened and explore how a new design between theory and practice can aid in remedying such questionable results.

I begin with a brief history of the introduction of the ethnography into American composition classrooms, explaining my own attraction to feminist ethnography assignments. I then describe my writing program's initial "ethical" designs for injecting the ethnography into its classrooms, ethical designs that I later discovered to be unsuccessful when I conducted archival research of nearly two hundred student-written ethnographies in the SU Writing Program. Upon this discovery, I considered the reason for such "unethical" results:

the politicized form of "ethnography" handed down to teachers through the intermediary step of institutional administration, a step that helps to separate theorists and practitioners. I conclude with recommendations to overcome this institutional imperialism of composition classrooms and enact a new ethics in the relation between theorists and practitioners, a relation in which both parties should be held equally responsible for talking to one another.

BACKGROUND OF "FEMINIST" ETHNOGRAPHY

When those of us in the academy transported the ethnography from the domain of anthropology into the various classrooms of the different disciplines, we were, in effect, transforming the ethnography from a field genre into a curriculum genre.[1] Many of us enjoyed the honeymoon period when ethnographies were a new form in our classrooms by encouraging our students to share in our excitement at the many possibilities for research and writing opened by this novel form. However, we too often did not pause to speculate that we had transformed a field genre into a curriculum genre,[2] and to question the best ways to effect this transformation within our individual fields. This challenge was exacerbated by the divide between the elite and the working class in the academy, that is, between the theorists and the teachers, a divide already discussed by theorists such as Louise Wetherbee Phelps in *Composition as a Human Science: Contributions to the Self-Understanding of a Discipline*. This divide is worsening with the academy's drive to diminish full-time tenure positions and fill the ranks with part-time and contingent labor, and this makes all the more possible, even desirable from an administrator's point of view, the institutional control of composition classrooms staffed by part-time teachers. Not only will such assignments as the ethnography become politicized, and eventually fossilized, but with newly imposed measures like outcomes assessments, institutional administrators can "own" the actual papers written by the students as well as the assignments handed out by teachers.

Thus, as we continue to hand the ethnography from professional anthropologists to undergraduate students, the need to bridge the divide between the elite theorists and the working practitioners is great. The ethnography is one illustrative study of this current challenge in our field, for with introducing the ethnography into writing classrooms, theorists offered to practitioners one grand, new possibility of guiding young writers to investigate "cultures," each loaded with the troublesome baggage of gender, race, and class. And if the teaching of the ethnography resulted unexpectedly in a lack of ethical outcomes, I present how one can subsequently optimize any ethical outcomes by becoming a genuine teacher-researcher; by applying the feminist theories of caring espoused by Nel Noddings, Janet Emig, and the like to break with the institutional prescriptions for teaching ethnography. This is a leveling move, for practitioners rise to the "heights" of theory while theorists visit the devalued realm of practice.

Moreover, the ethnography first appealed to me as a feminist teacher and scholar because the work of Wendy Bishop, Jacqueline Jones Royster, and other feminists showed the field the ways in which that genre could be a good tool to model interrogation of masculinist stories and ideas in American culture, and in our academic culture in particular. Royster, for example, in "Sarah's Story: Making a Place for Historical Ethnography in Rhetorical Studies," conducted an ethnographic analysis of the film *Amistad* to show how the life of one key participant, a young African American woman named Sarah, had been edited out. Bishop analyzed the ethnography in broader strokes in *Ethnographic Writing Research,* noting that when compositionists joined in the conversation on ethnography research and writing, its feminists such as Bonnie Sunstein suggested "new, ethics-oriented ways to evaluate the qualities of ethnographic texts" (147–48; 120–21). She takes care to present in an appendix a mini-ethnography, "Devan Cook: Considering Feminism, Pedagogy, and Underlife," that is a model of a feminist ethnography that interrogates the roles and challenges of women in a "masculinist" academic culture (212).

With all of this feminist appeal, then, imagine the surprise in discovering that the teaching of the ethnography in the Writing Program resulted in less than ethical harvests. Imagine finding that it resulted in students trumpeting the various chauvinisms of their cultures—an act that we would be hard pressed to argue benefited them. The answer not only points to the break in the "chain" of ethics starting with theorists and leading through our institutions down to practitioners and finally students. It also points to the pressing need to restructure the relations between theory and practice to dampen the force of institutional imperialism in our classrooms.

THE WRITING PROGRAM'S FIRST ETHICAL DESIGNS

The first-generation teachers of ethnography in writing programs had to struggle against many prejudices to successfully introduce this "new" genre. Writing courses are devalued sometimes as service courses; misguided administrators demand that TAs teach the revered classical forms of the essay, and so on. So the first-generation teachers worked hard to break through old molds, and they succeeded. As part of this process, they were also overreverent of the original anthropological model of ethnography, for it held so many possibilities for thought and research in our classrooms. The first-generation teachers urged students to explore the mating rituals in the laundry rooms of co-ed dorms, the social networking in the all-nighters pulled by our university's overworked architecture students, the female bonding that takes place through group watching of *Beverly Hills 90210* in student lounges, and so on.

As a second-generation teacher of ethnography, I had the luxury to critically assess this genre, now easily taught in our classrooms. I could perceive that
the content register, that is, the field matter covered in the ethnography, from
laundry rooms to Starbucks, is clearly a holdover from anthropology. This
needed to be interrogated, and modified, to better fulfill the goals of composition's own disciplinary concerns and theories. I still felt strongly that by selecting a site, engaging in observation and field noting, then formulating a claim
and writing the paper, the ethnography assignment teaches students to write
from their own research; it gives them what is often their first chance to experience the mutual evolution between research and writing. I therefore committed to the genre, for the ethnography assignment has these striking benefits for
the students, and on this level the teaching of the ethnography is fully ethical.
Yet I had also begun to perceive that this pedagogical triumph can be lost if the
undergraduate's work becomes content-driven, if the undergraduate becomes
enamored not of acquiring research and writing skills but of connecting with
the mating rituals in the dorm laundry rooms or daydreaming into her third
cappuccino at the Coffee Cave. While these concepts certainly are not binary,
the youth and peer culture that engulfs students just as certainly exacerbates
their infatuation with the "popular" and peer-approved content over the academic "inquiry" and writing skills. Worse, the teaching of the ethnography can
become unethical if the inexperienced and youthful students celebrate the cultural rituals, like binge drinking, that they find at these popular sites.

At the point of this realization, I ran into two conflicting goals of the
Writing Program. First, that the ethnography was content-driven for students
ran contrary to the theoretical goals of our individual Writing Program. In
"Writing (the) Studios: Composition Curriculum Development at Syracuse,
1986–1991," the authors quote the Writing Program's founder, Louise Phelps,
on the critical difference between "topic of inquiry" and "theme-driven"
courses: "a Studio designed around a topic of inquiry focuses more on the
processes of inquiry than on the actual subject" (49).

Phelps dubbed those concentrating on the "actual subject" as "theme-driven," her own phrase that, in the field, has since become "content-driven."
Phelps elaborated that the topic of inquiry encourages "inquiry *with* language
and *about* language." Yet, when the original anthropological model of ethnography lingers, it only makes it too easy for a student to write a theme-driven draft.

Second, the popular and peer-approved content aligned in a disturbingly
perfect way with the practical goals of the Writing Program. It is easiest to
teach the ethnography that way, for the students go wild over popular sites and
themes. Herein we see one of the results—and these results are benign compared to the results to come—of the institutionally created conditions of
employment throughout our field: composition teachers can minimize student complaints and optimize enthusiastic student evaluations with this
approach. Most teachers in writing programs are part-time and female ones

with tenuous job security, little to no real power, and the prospect of possible grief from administrators who range in their relationships with part-timers from those giving limited support to those boosting their egos by abusing the vulnerable part-timers below them. Given this teaching scenario, the ethnography assignment can easily slide down that slippery slope into a formula for quick success with undergraduates. In irony, during the time of my research, teaching in the Writing Program was one of the original theorists on writing-classroom ethnographies, James Zebroski. He cautioned against the ethnography becoming a "pre-packaged, pre-formed writing assignment" from his earliest discussions of its implementation ("Dialogue" 230). Zebroski condemned the superficial "slice of life" ethnography that students might turn out that "ignores the very sorts of social concerns of importance" (198) that the ethnography was designed to have them interrogate with rigor.

In addition, this "ease" in selecting a site—an ease never intended by the first and ethical theorists in this area—brought sharp criticism in the national press about the use of ethnographies in writing programs. In "Why Johnny Can't Write," Heather MacDonald attacks the "irrelevance" of writing instruction in higher education, singling out ethnographies at one point:

> [The personal essay] has been supplanted by "ethnographies." David Bleich's students at the University of Rochester conduct personal ethnographies on social relations in the classroom, observing how their gender, race, and class allegedly determine their response to literary worlds. *The most frequently assigned topic for student ethnographies, however, is popular culture—in other words, describe and respond to your favorite rock video* (italics mine). (11)

This growing criticism prompted some in the Writing Program to try to mitigate the tendencies toward a slice of life ethnography and adapt, somewhat, the anthropological ethnography for our purposes by asking students to draft a "language-interested" ethnography. We urged students to observe, and we hoped to subsequently honor, literacy in all of its ubiquity in human life. Our students ended up spending hours in dorm elevators, cafes, or smoking areas to observe "literacy" in action. When I tried to explore this literacy celebration, however, by conducting archival research of student-written ethnographies in the Writing Program, I was to discover that the language-interested ethnography was rare and rarely successful. Moreover, my research yielded disturbing findings on gender, race, and class.

ARCHIVAL RESEARCH/DISCOVERIES OF THE "UNETHICAL"

I read, tabulated content matter, indexed, then analyzed the content register of a variety of student-written ethnographies in the portfolios of student work held in the archives of the Writing Program. The work led to the discovery of a lack of success in guiding students to concentrate their ethnography research skills on language and the unexpected discovery of gender discrimination in student-written ethnographies, a discrimination accompanied by a disconcerting silence surrounding the issues of race and class.

I consulted the indexes of 196 student ethnographies from the classrooms of ten experienced teachers, spanning the eight-year period of 1993–2000 (which appeared to be the first and last years that work was systematically collected for the Odyssey archives). One of my first observations was that the content registry was, literally, all over the place—the chicken and pasta line in the cafeteria, bus stops, mosh pits, T.V. soap operas viewed in dorm lounges, designated cigarette smoking areas, the annual ice cream social for frosh, nursing classrooms, coffee houses, gyms, department stores, male or female cliques, fast food joints. Out of the 196 student ethnographies, 61 were on dorm sites (like elevators, laundry rooms, a weekly group of friends watching *Friends,* and so forth). The next largest group consisted of 26 ethnographies of trendy restaurants and businesses, such as coffee shops, most along Marshall Street, the popular place for S.U. students to congregate. There were 19 self-selected ethnographies of classrooms, most from subgroups of undergraduates who are particularly involved in their university work (like S.U.'s architecture students).[3] Then there came 16 on sports, 11 on general sites (such as a university bus stop), and so on down the line through t.v., music, partying, and so forth.[4]

Next, I discovered that any language-interested aspect present in the CCR ethnographies centered mainly on what students think is cool: slang, ska music, obscenities, rapping between friends, and so on. That "cool" themes dominate the CCR language-interested ethnographies gave pause for thought. Perhaps ethnography, when translated into a curriculum genre, is being used as a "school genre" in an insidious manner—students are writing in a "school boy" or "school girl" fashion. While these students were acquiring 'inquiry' researching and writing skills, I would argue that guiding them into a position not as a school boy writing on the guys talking trash on a dorm floor or as a school girl writing on the chit-chat over nonfat lattes at the Coffee Cave, but writing as new scholars investigating their current university, might connect the CCR ethnography activity more to the "real world," that is, those future professions in the public sphere in which students will become citizens. That move might do much to prevent the ethnography from lapsing—and potentially freezing—into a school genre.

As the archival work progressed, I wanted to analyze one class in-depth to assess the actual strength of the language content. I selected a class whose teacher had carefully designed a 'language-interested' ethnography by having the students read some literature by Deborah Tannen on male/female language use, then study this issue at their site. This teacher had designed one of the best assignments that I had seen for WRT 105 ethnographies, so I speculated that this teacher's students were among those encouraged to aim the highest in this work. There were fourteen students in this class, and thirteen ethnographies to study (as one portfolio was missing the ethnography paper). Of these thirteen papers, four of the papers had become so content-driven as to lose the language-interest focus entirely, a fact reflected in the teacher's comments. Three out of the four students who wrote papers that completely lost the interest in language explored local "food" sites—(1) Zopie's Coffeehouse, (2) the food court at the "in" mall, and (3) the central and huge S.U. undergraduate cafeteria; in these instances, the undergraduate lifestyle of congregational eating and socializing easily overtook the CCR goals for the ethnographic writing unit.

In yet another four papers, the language-interest theme was weak, a fact again reflected in the teacher's comments. The following two samples are typical of the teacher's comments on papers that had lost the focus on language: "The observations are very interesting, but I see very few people and *no* language" and "The focus shifted totally away from language. The study, however, is somewhat valuable, though not, strictly speaking, ethnography." One is prompted to ask, if the study veered "totally away" from language, to whom was the study valuable? To what classroom?

The teacher's comments on those papers with a weakened focus on language went like this: "Well done. However, you could have displayed more data, particularly with respect to language. What were the 'lines'? The conversations? You didn't *show* much." If this teacher's comments differed from others that I read in the archives, the difference lay mainly in the teacher's actively pushing the students to focus on language and reminding the students that they should have when they did not.

After these eight papers, there remained five out of the course's thirteen papers. I discovered that only one had a sterling concentration on and analysis of male/female language use; the other four made an average use of the opportunity. The one sterling paper was launched with a statement declaring the student's strong belief in gender equality—this female student being the only one out of the thirteen to commit openly to a nondiscriminatory study of gendered language.

This activity itself of studying, analyzing, and inventorying the student ethnographies raised yet another critical issue about the current ethnography assignment—that of gender discrimination. The most common theme in student ethnographies, a theme independent of the site studied, was gender. Students enjoyed exploring male and female language anywhere they came upon it. Out of the 196 ethnographies surveyed, 58 have a gender theme. This theme is unmatched in frequency by any other. Of the "gender" ethnographies, 32 were composed by female authors and 26 by male authors. Yet, females ranked as lowest priority when it came to the subject of these ethnographies. Eight studied "female" literacy in some aspect; 16 studied "male" literacy, and 34 studied the interaction of male/female literacy, covering subjects such as flirtation. The male authors either wrote on male literacy or male/female interaction while the female students might write on female literacy, male/female literacy, or male literacy, too (wanting to find out about the guys, so to speak). There was not one single cross-over interest of males into female language to match the females interest in male language. Clearly the larger culture's dominant male image and subdominant female images have been seeping into student writing, with the females liable to engage in the "dominant subordinate" behavior of studying and admiring the guys, with no reciprocity on the males' part (see Miller).[5] This has occurred in a writing program full of female and feminist teachers. Herein I had my first glimpse of the necessity of being a teacher-researcher: while an individual teacher might not notice a predominance of one or two ethnographies on male language in his or her class, the value of an inspection of student papers in the aggregate can clarify this bias to all teachers so that if it happens in one of their classes, the teachers can be quick to address it.[6]

Another disconcerting result of the archival research was the presence of even more aggressive gender discrimination in the student ethnographies. For students, reading Deborah Tannen's insightful work on male/female language was not enough to counter their lifetime absorption of the highly gendered images of the larger culture. Of the thirteen ethnographies in this class, in six a more pronounced form of gender bias—against females once again—was evident. One male student engaged in name-calling of the females on his dorm floor as "lounge rats . . . stuck in a seventh grade social state of mind," a name-calling that had no equal in any of the female papers discussing male subjects. This same student privileged the "really good arguments" of his friends, whom the reader could deduce were male, over the disparaged female conversations. Another student studied the construction of a kind of impromptu adventure narrative by five "persons." All five were male, but never was it noticed by the student that he might actually be studying the narratives of men, *not* "persons." This fact is more striking when one considers that the male author asked his male subjects to construct a narrative on a life-and-death adventure, a genre that theorists associate with males (see Gilbert). A third paper, by a female, claimed to look at the interactive literacy of the new "brothers" and "sisters" on her dorm floor, but the paper was dominated by an analysis of the males, five out of its six pages discussing these "guys." In a fourth paper, the writer claimed to be looking at the language of the "guys" versus the "girls" in two local bars, but he emphasized the sexually aggressive behavior of the guys. Furthermore, the girls sometimes consisted of women in their twenties or thirties, significantly older than the first-year male undergraduate writing this paper. Once again, out of these papers, the female engaged in the dominant subordinate behavior of focusing on the males, while the three males engaged in the dominant aggressive behavior of subordinating, or absenting, female subjects.

THEORY, PRACTICE, AND THE NEW ETHICS

Initially, I reacted as a "feminist" teacher to these findings in that I focused on the male teacher of this class of students. I wondered if this male professor did not know how unsettling to women might be the student's ethnography on male aggression toward females in bars. I was jarred out of this feminist frame of mind, however, when I was discussing this matter with a female TA who responded that she currently had a male student writing such sexist material on guys and bars for her and ostentatiously throwing it in her face. When I asked why she didn't say no to this male student, she averted her eyes and responded that she was not going to let him get a rise out of her. Having been subject to verbal assaults by aggressive male students myself, I felt much sympathy for this inexperienced TA who was, I knew, operating in a climate that did not provide her the needed support to be assertive. Yet I had another insight that was undeniable: the teaching of the ethnography is largely in the hands of female instructors in the Writing Program. I was one of those female instructors. How was I (and we) going to take full responsibility for my (or our) own teaching of the ethnography—despite the circumstances? How could we strive to rise above certain debilitating political and institutional conditions that we find ourselves mired in our female instructors and work rigorously to make our teaching of the ethnography as ethical as possible?

One thing my archival research of student writing had made clear: we like to think of our writing classrooms as offering the students a "rich flow of activity in a zone of proximal development" (Gee, Lankshear, and Hull 61), but the zone was not as rich as we had thought. My research bore out the unsettling conclusions of James Gee and colleagues in *The New Work Order*. He explains the ways in which the

> contemporary cognitive science replaced an earlier critique of school, based on the disproportionate failure of many lower socioeconomic and minority students, with a new initially rather startling critique: that it's not just minorities who fail. In actuality, all students do. . . . Even those with good grades do not "really understand" what they are learning. Students in traditional school, it is claimed, master only basic, rote, low-level skills at best. While such students may be able to pass tests and carry out basic computations, they really do not understand, in any very deep way, what they are doing. (Gee 54–55)

The Syracuse University Writing Program teaches a range of bright students, mostly white and affluent. They are the "good students," and they proved themselves adept at executing an assignment with skill but little depth of understanding.

I first, incorrectly, placed blame for this startling insight in one realm, but as it turns out, this realm was only valuable as it revealed the actual cause of

the results of the archival research. Upon discovering the high levels of cultural chauvinisms in the student work, I had speculated that the problem was
that we had not transformed the field genre into a curriculum genre with
enough care and forethought. In other words, a field genre has been designed
by professionals for *professionals*, for practicing experts in the field, persons
with years of training. In anthropology, the cultural baggage of gender, race,
class, and so forth would have been the focus of excavation and discussion for
years, in graduate school and in later professional activities. But a curriculum
genre is designed by professionals for professionals-*in-training*—for writers-
in-training, scholars-in-training, and so on. The work of dissecting—and
hopefully re-imagining—the cultural constructs of gender, race, or class has
only just begun for undergraduates. I concluded that this analysis of the content register of student ethnographies revealed the dangers that can lurk when
the ethnography is introduced into classrooms as a field genre, not as a curriculum genre for student writers.

I now saw that without meaning to, in fact intending the very opposite,
we had really made it easy for students to lapse into the 'folk theories' indicted
by Gee and colleagues:

> The problem . . . is that education does not remove or correct people's 'folk
> theories,' and people readily fall back on these folk theories when they have
> been, or are being exposed in school to "correct," or at least "better" theories
> based on disciplines. Even if they can answer school tests correctly, their
> school-based knowledge falls apart in the face of their well-entrenched, but
> unexamined, folk theories." (55)

The students cheered their "folk theories" throughout prescribed ethnography assignments.

The student enthusiasm for trumpeting their folk theories through our
assignment made me ponder if the central problem was not our ideas about
student "authority." I thought it ironic that one of the original appeals for
writing teachers of the ethnography assignment was that it might position
student writers as authorities: "Students assume authority as the experts on
their sites, taking this commitment seriously" (Zebroski "Ethnographic"
204). However, when a professional undertakes an ethnography, she brings
with her a certain *earned* authority from years of work. A student does not
yet possess this kind of earned authority. The student, then, has to imagine
his authority, and that is a risky business for undergraduates. In their late
teens, many WRT 105 students can misimagine authority in the worst way,
especially when they take their ideas of authority from the dominant and easily accessible images of gender, race, or class in the popular culture that has
engulfed them for years. We ended up with an ethnography that did not
become a tool for developing "critical consciousness" about the community

investigated (Zebroski "Dialogue" 229), but a tool to reproduce the larger culture in all of its biases and silences.

With our admirably ethical theorists and legions of well-intentioned teachers, how did this come to be? How did it reach this stage? Here I finally came to see, and to argue, that the institutions in which we work intervene in our theory and our practice in ways that are both enabling and debilitating. The SU Writing Program institutionalized, then politicized, the ethnography as a choice assignment for its teachers. As a positive consequence, teachers became acquainted with a way of teaching primary research and writing that will influence their practice in positive ways for years to come. As another consequence, however, teachers also became acquainted with constraints and politics imposed by the institution that will influence their practice in negative ways for an equally long time. In the Writing Program website on the teaching of ethnography, we find two sites—"What Students Get" and "What Students Do"—in which well-meaning administrators championed the ethnography as a way to lead students into "a genuine ownership and mastery over their own writing projects" and as a means for "owning and controlling a [writing] project" to the point that "the student is the expert." Such imperialistic language, the language of owning, controlling, mastering, and being the hierarchal expert, could only have results as debilitating as that language was intended to be enabling. It could only give students as many "wrong" ideas about doing an ethnography as it could give them the "right" ideas.

Yet, this train of thought dead-ends me—as a teacher and as a theorist. I begin to feel uncomfortably that I am still frozen in the old work order, and with this insight comes a glimmer of insight: are we keeping the students there with us? Somehow, both we and the students have the "fixed" freedom described by Gee and others (xvii–xviii). I realized that as long as we operate under key illusions, we are suffering from the symptoms of the deceptive new work order. So, I made a different move. The next time that I taught the ethnography, I openly shared the disturbing results of my professional research with my students. I told them of the gender discrimination and that out of the piles of ethnographies I had read, only a few had studied class, and only a few more—under ten—had studied race. Out of the latter authors, only one was white, and that person was a young white male from the Midwest describing his surprise at his discovery that there really were a lot of Jews in the world once one left the Midwest. Moreover, the Jews were nice people.

The students responded—within limits. One moment is not going to shatter their folk theories and inhibitions. They all set out to unearth race and gender relations on campus. Most came back in complete denial. All was well and friendly between races on campus. Out of the twelve groups, and forty-four individual students, in three classes, only three discussed race.[7] Of these three, it was hard for them to deny the glaring self-segregation of black, white, and Asian students into different corners of a certain study hall. Interestingly, these three white students wrote extensively of the segregating activity of black and Asian students, but had to be prompted repeatedly to describe the similar activity of the white students.

I took some comfort that overall the themes of these ethnographies were serious. This was a presidential election year, and some studied the voter registration booths on campus to note with dismay the apathy of the typical student. Others studied the campus bookstores to note that shot glasses and party paraphenalia were given far more prominence than notebooks and textbooks. Others studied the mail centers to note that the average student's "skim-and-toss" attitude toward campus mail was, regrettably, indicative of his or her attitude toward education. Some still studied gender, though these were still "Ethnography Lite."[8]

It dawned on me: I had shared the results of my archival research with them but not the processes by which I had arrived at the results. In discussing the categories, I had made the teaching of ethnography content-driven myself. I had to actually give them the thinking strategies of experts (Gee 58).

I had arrived at my archival research through certain acquired expert processes for making and sharing knowledge. Years ago, I had indexed my first book myself, and when an assistant director of the Writing Program had heard this, she had given me release time from teaching one course to begin indexing the student work in the archives. I realized that if I now made the students index their work, then consult it, I would not have to resort to direct lecturing on what themes were present and what themes were missing.

The plan of action went thus: the students would compile their ethnographies into a class journal, then mine the themes to create an index. It struck me that we often give students nebulous and even arbitrary directions for writing reflections on their work, whereas composing an index would be a concrete and professional task that would make explicit for the students the themes and ideas in their work. After indexing, the students would discuss the results, considering what knowledge was made, what knowledge was not made, and what knowledge they might want to make in the future. The group work would also eliminate the sting of self-indictment evidenced in the students' denials of racism. Finally, the students would be their own researchers. The problem was not that students lacked authority but that students did not know the processes to act with and gain authority as reflective knowledge-makers.

This worked well the first time that I piloted it. The students finally studied themselves and most arrived at the verdict announced by one young woman: "We live in selectively permeable bubbles." Discussions arose out of student capacity for focus and filtration, for the human mind to let in what it wants and shut out what it does not. The students had finally arrived at a meta-knowledge of themselves, as knowers, as thinkers, as subjective minds. I was finally satisfied that the ethnography had served one good purpose in my studios, and that had occurred when I myself had moved away from the themes of the ethnographies—be it race, gender, or, even, language—and concentrated on the expert processes of intellectual activity. It occurred when I became a real teacher-researcher, bypassing the institutional prescriptions of the ethnography assignment.

I used to think that whenever teachers taught content-driven courses, in, perhaps, the Rhetoric of the Vietnam War or the Rhetoric of Children's Literature, these were "hobbyhorse" courses. I know different now. The content is not the key. The key is the sharing of expert processes, for only then does true ethical reciprocity arise. If this relationship of ethical reciprocity is not established with our students, then in all courses we are riding our hobbyhorse. If we are ethical, however, then we are sharing our knowledge and crossing academic borders between and among ourselves and our students—we are dialoguing with each other and our students on how to be researchers, writers, knowledge makers.

NOTES

1. Ethnographies first moved from the field into actual classrooms—anthropology classrooms—when the work of its theorists like James Spradley and David McCurdy came upon the academic scene in 1972 (see works cited). The ethnography and its potential within the academy soon became realized, and its classroom use subsequently spread to other disciplines, like education, fairly quickly. Then, in 1986 and 1987, an outburst of theorists and teachers like Stephen North; James Zebroski and Nancy Mack; and Jeffrey and Judith Sommerfield proposed the new idea of benefitting from ethnographic methods in writing classrooms. Once more, however, in our initial honeymoon phase with the ethnography, we ignored the warnings emanating from the original sites of ethnographic studies. Anthropologists like George Marcus and Michael Fischer wrote extensively about turning the "experimental moment" in which the field of anthropology and its practices [like ethnography] were subject to self-reflexive critique into a moment of a "conventionalized" disciplinary debate with the resulting "accepted" ideas and approaches (vii–xi).

2. For an excellent discussion of "Curriculum Genres: Planning for Effective Teaching," see Christie.

3. One of the five teachers, who had redesigned the ethnography in the final years of the Odyssey Program, mandated that students do discipline-specific sites, making another 24 portfolios in this area.

4. Of the two sites that emerged as having slightly higher frequency than the others—dorm sites and Marshall Street sites—this also seemed to be the result of teacher encouragement, with one teacher responsible for the highest number in a certain category.

5. See Jean Baker Miller's *Toward a New Psychology of Women* for an analysis of the subdominant role of women in our culture.

6. At first, one might encourage females to focus on other females, but Nancy Miller's theories would remind one that the males concentrating on males is not a true "strength," just a narrowness of perspective, and the females willingness to study the entire human race, males and females, might show truer strength and open-mindedness.

7. Two more students noted potential discrimination in their field notes, but opted to address other themes in their drafts.

8. One group of four students noted in their field notes some horrid instances of gender discrimination at their site, but, as with the racial discrimination mentioned, none of these students chose to address this in their ethnographies.

WORKS CITED

Baker, Jean. *Toward a New Psychology of Women*. 1976. Boston: Beacon, 1986.

Bishop, Wendy. *Ethnographic Writing Research: Writing It Down, Writing It Up, and Reading It*. Portsmouth, N.H.: Boynton/Cook, 1999.

Christie, Frances. "Curriculum Genres: Planning for Effective Teaching." *The Powers of Literacy: A Genre Approach to Teaching Writing*. Ed. Bill Cope and Mary Kalantzis. Pittsburgh: University of Pittsburgh Press, 1993. 154–78.

Gee, James Paul, with Colin Lankshear and Glynda A. Hull. *The New Work Order: Behind the Language of the New Capitalism*. Westview, 1997.

Gilbert, Pamela. "Stoning the Romance: Girls as Resistant Readers and Writers." *Learning and Teaching Genre*. Ed. Aviva Freedman and Peter Medway. Portsmouth, N.H.: Boynton/Cook, 1994. 173–91.

Kahn, Seth. "Rethinking the Historical Narratives of Composition's Ethics Debate." *CCC* 52:2 (December 2000) 287–92.

MacDonald, Heather. "Why Johnny Can't Write." *The Public Interest* (Summer 1995) 3–13.

Marcus, George. "Ethnography through Thick and Thin: The Possibilities and Limits of Anthropological Writing after 'Writing Culture.'" Cornell University: Fourth National Writing across the Curriculum Conference. 5 June 1999.

Marcus, George, and Michael M. J. Fischer, eds. *Anthropology as Cultural Critique: An Experimental Moment in the Human Sciences*. Chicago: University of Chicago Press, 1986.

Miller, Susan. *Assuming the Positions: Cultural Pedagogy and the Politics of Commonplace Writing*. Pittsburgh: University of Pittsburgh Press, 1998.

———. *Textual Carnivals: The Politics of Composition*. Carbondale: Southern Illinois University Press, 1991.

North, Stephen. *The Making of Knowledge in Composition: Portrait of an Emerging Field*. Upper Montclair, N.J.: Boynton/Cook, 1987.

Phelps, Louise Wetherbee. *Composition as a Human Science: Contributions to the Self-Understanding of a Discipline.* NY: Oxford University Press, 1988.

———. *Feminine Principles and Women's Experience in American Composition and Rhetoric.* Pittsburgh: University of Pittsburgh Press, 1995.

Royster, Jacqueline Jones. "Sarah's Story: Making a Place for Historical Ethnography in Rhetorical Studies." Carnegie Mellon: Thirtieth Anniversary Conference of the Rhetoric Society of America, 5 June 1998.

Spradley, James P., and David W. McCurdy. *The Cultural Experience: Ethnography in Complex Society.* Prospect Heights, Ill.: Waveland, 1972.

"What Students Do." The Odyssey Project of the Syracuse University Writing Program. 31 July 2001. <*http://odyssey.syr.edu/curriculum/whatstudentsdo.html*>.

"What Students Get." The Odyssey Project of the Syracuse University Writing Program. 31 July 2001. <*http://odyssey.syr.edu/curriculum/whatstudentsget.html*>.

Zebroski, James Thomas, and Nancy Mack. "A Dialogue on Composition: A Composition on Dialogue." *Correspondences* (Spring 1987): 227–33.

Zebroski, James. "Ethnographic Writing for Critical Consciousness." *Social Issues in the English Classroom.* Ed. Mark Hurlbert and Samuel Totten. Chicago: NCTE, 1992. 196–205.

———. *Thinking through Theory: Vygotskian Perspectives on the Teaching of Writing.* Portsmouth, N.H.: Boynton/Cook, 1994.

———. "The Uses of Theory: A Vygotskian Approach to Composition." *The Writing Instructor* 5:2 (Winter 1986): 57–67.

Chapter Nine

CHALLENGES TO CYBERFEMINISM

Voices, Contradictions, and Identity Constructions

SIBYLLE GRUBER

It is 5:25 on a Wednesday evening. She is the teacher. She is the authority figure. Students are filing into the room for a five-hour class on the history and theory of composition studies. She is morphing. The brown Formica tables are
arranged in rows; microphones are waiting to be used. A disembodied voice
announces that the broadcast will start in five minutes. She tells the operator that
the camera needs to be focused on the students, not on her. She checks the computers, the pad camera, and the TV screen to make sure that students are also filing in at the other sites. *She is the technology expert.* While she listens to Maureen's
explanation of why she needs to hand in the paper next week, she also watches
the voiceless interactions of two of her off-campus students who apparently are
enjoying a joke—hopefully not about her. *She is a feminist but not essentially so.*
The theme song comes on, the students sit down, she moves to the podium, the
mikes are turned on, and the show begins. *Now she is also a performer.*
    The changed setting—an interactive instructional television (IITV)
room that uses various technologies to broadcast to four different sites in the
state simultaneously—raises some questions about teaching in general and
feminist pedagogies specifically. How do class dynamics change when you
cannot talk directly to your students but are instead restricted to email correspondences, phone calls, and short conversations before and after class? How

do our pedagogies and methodologies apply to a distance education course? And how do we—teachers and students—interact with each other and with the various machines in front of us? What combination of already morphed and still morphing identities takes on the challenge to continue and to redefine feminist practices while working within a traditionally defined academic system?

This chapter provides an account of how teaching in an IITV setting can amplify the fragmented and fractured feminist identities with which many teachers struggle in more traditional teaching environments. After discussing feminist issues in technology studies, I complicate my own role as a feminist teacher in online environments, calling attention to where and how feminist theories cannot adequately account for the pragmatics of this teaching situation. Next, I address how partially conforming to, and being complicit in, a traditional power structure does not necessarily have to be seen as opposing feminist ideas of working against a patriarchal system. I then focus on the perceptions and realities, including issues of objectification, with which feminist teachers are often confronted. I also look at how feminist pedagogies can become a part of a distance education course despite the difficulties presented by the technology-rich environment. In my conclusion, I foreground how we can use our sometimes conflicting and fractured identities to create feminist pedagogies that take into account our and our students' positionalities.

WHAT DOES IT MEAN TO BE A FEMINIST IN CYBERSPACE?

According to Lisa Gerrard, feminist pedagogy "guides students to reflect on their lives and to connect personal experience with ideology and social issues" (382). Furthermore, it looks at how power relationships can be equalized and how women's experiences and voices can be validated (383–84). Technology scholars interested in feminist issues have explored women's positions in an increasingly technologized world. They have discussed the virtual portrayal of women in online discussions and on the worldwide web, and they have looked closely at the underlying implications of computer technologies on race, gender, and economic issues in micro- and macroenvironments. We all are familiar with Donna Haraway's statement that "we are all chimeras, theorized and fabricated hybrids of machine and organism; in short, we are cyborgs" (191). Similarly, Allucquère Rosanne Stone argues that cyberspace is a place that allows for the "complex and shifting play of body, self, and community" (3). As a warning, however, she postulates that

> [t]o believe that in cyberspace everyone is equal merely because the codings that have attached themselves to voice quality and physical appearance have been uncoupled from their referents, and that this uncoupling provides a sensation that might be perceived as inherently liberatory, is to misunderstand how power works. (181)

Stone's warning is not the only cautionary note voiced by cyberfeminists. E. Laurie George, Pamela Takayoshi, and Laura Sullivan warn that patriarchal attitudes prevail (George), that "the argument that patterns of interaction deeply entrenched within a patriarchal system cannot be undermined simply by offering access to a new medium" (Takayoshi), and that the "virtual male gaze" can create a sense of cybersexism which inhibits women's participation in the "technology revolution." (Sullivan). Looking at computer technology as an artifact that is a recreation of dominant belief systems that reinforce the marginalization of nondominant groups by privileged groups leads Cynthia and Richard Selfe to label interfaces as the "cultural maps of computer systems" (485). The desktop, as they point out, represents modern capitalism, corporate culture, and professionalism, in its exclusion of representations from nonprofessional areas (486–87). In this sense, computer use is built on a number of expectations that reflect values ingrained in a class-, gender-, race-, and age-biased society.

Without doubt, the focus on corporate culture, economic modernization, efficiency, and technical as well as administrative issues influences and changes what I, as a feminist teacher, do in the classroom and how I do it. As Michael Apple and Susan Jungck have pointed out, one of the negative effects is that teachers often lose autonomy and control over their teaching and their work. Computer technologies, in their estimate, can undo many of the advances made by feminist teachers and scholars in the classroom. They can reinforce the loss of agency in teaching situations because of the scarcity of training programs for using computers, time constraints based on multiple other responsibilities, and administrative mandates to use computers without giving teachers any choice in how to implement new technologies in the classroom. Apple and Jungk see "deskilling" and "depowering" as consequences of enforcing technology use, since decisions about "what is actually to go on" are made by "someone outside the immediate situation."

Apple and Jungk's concerns about the impact of technology on teacher autonomy and teacher control—two tenuous concepts at best—are of great importance when looking at our positionalities as feminist teachers, our constructed identities for the many constituencies we need to appease, our fears about not doing the best job we could possibly do, and our anxieties about who we are, who we are supposed to be, and how we are seen by others. These positionalities become even more complicated if we look at distance education programs that use multiple technologies and that mediate between and also disrupt physical presence and virtual appearance. We take on the role of the cyborg, "a cybernetic organism, a hybrid of machine and organism, a creature of social reality as well as a creature of fiction" (Haraway 191). What is more, we become "a matter of fiction and lived experience that changes what counts as women's experience in the late twentieth century," because "we are all chimeras, theorized and fabricated hybrids of machine and organism" (191).

This openness of boundaries and shifting identities necessitates a willingness to accept the partiality of any perspective, including traditional feminist viewpoints. It also points to the need for combining a variety of perspectives to gain a less fragmented picture of the world, because "single vision produces worse illusions than double vision or many-headed monsters" (196). In other words, we must acknowledge difference, multiple and conflicting visions, and polyvocality as part of our complicated selves.

What comes next is a story of complicity and refusal to comply, a story of achieving a level of comfort with contradictions. It is a story that illustrates Haraway's concept of the cyborg but also points out some limitations of Haraway's cyborgian existence.

A STORY OF FRAGMENTATION

Although I can usually figure out who I am in certain situations (despite the multiple subject positions I inhabit), it is sometimes hard to comprehend who I am supposed to be in an IITV class. For one, I am an on-screen persona, a novice performer, seen by my students at four different sites, checked out by anybody who is interested in a taped version of the class. I am told to avoid sharply contrasting colors, busy patterns, noisy beads, necklaces, and reflecting jewelry. Being made conscious of this fact, I become self-conscious, hoping that my blouse is not too wrinkled and that my earrings do not jingle too loudly.

Next, I am the boss who needs to find out how to let the control room operator know that I really do not care to have my face splashed over four screens for five hours a week but that I had rather get the students exposed to the wonders of technology. My directives to the operator in these situations are short and to the point. Also, I am the technology expert, trying to figure out how the technological apparatuses in front of me can be coaxed into compliance. Unfortunately, it is sometimes not apparent that one site can see the computer images while everybody else is in the dark, or that the microphones do not work, and only after five minutes of lip-reading do my students' hand gestures alert me to the possibility of a technical glitch.

And, not to forget, I am the subject expert who supposedly had wisdom imparted to her many years ago and is now ready to return the favor. That is at least what my students think the first day of class. However, in my various teacherly personas, I am not curt, I do not like to give directives, nor do I propose to impart wisdom. This often causes lots of frustration for the first few weeks among my captive audience. My formal appearance and my curt interactions with the control room operator, and the general teacher-centered setup of the IITV classrooms, led them to believe that I would be authoritarian, unrelenting, and ready to tell them how it really is supposed to be. Instead of being excited that they can participate in "the making of knowledge," they are often disturbed that I am switching personas and have them do the thinking, the exploring, and the putting-it-together in the end.

This is what different contingencies at the university see: a woman dressed to perform and to be checked out, a person ready to get her way with the operator, and a teacher who practices various versions of critical and feminist pedagogies. What they often do not see, but which is invariably present, is a teacher who subverts the traditional paradigms of IITV teaching and a teacher who challenges the medium that tries to construct her in traditional ways. According to Haraway, I am "a condensed image of both imagination and material reality." I am "a matter of fiction and lived experience." I am an ambiguity, "theorized and fabricated" (191). I am an appropriation, and I appropriate myself. Not only do I create and recreate myself every time I teach, but my supervisors, students, and bystanders engage in a constant re-envisioning of my current identities. I am given roles to play, and I play my own roles. All these imaginations and theorizations—my own and those of others—constitute the tentative realities of my identity, realities that allow me to function in specific settings, discuss the injustices of current social and economic positions, argue for equal pay for equal work, and reconsider the ideological and political implications of my actions. In other words, I use my roles to create my own feminist identities sometimes in conjunction, other times in disjunction, with what it means to use feminist practices.

When I first started teaching IITV courses, I was only vaguely aware that I was getting ready for additional shifts in my already complicated identity construction. My readings about theory and practice in distance education (Holmberg), my exposure to the trends and opportunities in distance learning (Lau), and my interest in working with culturally and linguistically diverse students in a distance education environment (Feyten and Nutta) encouraged me to take on a new teaching challenge. I was drawn to the teaching opportunity because of my interest in the pedagogical and methodological implications of teaching in a "technology-rich" environment. What I did not immediately realize when I volunteered to teach an IITV course was that the teacher, despite all the technology surrounding her, has little control over the equipment or how it is actually used. Instead, the control room operator moves the cameras, switches from one medium to another, and decides—if one is not careful—who to display on the screen. My idea of being "in control" of the situation, of being able to teach according to loosely structured feminist ideas, was quickly replaced by an increasing sense of "being controlled" every step of the way. Instead of thinking of myself as a highly skilled teacher who wanted to be a critical user of technology in any situation, I started to experience the effects of deskilling—of losing my feminist identity in the classroom, of not being able to teach the way I wanted to teach because of who I was expected to become to fit the IITV image. My self-image started to become fainter, almost as if I were being erased, until I negotiated my way from a monolithic object position defined by others to a largely self-defined subject position and a position that I decided to manipulate myself.

I struggled—and still struggle—with my position as a partial object and partial subject, but I have also learned to live with and enjoy the multiple roles and identities I portray when I teach an IITV course. As a partial object, although not always of desire, I work toward transforming the objectifying gaze, deciding how to present myself and what to present, which allows me to move "along a continuum from objectification to representation" (Blair and Takayoshi). In addition, I do not think any longer that I failed as a feminist teacher because I play almost contradictory roles. I perform in front of a camera; I get fed up with external difficulties and technological glitches from time to time and forcefully express my displeasure; I let my students explore their own voices, endorsing expressivist ideas, and then I tell them that they need to move beyond a self-indulgent notion of writing as an individual activity and instead look at their participation in a social structure and a political system that influences their ideologies.

Moving inside and outside current power structures, knowing when to work with and when to work against an established hierarchy, is part of what I have begun to consider a move against dualistic thinking—us (the enlightened) against them (the reactionaries), tradition against transformation, subject against object, domination against subjugation. Not only are there multiple degrees of "us" and numerous versions of "them," but the boundaries between us and them are almost always blurred, making this easy distinction untenable. In other words, our complicity in continuing insiders' notions of power and control while also many times working against them should be obvious to all of us. We are members of powerful academic institutions and scholarly affiliations. We sign contracts and climb up the ladder of academic attainment, thereby institutionalizing differences between those who have made it, those who are still working on it, and those who are not in the running in the first place. Even if we do not like it, we struggle and fight to become an acknowledged member of the "field." We discuss working-class positionalities while often living a comfortable middle-class existence. Knowingly or unknowingly, we are part of them. And although I consider myself a cyberfeminist in many incarnations and mutations, my partial participation in oppressive structures also makes me an enemy of Haraway's cyborg. Although Haraway accounts for "the permeability of boundaries in the personal body and in the body politic" (212), she does not consider that parts of my shifting identities would work well within hierarchies and patriarchal systems, thus devaluing—and possibly demonizing—the partially complicit experiences of many feminist teachers and scholars.

We help write the master narrative, but our multiple self- and other-imposed identities can also help to change this narrative and to create a new experience, an experience that is based on our knowledge of our complicity but that is willing to reexamine this complicity to move beyond a stagnant interpretation of the various positionalities—feminist or otherwise—we supposedly inhabit. As Chela Sandoval (1994) would tell me, I am many things—an insider quite happy with the workings of how certain things are, an outsider who works within the system but is willing to take on the powers that be, and also an outsider who refuses to be part of the existing structure and tries to dismantle it with the tools of the revolutionary opposition. Whether I can tackle all these roles is certainly up for grabs, but at least I can try to work on some, as the next two sections on perceptions and transgressions should clarify.

TALKING ABOUT PERCEPTIONS . . .

Using critical and feminist pedagogies is hard work and can sometimes backfire, especially if these practices are used in uncharted territory. Here is an illustration: To establish connections between different members of my class and to foreground the importance of different knowledges and discourses from day one, I start with short introductions. I ask my students to tell us something that is important to our understanding of their interests in this class. In my first IITV course, a student, Mark, outright told me and the rest of the class that he hated taking a course via IITV, and if he had an option to fulfill his requirements, he would not be sitting here, being a pawn in the institution's badly run distance education program. Furthermore, he asserted that he paid his tuition to have the undivided attention of his instructor, not to have to compete with three or four other sites and a camera. And, in addition to all of this, Mark's friends had told him that taking an IITV course was a joke anyway and that he would only learn half of what others learn in traditionally taught courses. Mark did not explain what he considered "traditional" except to point out that one of his best classes was the one where the professor focused mainly on presenting important information to his attentive students.

Analyzing Mark's reaction is complicated. The negative feedback he received from his peers seems to play a large role in his dislike of distance education courses. Furthermore, Mark could have felt uncomfortable in exploring a different instructional environment, leaving behind a tested and tried atmosphere that fit his needs. He could also have been intimidated by the prospect of building relational networks—often emphasized in feminist classrooms—with his peers from the distance sites, or he could have just felt comfortable with the patriarchal structure that seemed to have dominated some of his other classes.

Many instructors point out similar attitudes in their students, and many of them dismiss these attitudes as unwarranted complaints and unsupported criticism. However, denying students' perceptions does not improve the situation. What is more, by teaching a distance education course, I can contribute to the problems in a system that students perceive as unresponsive to their needs. My proactive persona tells me that I can also change the system from within. I can use the media and turn this into a positive learning experience, or at least I can try. This was my perspective when I decided to continue teaching IITV courses after this first experience. As Gail Hawisher has emphasized several times in informal conversations, the technology is here and we cannot avoid it. But we can make a difference by being active and critical participants in the technology revolution and by trying to make some positive changes. Instead of accepting notions of technology as male-centered (Lisa Gerrard points out that *Time* magazine's "Man of the Year" 1982 was the computer [p. 380]), feminist teachers can explore the potential of new technologies for feminist pedagogies, and they can get into the middle of reinscribing different ideologies on the existing system. And into the middle I got, despite student concerns with the quality of their experience and despite the idea that IITV courses were considered to be academically undemanding, not only by students but also by colleagues and administrators.

I did not know about the supposedly "lower status" of IITV teaching on the hierarchical totem pole prior to engaging in this project. But a colleague of mine, Glenda, mentioned that she was told several times that the perception was that her colleagues were "teaching" courses, whereas she was "putting on a show" in the IITV classroom, thus devaluing her position as a teacher and her status as a colleague who needs to be taken seriously. Because, as Glenda pointed out, "women struggle to be taken seriously" already anyway, teaching an IITV course could undermine an already tenuous position in the department and the university. As soon as language such as "doing a show" is used, the person is not considered scholarly or as one who is providing education, but instead as one who offers entertainment. According to Glenda, "It's devastating! It's insidious!"

In addition to the problems created by being considered a less valuable teaching environment, IITV courses, similar to other distance education courses, are easily accessible for outside viewing. Glenda considers this issue of "open access," or what she calls "unauthorized observations," as the most problematic aspect of teaching via IITV. She told me that she was not even aware when she started to teach that almost everybody had access to her course. She only found out about these observations by accident when a university administrator came up to her and said, "Oh, I watched your course the other afternoon. You really get excited when you teach." This experience made her more conscious of her publicly accessible role, and it made her more cautious when discussing potentially sensitive or controversial topics with her students.

I also have colleagues standing outside my door watching me "perform" and afterward telling me that "it was a good show." I smile and ignore them, because that is not what I want to spend my time discussing in the hallways. I had much rather know that my students take me seriously and that they know that my camera role is only one role of many. My construction of my identity does not suffer from my colleagues' comments, and I do not mind having them think that they flattered my ego, although I would like to be much less polite in my responses. Yes, it is a form of objectification that I could live without and that I would like to squelch, and as a feminist teacher and scholar, I sometimes feel I should. But then I also think that I would satisfy a morbid pleasure in these particular colleagues if I stooped to explain why their perceptions of me do objectify me. Instead of changing their attitudes, I might very well contribute to intensifying the gaze that defines me in their eyes by providing them with new reasons for staring at my performance, talking about my attitudes, and speculating on my future in the department. I also know that the objectifying gaze does not disappear solely because I disapprove of it; it might shift to a less obvious but equally insidious position that I can no longer anticipate and deal with in my own way. In essence, knowing that somebody gazes at me through a window, however objectifying this action is, is far preferable to getting the feeling that I am the hot topic of secret office meetings.

Of course, my ambivalent attitude toward being objectified by my colleagues could change soon. Whether I need to address these perceptions in the future remains to be seen. My colleagues and supervisors, and their image of me as a performer instead of a teacher and scholar, could easily have impacted my tenure and promotion, and it could compromise a productive, successful, and safe working environment. Tenure, according to Fred Kemp, "thrives upon conformity and predictability." If these expectations are disrupted, then serious consequences could result. Teaching in an IITV environment that often involves innovation and taking risks while also suffering from preconceived notions about the educational value of these courses can certainly impede the smooth progression from untenured to tenured faculty member. This is confirmed by Carrie Leverenz who just recently pointed out that "the burden of proof rests on the untenured candidate to document why her (unconventional) work deserves to be valued" (144). If the majority opinion devalues teaching via IITV, the concerns that teachers have about tenure and promotion are certainly justified.

Furthermore, the issue of unlimited access to IITV courses provides much concern for teachers. In a recent publication, Michael Day voices concerns about the panopticon effect created through the uses of new technologies. The internet, according to Day, can become "an instrument of surveillance" (35). Evaluators, he points out, "may be watching us in ways we may not be aware of, and could be judging us by criteria that bear little relevance to our pedagogical goals" (33). Although Day refers to the internet, the same problems hold true for any course transmitted and recorded for broadcasting purposes. In effect, such surveillance can endanger a faculty member's academic status as well as her job opportunities. Women, often already in a more tenuous position than their male counterparts, are especially at risk in these situations. Eileen Schell found that women constitute 67 percent of all part-time faculty and only 33 percent of full-time faculty in the humanities (5). And even more disturbing, Theresa Enos points out that 80 percent of "non-tenure track, temporary full-time, and/or part-time [writing] faculty are female" (quoted in Schell 6).

Why am I still not overly concerned about my colleagues' opinions about my teaching in this environment and the institution's possible surveillance of my courses? To a small extent it is because I want to be naïve and not worry about the various implications of my actions and nonactions; in large part it is because of my solid record in my teaching, my scholarship commitments, and my interests in numerous college, university, and community services. My positioning as a productive member of the department is not an accident. It is well planned and well documented. It is my insider identity, my enthusiastic participation in the traditional academic roles of good teacher and productive researcher, that gives me the freedom to ignore intentional and unintentional attacks on my diverse subject positions. It also allows me to work against the system from within when necessary, and for the system when possible. Does that give me sleepless nights as the feminist I propose to be? No. I choose my battles carefully. I know about my fragmented selves and my perceived contradictions as a feminist teacher, scholar, and woman. I am not a revolutionary when it comes to "proving" or "defending" my worth as more than a performer to my colleagues and my supervisors. I do not think I need to justify myself because my actions and my yearly evaluations will do that for the time being.

Also, I am quite taken by a recent commentary by Fred Kemp. He suggests an attitude change and a change in our perspectives on tenure procedures. Kemp says:

> If you see your tenured professors as regal satraps dispensing favor from a
> boundless reservoir of power, then you approach the tenure matter a certain
> way. If, instead, you see your tenured professors as folk in transition clinging
> to the edge of a cliff kicking half-heartedly at what's climbing up below, then
> you see tenure in a different light. (115)

This gives me hope, albeit only for short spurts, that I do not have to prove and defend, but teach and teach well. And what gives me hope too is that most of my students know that there is more going on in the classroom than meets the superficial eye of the objectifying gaze.

TEACHING TO TRANSGRESS OR TRANSGRESSING TO TEACH

As a teacher who endorses feminist pedagogies, my idealistic goals include collaboration, cooperation, group projects, self-discovery, coming to voice, critical explorations of the connections between self and society, and discovery of political and ideological implications of actions. But, although I am by no means an advocate of the slogan that the medium defines the message, I have to concede that technology can have a severe impact on how to define feminist pedagogies, classroom dynamics, teacher and student positionalities, and communicative structures and forays. For example, because of the camera and the microphone, I was limited in my movements, and students were restricted to sitting at their desks with the microphones in intimate proximity. Furthermore, spontaneity, often encouraged in a regular classroom, became more difficult. Discussions were many times more restrained, not because students did not have anything to say, but because communication is mediated by cameras and TV screens. Somebody who does not want to be the focus of attention and have the camera zoom in relentlessly on her/his face is less likely to speak up than in a traditional classroom. Not only is everybody's gaze on the speaker, but the speaker herself gazes at her image on the screen. She is objectified not just by others, but she also tends to objectify herself—she is the image outside herself, watching herself while she speaks.

Furthermore, raised hands, a clearing of the throat, or looking up to show a willingness to speak are not enough for getting the attention of everybody else. Instead, it takes more initiative to be heard, such as speaking loudly, making one's intentions known by interrupting the previous speaker, dropping a book, or blowing into the microphone. Students not used to these interactive strategies or too polite to take such "rude" measures can become the silenced majority. Instead of presenting a reduced risk, the medium can increase the invisibility of already marginalized students at the distance education sites and it can lengthen the silence, a silence which can become "a marker of exploitation, oppression, dehumanization" (hooks 129). This undermines feminism's intent to provide safe spaces for all students that would allow them to speak up and be heard.

In addition to the difficulties in breaking the silence, interactions such as: "Yuma, can you hear us?" or "Can you speak into the mike. We can't hear you," become standard procedure in the IITV classroom and unfortunately take away from the discussions about the subject matter. Technological difficulties, more so than the actual teaching, can make it hard to keep the professional quality of the courses equal to those taught on campus, a problem about which students are well aware and with which teachers struggle constantly. Again, these problems can create an environment that hinders many of the positive interactions and easy communication endorsed by feminist pedagogies.

The logistical difficulties are almost always present. Perc Marland, for example, reports on a recent study of distance education students that showed only superficial student thinking and that "possessed few indicators of quality" (97). And according to Ellen Cronan Rose, feminist practices in distance education programs are rarely encouraged because "the educational philosophy animating distance education assumes a banking model pedagogy," which is Paulo Freire's way of saying that the teacher knows it all, and the students need to be filled with the information imparted by a lecturing teacher. If providers, not the teachers, of distance education think at all about pedagogy and teaching, they often look at it in terms of "delivering" education to students who "receive" the information in a largely passive form (see Holmberg, Lau, Van der Perre, for more information on this topic). Many feminist scholars have found this approach uninspiring, to say the least, and have argued that it reinforces traditional patriarchal power structures. Although "flexibility" plays an important role in the promotion of many distance education programs, such flexibility does not focus on methodology or pedagogy, but it centers on delivery systems: web-based, satellite delivery to your home or interactive instructional television. And the delivery systems are often seen as a one-way street: students in IITV classes are receiving signals, getting information from a screen, but they are often not able to send signals because the technology is not there for them to use. They are receivers, and this satisfies the university's idea about adequate access. It does not, however, satisfy my goals as a feminist teacher and scholar who considers "receiving" an education without appropriate student participation as an ineffective learning strategy.

My students did not know that I almost did not teach the course because of this interesting interpretation of access. Two weeks before the course was supposed to start I went to the administrators to inform them that the only way I could be successful as a teacher was to ensure that students could also become users of technology outside the classroom to access the library, to write their papers, to communicate with each other, and to email me. No, I did not want to be complicit in an existing structure where power/access was a one-way, no-return street. My indignant and revolutionary self wanted something that was at least the beginning of a different structure where it was no longer a privilege but students' right to access and use a computer as well as hone their technological literacy once they left the IITV classroom.

The fight left some ugly scars (and not just on me). However, the result, although not ideal, provided enough access for students to work on their papers, do their research, and collaborate online. It also set a precedent for future courses and for collaborations among the university, various community colleges, and high schools to ensure access for students at the distance sites. It did not ensure what Cynthia Selfe calls "critical technological literacy skills" to use the computers, but it provided the initial step to allow students to ponder this issue. Of course, after using a position of power to get what I wanted, after playing a game within the system's structure, my supervisors most certainly saw a reality, an identity, that told them that if she wants it she will fight for it. And even if she does not get it, she will at least have tried. Some would call this radical because I fought for those who would otherwise not have been given a chance to voice their opinions, much less have been provided with rudimentary access. I call it only a necessary step in the direction of more equity in the current technology empire, a goal that every feminist teacher, scholar, and researcher needs to support not only in theoretical explorations of the inequities concerning technology access but also by taking practical actions to ensure student access in specific instances.

Once the problem of access was partially solved, the other issue reverted back to the actual classroom experiences and the problems of silence. Instead of giving in to the media, letting the technologies define my message and the messages of my students, I refigured my ideas about an effective classroom environment. I knew that I was shifting my identity once again, portraying and becoming a new version of the old self. My experiences in the on-campus classroom had told me that it takes a lot of energy to make a certain pedagogy work. Furthermore, it takes the cooperation of the students to create an environment of intellectual curiosity, trust, and worthwhile interactions and discussions. Although the IITV classroom and the accompanying glitches with the technologies make this a harder task, I did not despair after my first experience with stony silence transmitted over the ether. Instead, I talked with my students about the strategies that I wanted to employ in teaching this course, and then I listened to some ideas from the students that brought up interesting changes in the classroom setup. They explained that because they were located at four different sites, each one tended to think that somebody else would respond. "What do you think?" turned out to be an ineffective way to start a general discussion about Mary Louise Pratt's explorations of contact zones because they did not think they were being contacted. And they did not respond to another student's comments right away because the visual cues for being finished did not get transmitted clearly. And in order not to be considered rude or pushy, they felt that they needed to wait until silence told them that it was now time to speak. However, since they also wanted to make sure that nobody else from another site would respond, the silence got prolonged beyond the point of my endurance. I had not read Pat Belanoff's 2001 article on the reflective powers of silence then. Even though, I volunteer to suggest that this silence was not "inhabited by meditation, reflection, contemplation, metacognition, and thoughtfulness" (422). Instead, it was the silence of not knowing when to speak, a silence of perceived voicelessness, that did not contribute positively to student interactions.

To create a more productive mode of interaction, we figured out that we needed some guidelines for the general good of everybody. My noninterventionist approach to teaching, my propensity for having students figure out who would talk next, needed to be altered because of the specific teaching situation and the specific issues that the IITV classroom presented. It meant that

I specified sites when I asked questions, that I called on people, and that I was more directive in my interactions with students. However, my perceived loss of direct student control of the interactive patterns I encourage in my on-campus classes did not deter me from my goals of creating a participatory learning experience. To encourage students to get to know each other, we created opportunities for group work that crossed sites and distances. For example, students from three different sites would discuss specific questions on a text read for class and then present their ideas to their classmates. Students started to interact with colleagues from other sites, and with that, they became more comfortable with the otherwise intrusive television cameras and microphones. Furthermore, everybody participated in on-line discussions that created another means to interact with each other. Students no longer identified themselves according to their sites; instead, they started to become members of the larger group and of subgroups defined by interests more than by location. As the semester proceeded, I no longer was required to take the responsibility for eliciting participation from all sites. Since the comfort level with each other and with the technology had improved, the class atmosphere also became more relaxed and conducive to critical learning and critical inquiry.

I could have given in to the superficial demands of the technology without trying to create a way to get students involved in the class. It certainly would have been easier to lecture and to give them what they initially wanted—wisdom as defined by their teacher. But to do that, I would have had to turn myself into a self that I did not want to become. Yes, I can make changes to my notions of what is acceptable, but I cannot adopt a teaching philosophy that makes me think of my student days and my inevitable nodding off when the lecture on the linguistic and phonetic variations between British and American English commenced. It also makes me think of the head, opened at the top, receiving pieces of information that get sucked into an unknown part of the brain, never to be recovered again. It is not part of my reality, and I do not want it to be part of what my students consider my reality or their realities.

AND WE DO IT ANYWAY

Now let me address some of the implications of creating and recreating our identities and realities in the image of ourselves, our students, our colleagues, and our supervisors. We are teachers. We are scholars. We are individuals. We are socially constructed. We are concerned about tenure and promotion. And we continue teaching in environments that are problematic to our understanding of what it means to be a teacher and that could potentially harm our rise in ranks because of increased preparation times that take away from scholarship, a higher risk of unsatisfying student evaluations, or colleagues' perceptions about the value of such teaching environments. However, if we did not get into the middle and did not take on the challenge, we would not have an opportunity to promote and create change.

Susan Jarratt in her introduction to the much-quoted book *Feminism and Composition Studies* suggests that we need to use new strategies, "other words" to look at the interconnections and the already existing integration between composition and feminist inquiry (4). She points to the "growing body of work on discourses and practices of difference, representation, and the social construction of knowledge and its subject"; she also addresses composition's investigations of the "gendered differences in language, teaching, and learning." What I would like to foreground, in addition to the intersection of composition studies and feminism, is the importance of recognizing the different subjectivities and positionalities that feminist teachers bring to the table. The social construction of our identities pointed out by Jarratt makes it necessary to pay close attention to the constructed realities in which we live and the assumed identities we take on. Although, as Stone points out, we might experience "our own senses of ourselves . . . like a universal constant, unchanged across space and time," we can be and are "quite plastic and malleable" (84). Acknowledging this plasticity and malleability, and revealing how in our various realities we might be complicit with existing power structures, might try to undermine them, or might call for radical change in institutional power relations is a step in moving toward a better understanding of how each one of us influences feminist inquiry and how each one of us participates in redefining what it means to be a feminist. I agree with Susan Hawthorn and Renate Klein that cyberfeminism has many tongues (1). I am many things at the same time. Understanding and gaining a level of comfort with my own morphed realities, my participation in positions of power, and my hope for instigating change is a first step in a long process that I started a while back.

My morphing abilities are not endless, however. They are hampered by my ideologies and by my need for agency in a world that often frowns on such agency. My fragmented and sometimes competing identities are capable of making choices and engaging in actions. I have also come to the point where I consider it necessary that we rethink our constructed selves, selves that are constantly changing while partly remaining the same. As my chapter shows, I have found that in order to come to a better understanding of what it means to be a feminist, to be influenced by feminist practices, or to endorse feminist ideologies, we need to revisit the often-told tales of power, authority, and identity. We need to encourage discussions and promote changes that enable us to see ourselves not as who we would like to be but as who we are when working in a technology-rich and largely traditional academic environment. As a cyberfeminist, for example, I am in support of minimizing hierarchical relationships, which are often seen as hampering feminist goals, but I also acknowledge that certain classroom practices sometimes require affirmation of hierarchies. I am for the ideal, but I also embrace—as well as question—the real.

I have come to understand that no matter how much we would like to see ourselves as noncomplicit with current power configurations, we are not outside the institutional structure. It is a bit more complicated. We practitioners who see ourselves as feminist teachers are sometimes part of it, sometimes apart from it, and always responsible for trying to change it by choosing our battles carefully. It is not our position as the outsider that connects us all, but it is our struggle for figuring out when it is more useful for our goals as feminist teachers to be insiders and when it is better to fight one of the many battles we need to fight. Even though we might have similar goals—to provide our students with a voice, to make them critical of their positions within a social and political system, to provide them with ways to make informed choices—we get there by different means. What is necessary, then, is to accept that there are many feminisms, to understand that feminists bring with them a wide array of ideologies, to be comfortable with the idea that feminisms cannot be confined to books but are lived experiences and always already fractured. Although you might think that I am who you see, you only see a small part of me.

WORKS CITED

Apple, Michael, and Susan Jungck. "'You Don't Have to Be a Teacher to Teach This Unit': Teaching, Technology, and Control in the Classroom." *Education/Technology/Power: Educational Computing as a Social Practice.* Ed. Hank Bromley and Michael Apple. Albany: State University of New York Press, 1998. 133–54.

Belanoff, Pat. "Silence, Reflection, Literacy, Learning, and Teaching." *CCC* 52 (2001): 399–428.

Blair, Kristine, and Pamela Takayoshi. "Navigating the Image of Woman Online." Available <*http://english.ttu.edu/kairos/2.2/coverweb/invited/kb.html*>. Accessed 1 May 2001.

Day, Michael. "Teachers at the Crossroads: Evaluating Teaching in Electronic Environments." *Computers and Composition* 17.1 (2000): 31–40.

Feyten, Carine M., and Joyce W. Nutta, eds. *Virtual Instruction: Issues and Insights from an International Perspective.* Englewood, Colo.: Libraries Unlimited, 1999.

Flynn, Elizabeth. " Composition Studies from a Feminist Perspective." *The Politics of Writing Instruction: Postsecondary.* Ed. Richard Bullock and John Trimbur. Portsmouth, N.H.: Heinemann, 1991. 137–54.

Freire, Paulo. *Pedagogy of the Oppressed.* New York: Seabury, 1968.

George, E. Laurie. "Taking Women Professors Seriously: Female Authority in the Computerized Classroom" *Computers and Composition* 7 (1990). Available <*http://corax.cwrl.utexas.edu/cac/archives/v7/7_spec_html/7_spec_3_George.html*>. Accessed 25 May 2001.

Gerrard, Lisa. "Feminist Research in Computers and Composition." *Feminist Cyberscapes: Mapping Gendered Academic Spaces.* Ed. Kristine Blair and Pamela Takayoshi. Stanford, CT: Ablex, 1999. 377–400.

Haraway, Donna. "A Manifesto for Cyborgs: Science, Technology, and Socialist Feminism in the 1980s." *Feminism/Postmodernism.* Ed. Linda J. Nicholson. New York: Routledge, 1990. 190–232.

Hawthorne, Susan, and Renate Klein. "CyberFeminism." *Cyberfeminism: Connectivity, Critique, Creativity.* Ed. Susan Hawthorne and Renate Klein. North Melbourne, Astralia: Spinifex, 1999.

Holmberg, Börje. *Theory and Practice of Distance Education.* New York: Routledge, 1989.

hooks, bell. 1989. *Talking Back: Thinking Feminist, Thinking Black.* Boston: Southend.

Jarratt, Susan. "Introduction: As We Were Saying . . ." *Feminism and Composition Studies: In Other Words.* Ed. Susan C. Jarratt and Lynn Worsham. New York: MLA, 1998.

Kemp, Fred. "Zen and the Art of Tenure." *Computers and Composition* 17.1 (2000): 109–15.

Lau, Linda, ed. *Distance Learning Technologies: Trends and Opportunities.* Hershey: Idea Group, 2000.

Leverenz, Carrie. "Tenure and Promotion in Rhetoric and Composition." *CCC* 52.1 (September 2000): 143–47.

Marland, Perc. *Towards More Effective Open and Distance Teaching.* London: Kogan Page, 1997.

Rose, Ellen Cronan. "'This Class Meets in Cyberspace': Women's Studies via Distance Education." *Feminist Teacher* 9.2 (Fall 1995): 53–60.

Schell, Eileen. *Gypsy Academics and Mother-Teachers: Gender, Contingent Labor, and Writing Instruction.* Portsmouth, N.H.: Boynton/Cook, 1998.

Selfe, Cynthia. *Technology and Literacy in the Twenty-First Century: The Importance of Paying Attention.* Carbondale: Southern Illinois University Press, 1999.

Selfe, Cynthia L., and Richard J. Selfe Jr. "The Politics of the Interface: Power and Its Exercise in Electronic Contact Zones." *College Composition and Communication* 45.4 (1994): 480–504.

Stone, Allucquère Rosanne. *The War of Desire and Technology at the Close of the Mechanical Age.* Cambridge: MIT Press, 1995.

Sullivan, Laura. "Cyberbabes: (Self-) Representations of Women and the Virtual (Male) Gaze." *Computers and Composition* 14.2. (1997). Available <*http://corax.cwrl.utexas.edu/cac/archives/v14/14_2_html/14_2_Contents.html#Sullivan*>. Accessed 25 May 2001.

Takayoshi, Pamela. "Building New Networks from the Old: Women's Experiences with Electronic Communications." *Computers and Composition* 11 (1994). Available <*http://corax.cwrl.utexas.edu/cac/archives/v11/11_1_html/11_1_Contents.html#Takay oshi*>. Accessed 25 May 2001.

Van der Perre, Georges. "Educational Innovation and Information and Communication Technologies (ICT): Revolution or Evolution?" *Virtual Instruction: Issues and Insights from an International Perspective*. Ed. Carine M. Feyten and Joyce W. Nutta. Englewood, Colo.: Libraries Unlimited, 1999, 107–26.

Part Four

Fractured Feminisms across Cultures

Chapter Ten

FEMINISMS AND MEMORY

Patriarchal Genealogy Translating and Translated in the Stories of Chinese/Chinese American Women

---

STUART H. D. CHING

When did this magnificent clan begin?
It started from Emperor Juen-Yuk of Ko Yeung.
A state was established during the Western Zhou dynasty.
Detailed genealogy was handed down from the Eastern Jin.
A stone in Guangzhou was inscribed with the name of a famed official.
Many virtuous men received high honors.
This is the branch from faraway Suzhou.
And has grown populous, long-lasting and strong.

THE GENEALOGY BOOK: A MYTHOLOGY

First appearing in the twenty-sixth volume of the Ching *Genealogy Book*,[1] the above poem partially records my family's history. The "famed official" represents Ching Shi Mang, who migrated approximately nine hundred years ago from China's coastal Suzhou to southern, coastal Guangzhou. Later, his son Ching Pak Fung moved farther south to coastal Zhong Shan. There Ching

Pak Fung had three sons, who, in turn, had five sons. Using the *Genealogy Book*, which records the names of sons in each generation, today the members of the Ching family in Zhong Shan trace their genealogy to "one of the five branches originating from these five great-grandsons of Ching Shi Mang" (Law 11). As an extension of the Ching family in Zhong Shan, Hawaii's Ching clan (my family) also traces its ancestry through twenty-six generations of this patriarchal genealogy to three Zhong Shan villages: On Ding, Tin Bin, and Hang Mei (Law 11).

My family's appropriation of the above genealogy exemplifies memory as an empowering cultural narrative. According to family lore, today a house in Zhong Shan County, On Ding Village, bears on one wall a picture of my father. My Uncle Tai Yau's, my Aunt Priscilla's, and my Uncle Herbert's pictures are also displayed, as is the wedding picture of my grandparents, Ethel Yuk Hin Ching and Hong Sing Ching. I have never been to On Ding, but since hearing this story, I have remembered the house with clarity.

My family's appropriation of the Ching genealogy illustrates how the above patriarchal lineage—like mythology—enables a community to imagine a place that the community could not otherwise articulate fully in the present. Through a kind of "prose work," or fragments arranged in symbolic narrative, the community reconstructs a story that precedes the community's memory.

FEMINISMS AND MEMORY

I have borrowed the term *prose work* from Hawaii poet and intellectual Donna Tanigawa, who, through her patchwork quilting metaphor, stitches together enabling feminist and cultural narratives of self. A useful metaphor in a collection such as *Fractured Feminisms*, the quilt, which bears lines and divisions, evokes the terms that Helene Cixous uses to revise patriarchal discourse: "fissure" (1235), "explode" (1240), "vibrations" (1234). In addition, the quilt signifies the conflicting identities resulting from feminism's intersection with cultural narratives. Addressing this intersection between feminism and cultural memory, I ask the following: How do feminist discourses enable students both to revise their world views *and* to affirm and appropriate culturally rooted narratives—specifically when these cultural narratives conflict with feminist values? This question especially addresses students who are positioned outside of dominant culture and for whom, because of this position, cultural maintenance is threatened. I respond by analyzing the stories and actions of the women in my family. Positioned within twentieth-century Hawaii—and within the discourses of American nationalism, the Hawaii plantation labor system, and its colonial legacy—the stories of the women in my family express competing needs. In one sense, these stories reproduce Chinese patriarchal lineage, staying cultural erasure, affirming cultural memory, and locating the community in a symbolic place. Conversely, they also transform place and memory, insisting on feminist translations and revisions of Chinese tradition. The feminism in these stories remains provisionally rooted within *and* partly resistant to Chinese patriarchal tradition. Supporting tradition and transgressing it, this feminism depends on Chinese patriarchal tradition to maintain cultural integrity and appropriates this tradition to define more empowering social roles for Chinese women.

At the outset, I summarize the versions of feminism informing this chapter, and then I suggest how attention to feminism's intersection with memory advances feminist and cross-cultural research in composition. In *Feminism and Deconstruction,* Diane Elam advocates a feminism that she calls a "groundless solidarity," an "ethical activism," and an "undecidability" (70–82, 84, 120). This feminism enables the community to act collectively and to exist provisionally. Eschewing essentialism, Elam resists entrenchment in one subjective stance. Figuratively representing her position as an abyss, or an infinite series of windows within windows, she advocates a feminism of continually shifting positions (26–32, 67). In agreement with Elam's argument, much feminist work in composition attempts to decenter the subjective self, or "I," and to invite students to embrace new perspectives (for example, see Lu; Caughie).

However, rarely have these valuable arguments fully explored the relationship between feminist goals and cultural discourses. Exploring this intersection informs current feminist composition research in three ways: First, this emphasis positions feminist composition theory within diverse local sites of cultural memory. That is, because of varied cultural histories, needs, and experiences, students translate and appropriate feminist texts differently within specific cultural and grassroots locations. Second, compositionists may more accurately interpret students' partial resistances to and appropriations of feminist theories. Resisting transformation, or "travel" (Clifford 2), may evidence critical consciousness if students' experiences outside of dominant culture necessitate rootedness or "dwelling" (Clifford 2) and "stay[-ing]" (Chang 23) within the home community's imagined borders. Hence, Evans questions "theories of deconstruction and decentering" that may unintentionally impede individuals' quests for "emancipatory identities" (274). Third, attending to both feminism and memory encourages a historicism already informing textual reclamation work in rhetoric. In revisionist textual analyses, scholars define the social matrices that have supported the traditional canon; simultaneously, these scholars locate the female rhetors who have conformed to and transgressed the patriarchal confines of their historical periods (see Lunsford; Glenn; Wilson; Ronald and Ritchie). Applying similar historicism to research in composition would enable students' cultural translations of feminism to reinform the theory guiding the field.

PASSAGE TO HAWAII: "SAILING FOR THE SUN"

My family's story is part of the larger narrative of immigrant hopes and dreams: Hawaii, Tan Heung Shan, or Fragrant Sandalwood Hills. According to historian Tin-Yuke Char, the first Chinese arriving in Hawaiian waters in 1788 were carpenters and craftsmen sailing aboard the British ships *Felice, Iphigenia,* and *North West America* (36–42). Years later in 1852, large-scale Chinese migration began when the first Chinese contract plantation laborers arrived aboard the British ship *Thetis* (Char 60). The cover of Arlene Lum's essay-and-pictorial anthology, *Sailing for the Sun: The Chinese in Hawaii 1789–1989,* bears an image of the early Chinese plantation laborers crossing the Pacific. In the picture, the Chinese coolies, their hair woven in queues, are gathered around the ship's mast. The background indicates a clear sky. The countenances of the men differ: some men look down at the ship's deck; others, their brows furrowed, look to the side. Three men, the picture's focus, gaze toward an area beyond the picture's frame, perhaps just above the horizon where the sun would be at daybreak. Their expressions suggest competing emotions: uncertainty, nostalgia, regret, hope. Sojourners, they sail between worlds.

Their difficult passage is well documented by historians and writers (Takaki; Char; Daws; Murayama). The laborers travel for approximately fifty-six to seventy days. During the day, they huddle below deck amid small pox and vomit. Near dusk, they are allowed on deck. The night air cools; the pungent salt air becomes tangible. They sleep on deck, on mats. They have already traveled a great distance, at first on foot or by sampans from their villages in southern China to the seaports of Macao and Canton and then by enormous open-water sailing vessels. The first ship of Chinese laborers comes to Hawaii from the Fukien port Amoy. At dawn, before being herded below deck again, they watch through breaking light their ship chasing the rising sun (see Takaki 29–34; Char 60).

They cannot yet know the history they will live and, through completing this difficult passage, enable and move their progeny to write about them: that one day the laborers will awaken on deck and see the cloud-misted peaks of the Hawaiian archipelago. They will disembark and enter a quarantine facility. Later, they will sign contracts binding them to a plantation for no less than five years. In the plantation system, each laborer will wear a bango, a small metal tag bearing a number, and in the fields, this number will be a new name, a new identity. The laborers will be exposed to opium and live among *luna,* or foremen, carrying whips and towering above them on horseback. The plantation will affirm their place in a social hierarchy: above them on a high hill, the manager will live in a mansionlike "big house"; on a second tier, the *luna* will live in well-kept cottages; and at the bottom, the laborers will reside. The plantation's sewage will pass through a network of ditches beginning at the big house on top and accumulating at the laborers' quarters below. In this way, the sewage system will become a metaphor for the manager's power and their relative powerlessness.[2]

After their contracts are completed, some of them will re-sign; others will leave and become merchants, rice farmers, or domestic servants. Many will migrate to Honolulu's Chinatown, where they will live in squalid conditions: cramped housing with inadequate sewage disposal, little ventilation, and an infestation of lice and rodents. In December 1899, they will suffer bubonic plague, and in January 1900, they will watch a fire that the government intended to sterilize one plague-infected area almost level Chinatown. And despite the prevailing white business community's anti-Chinese sentiment—and the economic and political sentiments and effects of America's 1882 Chinese Exclusion Act—during the 1900s the Chinese in Hawaii will gain a foothold in the islands' economic and political fabric.[3]

Within the imagination of Hawaii's Chinese community, these ancestors signify esteemed figures traversing a broad sea, figures who arrived in a new land and since then, even amid ruin, have risen from ash. In this sense, the Chinese story of "sailing for the sun" is heroic, even a mythology. And although my face and voice, shaped by Western consciousness, American allegiance, and Western education, would be strange to my ancestors, we remain connected through genealogy, and through story.

INSCRIPTION AND TRANSLATION

The Ching *Genealogy Book* seems to affirm that historically and symbolically women have rarely been prominent in and, in fact, have often been absent from this framing story. The wealth of material on my family's patriarchal lineage reminds me that within Chinese genealogy, the story of Chinese women is largely forgotten. However, within the smaller, more fluid site of family oral record, Popo, or Grandmother, Ethel Yuk Hin Ching, inscribed her life indelibly in my family's memory.

Popo grew up on the island of Oahu in Manoa Valley during the early 1900s. In contrast to the suburban enclave that Manoa Valley is today, in the early 1900s, Manoa was largely agricultural wetland irrigated by water from the Koolau Mountains. Popo, then a young girl, assisted her family in running a taro farm. Later, as a young woman, Popo married Hong Sing Ching, and together they purchased a house in Kapahulu, adjacent to Waikiki Beach, then an undeveloped swamp. Years later, landfills and sewage infrastructure would redirect water and enable the area's urban development.

Popo took several jobs. She worked as a salesperson at Shanghai Store in Chinatown, and she trimmed pineapples at the Dole Cannery. However, her primary job, which she embraced fully, was Chinese mother: traditional caregiver and nurturer. As a child, she awakened daily at 4:00 A.M. on the Manoa farm and did the family chores. Because her mother was severely limited by bound feet, Popo helped raise her eight younger siblings. When her mother was giving birth, Popo tended the outdoor fire for boiling water and then ran for the midwife. In addition, the Manoa house was built on low stilts, and before the women harvesters with infants would wade bare-foot into the wetlands for the day's harvest, they would wrap their babies in cloth and leave them in the shade beneath the dwelling. As a child, Popo, would care for these infants during the work day. Years later in Kapahulu, as a mother herself, she was the one who painstakingly washed, starched, and ironed clothes. She told her son Herbert to stop shining shoes for the sailors at the Royal Hawaiian Hotel. She smashed taro leaves, a home remedy that she would paste to the chest of her asthmatic son, my father, Wilbert. She also rubbed peanut oil and Vicks on my father's chest. She was the one who, years later, would rub Vicks on the chest of her youngest grandchild, me, in the same way. She prided herself in raising her children, her grandchildren, and the children of relatives and friends. She also embraced the name that the entire neighborhood gave her, Popo Ching, or Grandmother Ching.

Popo was traditional in other ways. My mother marveled during her visit to China that "walking through the arts and crafts shops in Beijing was like walking through Popo's living room." Popo also passed on family cultural tra-ditions and beliefs: among these, Baisan, or Clear and Bright Festival, in honor of the deceased; tea-pouring customs; cultural home remedies; and wedding and birthing traditions.

In addition to affirming culture, Popo revised tradition. While many eth-nic communities of her era preferred the cinema of their native languages, she loved Western movies and plays, especially musicals. She also advocated inter-racial marriages. Speaking in her Cantonese dialect and accent, she would advise, " So what . . . never mind . . . as long as they're happy . . . don't always have to marry a Chinaman!"

Instrumental within this revision was her redefinition of women's social roles. My mother, an Okinawan American who married into the Ching fam-ily, insists,

> I have been told that the Chinese woman is the first liberated woman. And, when I think of Popo, it's easy for me to agree with that belief. She was a confident woman who did not feel she—or any woman—was born to serve a man. However, she was an excellent wife and a wonderful mother who would do anything for her family—because she wanted to, not because she had to.

Crucial in this description is Popo's agency and choice. Through this redefinition, her role as caregiver becomes both reproduction of and resistance to patriarchal tradition. In addition, although Chinese culture even today traditionally values sons who must carry on the family name, Popo highly valued daughters, insisting that daughters would stick by their mothers' sides. My mother recalls that prior to my birth, Popo hoped I would be a girl. When she would carry me during my infancy, she would affectionately say, "You should have been a girl."

Popo also insisted that women should aspire to public leadership. She encouraged my Aunt Priscilla and my mother, who were both school teachers, to be administrators. Popo would insist, "We better have at least one principal in this family." Furthermore, when my mother proposed graduate study in Arizona, Popo promised to help raise my brother and me during my mother's year-and-a-half absence. As my mother recalls, "My friends thought that was pretty amazing for 'those days.' Other mothers-in-law would have strongly disapproved and probably criticized me to their friends." Traditionally, women were subservient to men, but Popo encouraged my mother to exceed my father's education, fully realizing that my mother's graduate degree would enable my mother to become a public leader. With Popo's approval, my mother became a university professor and then administrator.

Hawaii's historical context in the mid-1900s further accounts for Popo's competing actions. Interaction with other plantation cultural groups, a growing sense of American allegiance, and introduction to Western education must have changed Popo. In contrast, political pressures to assimilate completely into Western culture likely provoked resistance. As noted elsewhere in this chapter, the plantation labor system and Chinese exclusion legislation threatened Chinese identity. In addition, other historical events threatened Chinese culture: stigma against Hawaii-Creole English and its origins in the plantation labor class; English Standard Schools, which accepted standard English speakers and excluded others; the social-sorting effects of this governmentally implemented educational system; and the urgency of "Americanization" following the Japanese attack on Pearl Harbor (Kawamoto 201–03; Sato, "Sociolinguistic" 651–58; Sato, "Language" 132–37; Tamura 52–61; Dotts and Sikkema 104–05). According to Lisa Lowe, from the late 1800s to the present, American immigrant legislation, labor needs, and global economic and diplomatic policies have both given Asians access to America and paradoxically cast them as strangers within the nation. This exclusion has resulted in alternate sites of culture within American memory (1–36). These political and economic factors—along with the landmark Massie and Fukunaga murder cases in which the Hawaii judicial system favored European Americans over the local population[4]—likely created among Hawaii Asian communities an equally strong desire for resistance.

Hence, Popo's stories and actions reflect the competing desires to stay and to travel, to remain rooted in an imagined place and to create this place anew. While Popo maintains identity through a patriarchal discourse, she also changes women's social roles within this tradition. The emergence of a feminist stance composes a significant part of this transformation.

"JOY LUCK MOTHERS": FEMINISM, MEMORY,
AND CROSS-CULTURAL COMPOSITION PEDAGOGY

Interdisciplinary research on memory figures prominently in cross-cultural composition pedagogy and theory. For example, analyzing the fiction of Lois-Ann Yamanaka, Morris Young argues that the language of "home" liberates Hawaii Creole English speakers from colonial control (422–23). Similarly, scholars have associated cultural memory with power in African American, Native American, and Latina/Latino contexts (Villanueva; Evans; Gilyard; Lyons; Frijalva; Pratt; Canagarajah). For example, Keith Gilyard and Victor Villanueva emphasize the recovery of cultural memory and, conversely, lament what Richard Rodriguez calls the "hunger of memory" coinciding with memory's erasure. Ruth Behar notes that memory's erasure is death made absolute: "to die without being reborn in historical memory" is "to die once and for all" (42). Collectively, the above perspectives suggest that cultural memory— enacted through language, story, and a critical dialectic between home and institutional perspectives—enhances self-determination in institutional contexts that demand conformity to dominant culture.

However, as I have noted above, drawing from cultural memory becomes problematic when patriarchal cultural narratives subvert feminist causes. The narrative landscape of Asian America exemplifies this tension between feminism and memory. Discussing Amy Tan's *Joy Luck Club*, Wendy Ho argues that the "Joy Luck mothers teach their daughters that personal and cultural identity need to be maintained . . . through the preservation of Chinese heritage"; at the same time, these mothers promote a feminist "active, fluid, multidimensional agency that can negotiate the fluctuations of oppressive social, cultural, and historical processes [comprising both race and gender]" (333). Furthermore, while the Joy Luck mothers' stories partially reproduce patriarchal authority, the women simultaneously teach their daughters strategic "interventions" that "counter patriarchal and imperialist systems" in China and in the United States (333). Shirley Geok-Lin Lim notes similar competing strategies in Maxine Hong Kingston's *Woman Warrior*, in which female characters affirm patriarchal traditions in order to preserve identity and partially resist these traditions in order to gain agency and revise the very landscapes of the culture that sustains them (274, 279).

Like Popo, several characters in these narratives realize their feminism within the cultural memory that, paradoxically, at once limits, enables, and advances their critical perspective. For example, in both the women's stories in my family and Tan's novel, feminism depends on cultural tradition for articulation. This assertion acknowledges the cultural borders that limit ideological travel; at the same time, this assertion suggests that the tension between culture and feminism may lead to new hybrid discourses that facilitate transformation.

Drawing from feminist theory and Paulo Freire, Joy Ritchie advocates a feminist classroom out of which feminism may continually emerge, or a site that "constantly connects intellectual activity—the study of literature, language, and ideas—to the history and experiences of people's lives" (271). Applying the ideas of Gayatri Spivak, Ritchie argues that "any claim of women's identity must be analyzed in light of the multiple historical and social circumstances in which women live their lives" (256). Her argument suggests that feminisms must emerge from a dynamic space that invites critical dialogue among texts and cultural narratives. In these ways, students may compose their lives, at times, through affirming the myths that sustain their cultural existence and at other times, through questioning these myths and moving toward a new consciousness.[5]

Ritchie's statement is crucial because it connects feminist discourses and the histories (or memories) of communities. Feminisms remain rooted in imagined and remembered local sites both beyond and evoked by students within the classroom. Gender, culture, place, memory, story, language, and critical thought remain complexly interwoven. Extricating one from the others is questionable. Alternatively, the feminist, cultural project of contemporary feminist rhetors—students and instructors alike—is a dialogic and organic endeavor. As we construct and reconstruct ourselves through composing, we turn our gazes both homeward and abroad, clarifying, claiming, and generating the narratives that will sustain us within and across the borders of time and space, gender and culture.

CHUNG CHUN NGIT: PASSING THROUGH CHINATOWN

The patriarchal genealogy connecting my family to On Ding Village in southern China grounds family members in an imagined, symbolic place. In this way, patriarchal genealogy counters cultural erasure and what Peter McLaren has called a "fragmented post-modern consciousness" (198–99). At the same time, this chapter values counterfeminist narratives that challenge and revise patriarchal discourses across several generations. The intersection between cultural memory and feminism that I have described necessitates a pedagogical practice of remembrance that enables communities to reinvent culture while maintaining the integrity of its borders, to travel from within while remapping the cultural landscape.

My family's historical and political context necessitates this critical turn inward. Jeff Chang insists that because of Hawaii's colonial history—and the emergence of a panethnic local identity that resists this colonialism—political change in the islands must emerge from within local communities' cultural borders. Dismantling these borders would subvert an enabling solidarity, but solidarity without critique is equally disabling. Chang argues that the islands' greatest hope for ethical renewal is a turn "inward": "Would not the islands be better informed by an inward turn? . . . For on this 'borderline of history and language,' in the flux of time, the islands cry for their own translations and transformations" (23).

This inward turn informs composition research in the following ways. First, it reminds us that in composition classrooms, feminisms are enacted among and within many intersecting sites of memory, both public sites of memory and private, sovereign spaces of remembrance (shared only by cultural insiders). Second, this critical framework provides a lens for recognizing and interpreting feminisms that gain articulation while simultaneously evoking patriarchal traditions and mythologies. Third, while current feminist theories importantly advocate decentering the subject "I," the stories of the women in my family suggest that recentering the self—or engaging in myth-making—may be equally empowering for some students whose cultures exist on the margins of dominant society. Last, in agreement with postcolonial feminist perspectives, this critical framework assumes that latent feminist narratives exist in all traditionally patriarchal cultures, as they have in Chinese culture. Thus, although the feminist theories informing composition studies may fracture—may even become limited on various fronts—upon entering into conversation with these patriarchal narratives, feminist texts may also illuminate, affirm, clarify, and extend those latent and partial feminist narratives emerging from students' experiences and calling for dialogue and articulation.

In the acclaimed *Woman Warrior*, positioned on the borders of gender and culture, Maxine Hong Kingston recovers the story of an aunt, a "No Name Woman," whom her family has exiled from memory (3–16). This absence, or "silence," Hong Kingston's elders wish to reproduce in the next generation. But in "devot[ing] pages" to her aunt's story, Hong Kingston resurrects her dead aunt, saving her from erasure. Ruth Behar has named this kind of erasure the "death of memory," or death made absolute (42–43). A landmark contribution to the literary canon and positioned on the borders of cultural and feminist studies, Hong Kingston's text functions as both a powerful cultural narrative and an enabling feminist discourse. Patriarchal and feminist discourses remain interconnected rather than run parallel, each enabling the other's articulation, each necessitating the other's presence, the former provoking the latter's emergence.

There is a story passed on by the women in my family that similarly marks the emergence of a feminist consciousness within the boundaries of culture. I have this memory:

Once in Hawaii at the turn of the century there lived a woman named Chung Chun Ngit. When she was still a young girl, her parents, without telling her why, sent her back to China to have her feet bound. In this way, at an early age, she was destined to live her life only in semifreedom. In Guangdong, at night, while the

*rest of her body and spirit grew, her feet remained encased in cloth, her toes curled
inward, her bones crushed in the shape of a deer's hoof. She knew, intuitively, that
her chance of achieving a life of great distance was greatly diminished. But her
tongue remained free, unbridled, and so after she returned to Hawaii and when
she became a mother, she began her story to her daughter this way: "If I had known
I was being sent back to China to have my feet bound, I would have run away ..."*
    *Her daughter, Ethel, remembered these words and became a strong woman.
It is said that her spirit was as steadfast as a pillar, her tongue as powerful, grace-
ful, and elegant as a warrior's sword. And though she came from a lineage of forgotten names—women with no names, women whose names had been erased from
the book of memory, women whose names were devoured by the names of men—
she used the power of her words to write herself into the memory of her children,
and their children, and all the children thereafter.*

My great grandmother, or *taipo,* Chung Chun Ngit, told her story of
foot-binding to her daughter, Ethel Yuk Hin Ching, who then told my
mother, who has since passed the story to me. Each generation has translated
the story with some variation, depending on the storyteller's and listener's
experiences and intentions. I am the first to translate this part of my family's
oral history into a literary discourse. In this way, each generation, translating
and being translated within a new historical context, inscribes its image in its
progeny. This inscription remains essential to the community's reproduction.
Within this form of remembrance, the emergence of a feminist position is
clearly visible and remains central to the story's revisionist purposes.

    Sometimes during my most quiet moments, I imagine Taipo: I see her *en
medias res.* On extremely reduced feet, she is shuffling amid throngs of people
and past open Chinatown storefronts, among vendors with wicker baskets
bearing vegetables and blackened duck eggs. On Honolulu's crowded Chinatown sidewalks, her movements are tenuous. Each step seems an impossible
distance. Still, she presses forward. Miraculously, she balances. Despite the
brutal tradition that has crippled her feet, Taipo walks. She travels. Years later,
though I have never known Taipo save through story, I see her this way in the
present tense of remembering: Simultaneously returning to Chinatown and
crossing its metaphorical boundaries, she is on the verge of taking another
step. One step, in memory, becomes a mythical journey that both begins and
ends here—with Taipo passing through Chinatown and never leaving.

NOTES

    1. The poem's translation is by scholar Yip-Wang Law and appears in
The Genealogy of the Ching Family in Nam Long (51).

    2. On sugar plantation life, see Takaki (57–98, 127–34); on plantation
hierarchy, see Murayama (28) and Takaki (92).

3. On the Chinatown fire, see Char (101–10); on Chinatown's political and social context and living conditions prior to the fire, see Daws (302–04).

4. On the Fukunaga case, see Ogawa (109–46); on the Massie case, see Daws (319–28).

5. This claim is also informed by writers and scholars such as Gloria Anzaldúa, bell hooks, Dorothy Allison, Roger Simon, Minnie Bruce Pratt (see Bulkin), and Peter McLaren, who enact or theorize memory as a pedagogical tool that enables individuals both to reclaim and to critique myth as well as to deliberate morally between affirming and revising tradition. The myth-maker and traditional storyteller construct a compelling and seamless narrative that strengthens the boundaries of the community, while the cultural critic reveals seams in legend and provokes critical exploration into the workings of myth. A pedagogy of critical remembrance would encourage students to act as both myth-makers and cultural critics. My discussion is also largely informed by John Gardner's analysis of traditional and postmodern narrative, in which he claims that the "continuous" "dream" is most important in traditional fiction, while the "breaks" in dream, or the spaces of inquiry, are equally important in deconstructive narrative (31, 87–88).

WORKS CITED

Allison, Dorothy. *Two or Three Things I Know For Sure*. New York: Plume, 1996.

Anzaldúa, Gloria. *Borderlands/La Frontera: The New Mestiza*. San Francisco: Aunt Lute Books, 1987.

Behar, Ruth. *The Vulnerable Observer: Anthropology That Breaks Your Heart*. Boston: Beacon, 1996.

Bulkin, Elly, Minnie Bruce Pratt, and Barbara Smith. *Yours in Struggle: Three Feminist Perspectives on Anti Semitism and Racism*. New York: Long-Haul, 1984.

Canagarajah, A. Suresh. "Safe Houses in the Contact Zone: Coping Strategies of African-American Students in the Academy." *College Composition and Communication* 48.2 (1997): 173–96.

Caughie, Pamela L. "Let It Pass: Changing the Subject Once Again." *Feminism and Composition Studies: In Other Words*. Ed. Susan C. Jarratt and Lynn Worsham. New York: Modern Language Association, 1998. 111–31.

Chang, Jeff. "Local Knowledge(s): Notes on Race Relations, Panethnicity and History in Hawaii." *Amerasia Journal* 22.2 (1996): 1–29.

Char, Tin-Yuke. *The Sandalwood Mountains: Readings and Stories of the Early Chinese in Hawaii*. Honolulu: University of Hawaii Press, 1975.

Cixous, Helene. "Laugh of the Medusa." *The Rhetorical Tradition: Readings from Classical Times to Present*. Ed. Patricia Bizzell and Bruce Herzberg. Boston: Bedford Books of St. Martin's, 1990. 1232–45.

Clifford, James. *Routes: Travel and Translation in the Late Twentieth Century.* Harvard University Press, 1997.

Daws, Gavan. *Shoal of Time: A History of the Hawaiian Islands.* Honolulu: University of Hawaii Press, 1968.

Dotts, Cecil K., and Mildred Sikkema. *Challenging the Status Quo: Public Education in Hawaii 1840–1980.* Honolulu: Hawaii Education Association, 1994.

Elam, Diane. *Feminism and Deconstruction.* New York: Routledge, 1994.

Evans, Henry. "An Afrocentric Multicultural Writing Project." *Writing in Multicultural Settings.* Ed. Carol Severino, Juan C. Guerra, and Johnella E. Butler. New York: Modern Language Association, 1997. 273–88.

Gardner, John. *The Art of Fiction.* New York: Vintage Books, 1983.

Gilyard, Keith. *Voices of the Self: A Study of Language Competence.* Detroit: Wayne State University Press, 1991.

Glenn, Cheryl. *Rhetoric Retold: Regendering the Tradition from Antiquity through the Renaissance.* Carbondale: Southern Illinois University Press, 1998.

Grijalva, Michelle. "Teaching American Indian Students: Interpreting the Rhetorics of Silence." *Writing in Multicultural Settings.* Ed. Carol Severino, Juan C. Guerra, and Johnella E. Butler. New York: Modern Language Association, 1997. 40–50.

Ho, Wendy. "Swan-Feather Mothers and Coca-Cola Daughters: Teaching Amy Tan's *The Joy Luck Club.*" *Teaching American Ethnic Literatures: Nineteen Essays.* Ed. John R. Maitino and David R. Peck. Albuquerque: University of New Mexico Press, 1996. 327–45

hooks, bell. "Representing Whiteness in the Black Imagination." *Cultural Studies.* Ed. Lawrence Grossberg, Cary Nelson, and Paula A. Treichler. New York: Routledge, 1992. 338–46.

Kawamoto, Kevin. "Hegemony and Language Politics in Hawaii." *World Englishes* 12.2 (1993): 193–207.

Kingston, Maxine Hong. *The Woman Warrior: Memoirs of a Girlhood among Ghosts.* New York: Vintage Books, 1989.

Law, Yip-Wang. *The Genealogy of the Ching Family in Nam Long.* Honolulu: Ching Clan Benevolent Society of Hawaii, 1997.

Lim, Shirley Geok-Lin. "'Growing with Stories': Chinese American Identities, Textual Identities." *Teaching American Ethnic Literatures: Nineteen Essays.* Ed. John R. Maitino and David R. Peck. Albuquerque: University of New Mexico Press, 1996. 273–91.

Logan, Shirley Wilson. *With Pen and Voice: A Critical Anthology of Nineteenth-Century African-American Women.* Carbondale: Southern Illinois University Press, 1995.

Lowe, Lisa. *Immigrant Acts: On Asian American Cultural Politics.* Durham: Duke University Press, 1996.

Lu, Min-Zhan. "Reading and Writing Differences: The Problematic of Experience." *Feminism and Composition Studies: In Other Words.* Ed. Susan C. Jarratt and Lynn Worsham. New York: Modern Language Association, 1998. 239–51.

Lum, Arlene, ed. *Sailing for the Sun: The Chinese in Hawaii 1789–1989.* Honolulu: Three Heroes, 1988.

Lunsford, Andrea, ed. *Reclaiming Rhetorica: Women in the Rhetorical Tradition.* Pittsburgh: University of Pittsburgh Press, 1995.

Lyons, Richard. "Rhetorical Sovereignty: What Do American Indians Want from Writing?" *College Composition and Communication* 51.3 (2000): 447–68.

McLaren, Peter. "Multiculturalism and the Post-Modern Critique: Toward a Pedagogy of Resistance and Transformation." *Between Borders: Pedagogy and the Politics of Cultural Studies.* Ed. Henry A. Giroux and Peter McLaren. New York: Routledge, 1994. 192–222.

Murayama, Milton. *All I Asking for Is My Body.* Honolulu: University of Hawaii Press, 1988.

Ogawa, Dennis M. *Jan Ken Po: The World of Hawaii's Japanese Americans.* Honolulu: University of Hawaii Press, 1973.

Pratt, Mary Louise. "Arts of the Contact Zone." *Profession* 91 (1991): 33–40.

Ritchie, Joy S. "Confronting the 'Essential' Problem: Reconnecting Feminist Theory and Pedagogy." *Journal of Advanced Composition* 10.2 (1990): 249–73.

Rodriguez, Richard. *Hunger of Memory: The Education of Richard Rodriguez.* New York: Bantam Books, 1983.

Ronald, Kate, and Joy Ritchie. "Riding Long Coattails: The Tricky Business of Feminists Teaching Rhetoric(s)." *Feminism and Composition Studies: In Other Words.* Ed. Susan C. Jarratt and Lynn Worsham. New York: MLA, 1998. 217–38.

Sato, Charlene. "Language Change in a Creole Continuum: Decreolization?" *Progression and Regression in Language: Sociocultural, Neuropschological, and Linguistic Perspectives.* Ed. Kenneth Hyltenstam and Ake Viberg. New York: Cambridge University Press, 1993. 122–43.

———. "Sociolinguistic Variation and Language Attitudes in Hawaii." *English around the World: Sociolinguistic Perspectives.* Ed. Jenny Cheshire. New York: Cambridge University Press, 1991. 647–63.

Simon, Roger I. "Forms of Insurgency in the Production of Popular Memories: The Columbus Quincentenary and the Pedagogy of Counter-Commemoration." *Between Borders: Pedagogy and the Politics of Cultural Studies.* Ed. Henry A. Giroux and Peter McLarren. New York: Routledge, 1994. 127–42.

Takaki, Ronald. *Pau Hana: Plantation Life and Labor in Hawaii 1835–1920.* Honolulu: University of Hawaii Press, 1983.

Tan, Amy. *The Joy Luck Club.* New York. G. P. Putnam's Sons, 1989.

Tamura, Eileen H. *Americanization, Acculturation, and Ethnic Identity: The Nisei Generation in Hawaii.* Urbana: University of Illinois Press, 1994.

Tanigawa, Donna. "Trying Fo' Do Anykine to Donna: Fragments of a Prose Work." *Social Processes in Hawaii* 38 (1997): 62–69.

Villanueva, Victor, Jr. *Bootstraps: From an Academic American of Color.* Urbana: National Council of Teachers of English, 1993.

Young, Morris. "Standard English and Student Bodies: Institutionalizing Race and Literacy in Hawaii." *College English* 64.4 (2002): 405–31.

Chapter Eleven

COMPOSING SELF

An Intercultural Curriculum
for First-Year College Composition

M. DIANE BENTON

> In the end, it is words that enable us to make some sense of our
> existence by allowing us to stand aside to narrate it. We die. That
> may be the meaning of life. But we do language. That may be the
> measure of our lives.
>
> —Toni Morrison

As we begin to revisit feminist theory and address the issue of the fracturing
of feminism into "feminisms," we are offered the potential and possibilities of
crossing boundaries and exploring and connecting with other disciplines such
as rhetoric and composition studies. At the same time, we are able to explore
the often overlooked practices of African American feminist rhetoric, one of
the shards of a fractured feminism. This revisitation of feminist theory is not
feminism revised but feminism revisioned. From its beginning in the 1600s
African American rhetoric has perceived itself as open to change, alteration,
and self-questioning and at the same time, provided a powerful rhetoric that
would lead us to fundamental social change. African American feminists,
though often disregarded, have been a part of this change from the early days

195

of the struggle for the abolition of slavery to the days of the Civil Rights movement of the sixties and seventies and to the rhetoric of hip hop today.

Within this change African American rhetoric has challenged itself from the inside and rejected prescribed identities (stereotypes) to form new identities as well as establish new voices using the African American rhetorical practices of social responsibility, self-authorization, and call and response. These practices may not be uniquely those of African American feminists. After all African American men use these practices also and consider them vital strategies as I show in this chapter. Yet, because it is African American feminists whose voices are often lost, they use these strategies often to establish those voices. African American feminist rhetoric poses critical potentialities for pedagogy: It is both an example of a fracture from mainstream feminism and an example of a growing and critical form of feminist thinking. It claims a past in African American rhetoric and feminist thinking while not wedding itself to either group alone as it articulates its politics. As I write about these potentialities, I will move beyond the simple inclusion of African American writing in the classroom. I will consider the strategies we learn from the readings of African American rhetoric.

Drawing from the work of Jacqueline Jones Royster, Juanita Rodgers Comfort, and many others in the history of African American rhetoric, this chapter will examine the importance of personal writing in composition based on these rhetorical practices and how it can be applied to all students, regardless of gender or race, creating an intercultural approach to composition. Based on the premise that African American feminist rhetoric, just like Euro-American feminist rhetoric, should not be segregated or marginalized or set at the boundaries of the borders, I will reveal what African American rhetoric can teach feminist thinking and how it might inform feminist practice in our classrooms. This chapter presents an intercultural approach that shifts the center—unsettling the power structure of rhetoric from Euro-American male rhetoric—to embrace rhetorical strategies from all cultures, asking how African American feminist rhetoric specifically can help us reach that goal.

This intercultural approach stems from my experiences as a professional and as a feminist. As an African American teacher and as a scholar, I found myself often raising questions that were not addressed in graduate classes or in the major scholarly works of rhetoric and composition studies. I often reflected on my history as an African American female who both valued feminist practice and valued my African American heritage. As someone who came of age during the women's movement, I found that in my professional life my very presence became a challenge to the status quo. As the administrator for the sexual harassment policy at a large university, aspects of my work had allowed me to voice my feminist concerns in support of both women and men who faced harassment. For a little over ten years I have taught at a community college, a university, and a private high school. During this period, I have encountered students who came from many different cultural backgrounds and who were not always open to feminist views. Yet, overall, these experiences confirmed that the laws and social practices that feminists fought hard for could benefit and, at times, did benefit everyone in the workplace and in the classroom. I witnessed time and time again that those who could use words, as Morrison suggests, to "make some sense of their existence" were more successful in claiming their identities in the face of harassment or a push to the margins.

In my work as a teacher, I have seen students struggling internally with their identities, witnessed them react to cultural norms as they attempt to develop their voices as writers within the confines of narrowly defined rhetorical strategies. As I reflect on teaching, I think about the voices of my many students from different cultures and backgrounds who often struggle with their identities as writers. Over the years the majority of my students have been European Americans. Yet many have been from other countries such as Japan, Korea, People's Republic of China, India, Venezuela, Nigeria, and Somalia. Some have been middle class; some have been poor. Some have been in a boys' prison and come from very troubled backgrounds, and some have emerged from very wealthy and privileged backgrounds. Most have been women, and fewer have been African American men or women. Almost all have had to struggle with identity, with finding a voice, with feeling as if they have something valuable to say.

As I have read their papers, I have seen them grapple with the question of which voice to claim. Many have been taught through experience, whether in prison or in private high school or while working their way through college, that the voice—the identity they must master—should reflect that of the powerful in our society. That identity is usually white, male, heterosexual, and upper class. Likewise, most of these students have perceived composing as an activity limited to assignments in a classroom environment. They enter the classroom to "do the teacher's writing assignment" without thought of seeing themselves as writers who have something worthwhile to say. As one white, male, working-class student wrote: "I never thought anyone would be interested in anything I had to say." Often, regardless of differences in race, ethnicity, class, and gender, my students have not trusted their identities, their voices. I have found that I have to struggle with students to see that they do indeed have something to say.

Both Jacqueline Royster and Juanita Comfort confirm this view, as they perceive students as thinkers who can explore and interpret their experiences within the larger context of social and political experiences. Both also draw on the work of African American women rhetoricians. Comfort taps the experiences of African American women essayists who move from the margins to establish a space for their voices, viewing the essay as "an important space for continually re-forming, re-visioning, and renegotiating personal identity in light of the past and ongoing experience that shape their lives" (554).

Such attention to issues of identity and personal experience might lead to pure expressivism, the presentation of experience without any critical examination. Such a view often maintains that personal experience is not mediated by cultural context, history, or social formations. Yet we move beyond expresssivism when, as Morrison contends in the epigraph to this chapter, students stand aside and narrate their experiences, coming to understand how they are socially and culturally constituted. At such moments, students are able to examine, "re-form and re-vision" their lives and develop their voices. They are then able to utilize composition to their own ends, to learn, to create, and to re-create. They are able to compose and "re-compose" their identities.

The flip side of expressivism, of course, occurs when teachers dictate students' interactions with curricula entirely. Comfort addresses this issue, implying that some teachers believe that students are "incomplete knowers" who must first earn the right to speak (550). Yet Comfort firmly asserts that students should be given an opportunity to explore and interpret their experiences, past and present, and to recognize, define, and develop distinctive intellectual voices. They should be able to perceive experiences in cultural contexts and understand how their identities are constructed for them by social forces—as well as how they can build them themselves. Comfort calls this voice the "writerly self." Comfort further acknowledges the need for establishing a credible voice and maintains that the work of African American woman rhetoricians can contribute to our understanding of that need as well as how to fulfill the need. Likewise, using this culturally grounded theory, Comfort's work suggests, will allow our students to draw on their own cultural identities. As with African American feminists, their identities are based on race, gender, and cultures.

Comfort considers the writerly self representative of the rhetorical practices of African American women. She traces how in the 1800s, when women were fighting for their rights, African Americans stood beside their European American sisters in defying the sociopolitical standards of the time. They challenged the prevailing rhetorical constraints of a "woman's place" that did not afford women political voices in public settings. It is thought that an African American woman, Maria Stewart, may have been the first American woman "to step onto a lecture platform and speak her political mind" before an audience of both men and women (Gates and McKay 201). Through the fractures of today's feminisms, we can and should build on the work of our foremothers. Doing so will provide our rhetoric and composition classrooms with more politically viable pedagogical practices, ones that work toward inclusion and dialogue, rather than exclusion and monologue. Doing so will ultimately inform both feminist theory and African American rhetoric, suggesting new opportunities for both.

Arguing for the credibility of this practice, Comfort affirms, "What is most memorable about both the professional essayists and my student is what

I believe most college writers can be convinced of —that, as Halloran asserts, 'the rigor and passion with which they *disclose their world* to the audience, is their *ethos*'" (550). Royster proffers a rhetorical stance of self-authorization, indicating that the writer's knowledge and experience can develop insight in a number of ways based on what Comfort calls the writer's "multiple locations of voices," that knowledge and experience create multiple locations based on race, gender, and cultures. Self-authorization can best come through an interrogation of one's selves and their cultural practices within the complex web offered by doing so in conjunction with other voices. Royster's and Comfort's concepts support encouraging students to begin with writing personal essays in their composition classes. Such essays would invite students to draw upon their experiences and backgrounds as well as to constantly revisit these in light of their own texts, the reactions of their audiences, and the writings of others.

In recognizing the value of the African American feminist approach articulated by Comfort and Royster, it is important to understand the cultural context of their research. The scholarship of both of these authors stems from a long history of African American rhetoric establishing an authoritative, socially responsible voice that spoke to a larger audience. When captured and enslaved, African men and women were faced with two rhetorical dilemmas. The first dilemma was that they had no common language through which to communicate with each other and likewise that they could not convey their thoughts within the dominant cultural modes. Forced to live with other African ethnic groups, all of whom spoke different languages and often enacted different cultural practices, enslaved Africans were unable in the beginning to communicate with each other and form communities. Simultaneously, African slaves had to contend with captors who spoke different languages, also practiced different cultural norms, and exerted the power of life and death over the captured Africans. Several scenes in Steven Spielberg's film *Amistad* aptly depict this dilemma as the Africans attempt in vain to communicate with each other, with their captors, and with those who sought to help them, the abolitionists. As a group, they were necessarily forced to draw upon similarities from their African homelands and upon their common experiences to build tentative, often temporary communities that had a common goal of fighting for their freedom and human identity.

Second, they were confronted with the power of rhetoric used to keep Africans enslaved physically, socially, and psychologically through laws and social practices. Additionally, enslaved Africans were forbidden to speak their native languages. Since language has historically acted as an outcome of knowledge and has also been used to organize reality to create new knowledge, these Africans were effectively but temporarily stripped of knowledge-producing power. As these Africans were denied the use of their native languages through which they might form some type of order, they faced extreme chaos and utter disempowerment. Likewise, they were denied rhetoric in its most potent forms: reading, writing, and free speech. In fact, to date, African Americans as a people have lived longer under this condition, a three hundred year period of exile from language use, than they have lived free to read, write, and speak, owners of their own discourses.

Nonetheless, out of this rhetorical lineage, African Americans developed strong rhetorical strategies in order to form powerful rhetorics. This power is evident as early as the first published slave narratives offered by both men and women, through the first African American Literary Renaissance of the1850s, the Reconstruction era and the Harlem Renaissance, and now into more contemporary works in African American literature. The narratives of African men and women, for example, carefully recounted the conditions of slavery and how slaves gained their freedom. These narratives now provide us with a window into how many slaves became literate in the language of the dominant culture, while at the same time maintaining their own languages. This practice of maintaining dual linguistic identities, often called "code switching," was as common then as it is today. Olaudah Equaino's 1789 slave narrative, an international best seller, represents such variation in rhetorical strategy, commencing with its title *The Interesting Life of Olaudah Equaino or Gustavus Vassa, the African.*

These early examples bear witness to the self-authorized voice through the use of rhetorical double consciousness—African Americans' historical awareness of oneself and one's own cultural identity while at the same time being aware of audience and her or his cultural identity. Ultimately, this form of double consciousness relies on one's own experience within a social context. This awareness has often relied on understanding one's race and gender in rhetorical relationship to the audience. Frederick Douglass's narrative stands as a superb example of this emerging double consciousness. In *Narrative of the Life of Frederick Douglass,* Douglass recounts how, when his master caught his wife teaching Douglass how to read, an illegal act, the master argued, "A nigger should know nothing but to obey his master—to do as he is told to do. Learning would spoil the best nigger in the world" (Douglass 325). Yet Douglass became doggedly determined to learn how to read and write. He studied Richard Sheridan and *The Columbian Orator,* a book of poems, dialogues, plays, and speeches. Douglass eventually escaped to freedom and became a great international figure, resisting the attempts of whites to deny him what Audre Lorde terms the tools to dismantle the master's house. Language remained key in his life, as an orator, newspaper publisher, author, and politician.

Douglass's experiences as well as how he conveys them rhetorically make it clear that language is used by the powerful to dominate, but they also reveal something perhaps more crucial: Douglass does not see himself as a victim. Instead, he uses language as a means to define his identity and to establish the possibilities for his own freedom. Often viewed as Douglass's counterpart, Sojourner Truth uses a somewhat different approach. She establishes voice and identity through the vernacular rather than the literary, weaving together the nontraditional voices of vernacular with the sanctioned voices of white culture. Truth was also more supportive of communitarian interests than Douglass—whose work centered more on individualistic interests (Gates and McKay 197).

Narratives such as those offered by Douglass, Truth, and Equaino as well as Harriet Jacobs and Harriet Wilson employed language to deconstruct a dominant reality—one that cast African Americans as only fit to exist as chattel in slavery, one that cast African Americans as having no rhetorical power of their own. With its consistent use of social consciousness, support of political awareness, and call for participatory action, African American rhetoric helped to create and sustain this rhetoric of freedom. Such narratives further used language to construct selves and identities alongside new conceptions of reality that spoke to the human condition of all Americans. Thus, these narratives provided the possibilities for later establishing the African American feminist rhetorical practice that Comfort describes as the valuation of the "writerly self" and Royster characterizes as the "self-authorized writer."

At the same time, these early African American narratives established the practice of the writer's social responsibility to place his or her background and experience into a social context and grapple with the social issues that interaction might yield. From its inception, African American rhetoric has depended on the responsibility of the African to address social issues, giving perspective and honestly acknowledging the cultural nature of that perspective to an audience. At the same time, however, African American rhetoric has also almost always demanded a response from that audience. Whether in the speech of call and response or the rhetorical interaction between writer and audience, African American rhetoric builds knowledge together through the rhetorical interaction of rhetor and audience.

There is no denying the importance of African American rhetoric's historical attention to social concerns. Keith Gilyard has also identified this crucial feature of African American rhetoric ("Social"). He emphasizes:

> Writing is not an activity that features social responsibility as an option. Writing is social responsibility. When you write, you are being responsible to some social entity even if that entity is yourself. You can be irresponsible as a writer, but you cannot be nonresponsible. (21)

Accepting the 1993 Nobel Prize for literature, Toni Morrison echoes Gilyard's description of the importance of power and its connection to responsible language use. Morrison contends, "In the end, it is words that enable us to make some sense of our existence by allowing us to stand aside to narrate it. We die. That may be the meaning of life. But we do language. That may be the measure of our lives." "Standing aside to narrate," we understand a bit better who we are. Morrison invokes the power of language and the responsibility associated with its use. In "doing language," she indicates, we must be responsible for how we use it to make sense of our lives.

Citing Alice Walker, Royster also indicates the historical importance of the African American writer's responsibility around the use of language. One must be "courageous enough to go deeply into one's own mind, heart, soul, and experience and to bring forth language with social and persuasive intent in the interest of touching, teaching, and deeply affecting others" (27). Today these writers carry forward the rhetorical traditions of their foremothers and forefathers, a tradition that we see firmly in place in African American feminist rhetorics. African American feminist rhetoric takes with it this long history of marginalization based in racist and gender-biased discourses and works to empower black women as a way to empower all people. Such African American feminist rhetorical traditions can be taken into the classroom so that students, regardless of gender or race, can develop their writing identity, just as we expect students regardless of gender or race to use Euro-American rhetoric.

The act of using language courageously and responsibly is also heavily tied to bell hooks's work in *Teaching to Transgress:* the classroom must be grounded in a safe learning environment but also one that challenges passive learning (14). All students should feel a responsibility to contribute to the environment. hooks considers this environment to be based on engaged and transformative pedagogy, teaching that transforms and engages the writer (1–22, 39). Students and teachers work together to construct knowledge, knowing that such constructions are temporary and will be challenged by the discourses of the students in the class themselves. Together, knowledge will be constructed, challenged, and reformed over and over again in a synergistic spiral of call and response.

As hooks suggests, we as teachers need to transform our classrooms. My experience in the classroom in all settings suggests that for students to make sense out of their worlds, they need to constantly display such worlds and their relationships to them. We need to make African American feminist practice, an intercultural mode of rhetoric altogether, a greater part of our classroom environments.

Concentrating on the writerly self and transformative pedagogy can be critical. Nearly two years ago I witnessed this while teaching an African American literature class in a community college in a boys' prison. Students in this prison for boys, ages fourteen through twenty-one, face even greater obstacles to the use of rhetorical strategies. Not only may they be marginalized outside the walls of the prison for issues related to race, ethnicity, class, sexual preference, or age, but being removed from conventional society further marginalizes them. Many of these students have been incarcerated for a long time, not attending a "normal" school setting since earlier than eighth grade. Some of these students come from native discourse communities in which very few people are familiar with academic discourse. As a result, they may have little to no sense of these discourse conventions, how they work, what they mean, or why they might be important. Even more difficult, the conventions of their native discourse communities may be shunned or even rejected by the academic discourse communities. Finally, in many cases, students' own experiences in academic communities might have invalidated and rejected their native discourse conventions as well as their communities. Thus, the overlap between their discourse communities and those of academic discourses can oftentimes be narrow or nonexistent, leaving students little with which to work when encountering writing in a first-year composition class. While a few of these students did imagine themselves in college, they still had tremendously low expectations about their ability to succeed there.

On the first day of class, one young man, Alan, told me that as a child, in large part because of his family's involvement, he had been a member of the Ku Klux Klan. Alan then revealed that he was no longer a member. While for many Americans the KKK may hold of a place of shame, for an African American woman—for me—the KKK undeniably holds a place of fear. As I read Alan's writing, I chose to draw upon one of the key principles in African American rhetoric concerning "hearing someone." To "hear" someone goes beyond listening to his or her words. It requires hearing the intangible feeling behind these words. It requires witnessing someone's testimony. What I heard in Alan was his own fear of finding acceptance. It is not surprising that Alan's fear was making him test how I would respond to his statement. I heard his desperate need for a safe environment in which to learn, and I heard his desire for some mode of valid self-expression. Taking this rhetorical tactic from African American feminist rhetoric, I never felt threatened, nor did I fear him. Instead, I was more curious than anything else about his narrative and where he would take it. I wondered, and I hoped. Could this white supremacist student write a new narrative for himself, using the same techniques that African American rhetoricians had utilized in the past? And if he could do so, would this not benefit not only his own personal history, rewriting it substantially, but also serve the rhetorical ends of African American rhetoric itself?

In addition to the reading assignments and exams in the course, students were required to write reader response journals. These journals were a place students might use to explore some specific aspect of the reading and class discussion. The response could be personal, but it also needed to be grounded in the class work. It needed to be contextualized. I always furnished suggested topics, but I often left the assignment open so that students might explore the various voices used in this literature.

For the first journal assignment in the class, Alan wrote about how the Bible justified slavery. While no longer a member of the KKK, his white supremacist beliefs clearly remained fully intact. My first response was surprise and disbelief. I sensed that a very traditional rhetorical strategy, one based in hatred and bigotry, had been thrown at my feet. One critical aspect of rhetorical strategy is developing a rhetorical stance that is representative of "self." One has to recognize the authority of one's own authorship, what Comfort calls accepting the "writerly self," so that we use our gender, race, and culture as part of the strategy. However, Alan used what some might consider a rather conventional racist rhetorical strategy that has a long and disturbing history—deploying the Bible as authority to justify beliefs that did not seem humane let alone spiritually viable. He had also used this strategy, the invocation of an expert source read literally and outside of its historical context, as a way to lend his oppression of African Americans credence.

As an African American feminist teacher, a crucial question faced me: Was I going to legitimize this kind of rhetoric by addressing his argument? Would I try to view Alan's journal as simply a thoughtful challenge to the perspective of the course literature? Or would I also have to perceive his written work as a challenge to my own legitimacy, authority, and identity as his teacher? I could not help but do a bit of all three—to acknowledge Alan's valiant attempt to make an argument, to encourage Alan's critical exploration of African American literature and his own identity, and to acknowledge privately to myself that the rhetoric this student was using challenged me as a teacher and a scholar of African American rhetoric. This is the true value of what African American feminist rhetoric holds—a willingness to both put forward its own critical tenets and yet be open to challenge, dispute, dialogue, and change.

It is interesting that holding all of these possibilities open, coupled with Alan's own willingness to explore his writerly identity, led to some truly powerful results. By the middle of the semester, Alan's writing began to change in rather astounding ways. We had read narratives, short stories, and poetry of enslaved African Americans. We had examined each writer's voice within the sociohistorical context of the work. We had explored how the writer's voice might be viewed in our current sociocultural and historical context. We had considered the rhetorical context given the audience and the writer's message. And we had investigated how African American writers structured their voices in light of changing sociohistorical contexts. We heard African American male and female voices using the traditional linguistic form to argue against the traditional view of the writer and to assert the importance of full human rights and acceptance. Many such voices utilized traditional religious arguments as well as political arguments to support their views. We also heard many African American male and female voices using African American vernacular to resist the traditional language and rhetoric that had been imposed on them. On a daily basis, students from all racial and ethnic backgrounds resisted the rhetoric of the conventionally established "powerful"—practicing the power of African American rhetoric as a strategy for reclaiming an identity.

It was in the midst of this that Alan wrote about the impact of the poem "We Wear the Masks" by Paul Laurence Dunbar (1872–1906). Alan indicated that he was surprised to learn that he could ever have "believed or agreed with something written by a black man." But somehow Dunbar's poem broke the doors open wide for Alan. In an environment based in African American feminist principles, free exchange and self-reflection were the dominant modes of inquiry. Dunbar's poem forced Alan to think about himself and the mask Alan himself wore. In his poem Dunbar invites his audience to join him, using "we." In fact, Dunbar does rhetorically encourage everyone since he never overtly reveals his own race or gender. Dunbar strategically utilizes rhetoric to engage his audience, whether black or white, and this student, years after Dunbar conceived of this poem, responded.

By the end of the semester, Alan was deeply engaged in African American literature. He began to notice and seek the multiple voices African American literature utilized for his own rhetorical purposes. These texts continued to raise questions about identity, and many texts resisted the prescribed identities for males in American culture. Such readings prompted Alan to read beyond the course texts themselves. Alan took up one unassigned poem about homosexuality, Essex Hemphill's "XXIV." After reading this text, Alan wrote in his journal about his traumatic experience of sexual abuse by his stepfather. After describing how this experience had shaped his identity, Alan courageously revealed his own homosexuality, something about which I had been entirely unaware until this point. Somehow, this poem helped Alan to deal with his abuse and to openly write about his own homosexuality; Hemphill's voice invited Alan to reconsider his place in society as a gay man. This change in Alan's responses flew in the face of his earlier rhetorical strategies and his identities as a member of the KKK as well as his justifications for his beliefs. Suddenly, Alan was seeing his identities as multiple. He was finding his own voice, contextualizing it, and allowing his multiple selves to talk to and to question each other.

Clearly Alan responded to Dunbar's call. He was open to the ideas of others himself. This led to Alan becoming confident enough to explore ideas that contradicted not only his own identity convictions but also those of the dominant culture. During the next semester when I had Alan for a communications class, I saw further growth in his writerly self. In one writing assignment, for example, students had to write a letter to the editor responding to an article about antigay political rhetoric and legislation. Alan's writing was more prolific and more confident in responding to this antigay rhetoric than it had ever been before, and Alan left the class vowing to continue to pursue gay rights on behalf of the gay community.

The social responsibility that comes with African American feminist rhetoric includes honestly dealing with one's race, gender, and cultural perspective as well as speaking to that perspective. This use of African American

rhetoric also requires the courage to inquire and challenge the single identity
to which society may relegate you alongside a willingness to explore the multiple traditions and voices available to writers. Alan chose to accept that challenge. His experience as a member of the KKK will always be a part of his
identity. He can choose to embrace it or challenge and understand it in the
face of his other identity as a gay man. He can draw upon those identities in
his writing voice and in his voice to the world.

Such complexities of identity not only occur in prison teaching situations,
however. I also recently witnessed a similar struggle for identity in a first-year
composition class that I taught at a large university. The class members were
from very diverse backgrounds in terms of race, ethnicity, and gender. Most of
the students, however, came from working-class and middle-class homes.
Their lives intersected many discourse communities. The university itself is
located in an area that is predominately working and middle class but next to
a more affluent, medium-sized city.

In this class our primary text was Gilyard's *Voices of the Self,* a book that
alternates between chapters of narrative autobiographical text and chapters
that analyze sociolinguistic and cultural aspects of that text. While the class
enjoyed the autobiographical chapters of the book, they struggled with the
theoretical chapters. These chapters were written in a more traditional, academic discourse. Likewise, even some of Gilyard's autobiographical chapters
raised questions for the students. For many students, the specific discourse
community that Gilyard discussed was unfamiliar. Still others who hailed
from communities similar to Gilyard's found his characterizations questionable—their experiences were not anything like his experiences. Working
within a working-class, urban African American community, Gilyard discusses the dominant culture's rejection of such community discourses. Gilyard
reveals that, like Dunbar, Zora Neale Hurston, and others before him, he
embraces this stigmatized discourse and culture while also acknowledging and
working within dominant white discourse to reform it.

Despite their differences with Gilyard's text and perhaps because of
them, the students in the class were able to use strategies from the book to
compose essays about the various aspects of language in their communities
and their identities in those communities. Almost every student found the
experience of struggling to comprehend other cultures as well as her/his own
very beneficial.

The experiences of two students in particular stand out. Both were African
American males from a medium-sized, economically depressed city with a large
African American population. One student, Ryan, focused on what he considered the positive aspects of his culture. He wrote about how many students from
various cultural groups in his high school spoke black English in classroom settings. Ryan described how some teachers reacted negatively to this practice.
And, in some cases, teachers themselves would be drawn into speaking vernac-

ular as well and were not sure whether that was a valuable practice for their students or not. All the same, Ryan felt that vernacular was an important part of his community and identity. He championed its use, feeling as though it was a unique aspect of his identity and community, that it gave a political perspective to the work of his community. While it was not a rhetorical strategy that fit in all settings, Ryan acknowledged, perhaps it held the potential of empowerment and challenge to dominant modes of speaking and writing.

Ryan's friend, Kenny, wrote about the stigma of being black. He struggled with why being black is a stigma, blaming both society and African Americans in turn. White-dominated society did not support or value African American achievements enough, he contended, and African Americans did not value themselves. Kenny also briefly discussed the critical need to change his rhetorical choices to adapt to different cultural settings. Kenny's writing was less fluid than his classmates' and he was less confident about his writing altogether. As a result, his text was somewhat halting. Despite his argument against supporting the use of vernacular, Kenny's own identity in the world seemed to refute his very claim. His dress and speech clearly indicated that he identified with popular, urban African American culture. Yet Kenny rejected his African American identity almost in the same breath as he articulated it. For Kenny, reshaping his rhetorical choices to fit the rhetorical situation came with a price. The "price of the ticket," as James Baldwin would say, was himself—his own language and his own identity.

I realized something critical as a teacher as a result of this experience. I wanted students to be aware of the tradition of African American rhetoric. I wanted them to understand the complexities of double consciousness and polyvocality that is part of this heritage. Part of this is understanding one's audience as valuable. But Kenny was willing to value his white audience almost over and against African American rhetoric itself. I wondered whether teaching audience awareness goes too far. I wondered when and how teaching rhetorical situations could become too overbearing—when and where could it compromise identity and student voice? African American feminist teaching practices made me rethink my own approaches to teaching African American rhetoric itself. How might teaching rhetoric at the expense of voice lead to confusion over how important audience reaction indeed was?

It is interesting that in their final reflective essays both Ryan and Kenny wrote that they had planned to drop the class because of the focus and the difficulty of the work. However, they explained that they were glad that they had not. Ryan helped Kenny to understand that audience should not challenge his fundamental relationship to his community. Vernacular was valuable. It was part of their identity, their community, who they were in the world. In turn, Kenny helped Ryan to see that sometimes understanding one's audience was critical to being persuasive, that rhetorical tactics, setting, and place impact how others receive what we say.

For their final public project, the two students brought their interests together. Ryan and Kenny constructed a black English dictionary for their colleagues and faculty. They utilized their experiences in their communities, as well as in the university, to write it for a specific audience, those who work within the academic discourse of the university. They took responsibility for their experiences and knowledge through their research. Ryan and Kenny broadened and contextualized the foundation of their experience and knowledge as well as presented it to an audience for response. They, like Alan, transformed their learning experience, taking responsibility for active learning as hooks suggests, inquiring and discovering the authority of their own voices, and through research creating knowledge for a larger audience.

African American feminist practices have the possibility of empowering not just African American students but all students. Such pedagogy might start with two basic African American feminist rhetorical strategies: developing a writing identity and the social responsibility of writing. Students in first-year composition classes are at the point in their lives during which they are developing and establishing new identities. For the traditional eighteen-year-old students, this is an opportunity to try new personae now that they are often away from parents and even old friends. Even if they are at home, because of the freedom and choices they must make, college still offers this opportunity for change, a revisiting of self. It is appropriate to start with exploring who they are today and who they can become and to place that re-forming in the context of social responsibility.

While using this traditional frame, the curriculum might usefully focus on developing and sustaining the writer's identity, an expected interaction and understanding of audience, and developing a variety of organizational and investigative approaches. These are teaching strategies I have used with students from a wide range of cultural, racial, and ethnic backgrounds, from those at the prison to those in the private high school. The proposed curriculum would focus on the following:

1. The writer is self-authorized; knowledge and understanding are grounded in experience.
2. The thinking is exploratory, questioning, unfinished, open-minded.
3. The writer recognizes a listening audience, considers the position of the audience, and expects a response.
4. The cultural backgrounds of the writer and the audience along with the social issues create the context.

Employing African American feminist rhetorical practices, one of the goals of this curriculum is to develop an ethos, a rhetorical stance, a writerly self that is complex and multilayered. Such an approach foregrounds the creation of work and encompasses responsibility for that work. It uses strategies of inquiry, particularly those that center on the intersections of culture and identity. While the curriculum emerges from the tenets of African American feminist rhetoric, this does not mean that the curriculum can only work with African Americans or female students as can be seen by the examples I have provided. Rather, this critical approach for all students encourages exploration of the "other" as a way to come to terms with the "self." In fact, if we look at this rhetoric as defined by Alice Walker, we understand that this rhetoric is "committed to the survival and wholeness of entire people" (xi). Of course, Alan, Ryan, Kenny, and other students from other ethnic backgrounds will be able to draw upon these strategies to develop their writerly selves so that they can "do" language as a measure of their lives.

African American feminist rhetoric necessarily raises critical questions about monocultural, multicultural, and intercultural strategies. As one explores African American feminist rhetoric in detail, one also begins to pose other questions about other cultures. What else might the fractures in feminism reveal? What have they contributed to the story of rhetoric, and what can we learn from them? Our students often become knowledgeable and skillful in Euro-American rhetoric. Yet is Euro-American rhetoric in any way capable of addressing the experiences of all students? Is African American rhetoric alone capable? While this is the approach I explore here, clearly an intercultural approach that examines a wide range of options may be the most helpful to our students in the future.

Rhetoric and composition studies has a strong history of examining this question. Other theorists and rhetoricians have incorporated multicultural rhetorics into the composition curriculum. In the last few years Mary Louise Pratt's contact zone model that honors other rhetorics by creating a classroom environment where conflicts with other cultures are acknowledged and engaged has been discussed at length. At the same time, other theorists and practitioners, such as Maxine Hairston, Laura Gray-Rosendale, and Richard Miller, have raised the issue of students' and teachers' ability to grapple adequately with the cultural conflicts in this model of the contact zone. These cultural conflicts are often directed at the cultural authority, and this cultural authority is something that many students desperately need. Hairston, in particular, raises questions about what she considers the overtly "political nature" of the contact zone. She argues that students are not ready for "politicized" diversity and curriculum oriented to specific kinds of causes. Instead, they should write about something they care about in a low risk environment and should not be subjected to a prescribed political context. Miller and Gray-Rosendale have raised similar kinds of questions, asking whether teachers are setting the agenda of the contact zone at the expense of their students.

I agree with such scholars that students may not be ready to grapple with what some view as the cultural wars. Like these authors, I find that the complexities of the historical, social, and economic issues are too much to cover adequately in one semester. Furthermore, belief that the concept that real diversity emerges from students themselves in a collaborative classroom is a sound pedagogical practice.

Despite the challenges inherent the contact zone model the idea of these nondominant rhetorics is important. The focus on one dominant set of rhetorical strategies reflects a monocultural approach. It is the focus that we find in most of our classrooms where Euro-American rhetoric is the center of the discourse and considered the norm. A monocultural curriculum based on the dominant culture can silence critical thinking to an unchallenged acceptance of the status quo, the constructed monolith, and it can eradicate the culture, language, and identity of students of nondominant cultures. Moreover, some researchers would argue that the psychic price paid by students not of the dominant culture is high and often drives them out of the school doors (Gilyard *Voices;* McLaughlin). In addition, a monocultural approach eradicates for students of the dominant culture a critical lens on their world that will allow them to accept, reject, and, ultimately change rhetorical strategies as needed.

If we offer students only Euro-American rhetorical strategies, we furnish what some researchers describe as a linear thesis-driven approach in which the writer's role is viewed as authoritative and the audience is perceived as passively receptive (Lisle and Mano; Scollon and Scollon). This model may be appropriate for some writing strategies. But this rhetorical stance is only one of many rhetorical stances that may act as models for student writers as well as all writers. Rhetoric has so much more to offer once we cross borders and venture into rhetoric within other cultures, letting different rhetorical strategies inform and re-form our practices. If we can do this as teachers, we will also have a great deal more to offer our students when we bring these strategies to our classrooms.

Researchers such as Mano and Lisle, the Scollons, Henry Louis Gates Jr. ("Signifying"), Geneva Smitherman ("Talkin"), Elaine Richardson, John and Russell Rickford support these "other" strategies. In order to provide a clearer overview of the kinds of teaching possibilities that their work might offer us, I provide a graphical overview of these strategies.

Without doubt, the characteristics in this table are generalizations and, as Mano and Lisle point out, are not inherent qualities based on an individual's ethnicity (20). Yet these characteristics can supply a holistic picture of rhetoric and its possibilities. While Euro-American rhetoric is considered to represent the "culture of power," we should also consider that even Euro-American rhetoric is not universal. There are differences within that which has come to be viewed as "dominant discourse." It has been and will continue to be affected by other cultures, and, consequently, will always change. At the same time, other cultures have rhetorical lineages, as well. Such a holistic view supports an educational goal of diversity—to help students understand where they fit within what the world looks like today, what has preceded them, and what the future might be.

TABLE 1. In Progress Comparison of Rhetorical Strategies

	Speaker/Writer	Audience	Rhetorical Strategies
African/African American feminists	One with the audience, speaking a collective voice, nommo. Self-authorized; exploratory, open-minded	Responsive, one with the speaker/writer	Inductive, poetic, word play/performance, voice merging, establish verbal prowess, metaphor and rhythm, sound, repetition, double-voiced, signifying
Arabic	Verbal artistry	Collaborative	Inductive, poetic, metaphor and rhythm, sound, repetition, religious references
Asian	Not determined	Communal, responsive	Inductive
Chinese	Harmony and social inclusion	Communal, responsive	Onion-layered whose outer layer begins with a universal truth
Korean	Not determined	Communal, responsive	Includes a tangential subtopic
Japanese	Not determined	Expects the audience to work at understanding allusions	Uses allusions
Euro-American	Individualistic, separate from the audience	Individualistic, separate from the speaker/writer	Deductive, distinction and division, one central story, thesis driven and linear
Native American, Pueblo	Communal—Connections and inclusiveness, one with audience	Communal, one with speaker/writer	Inductive, one story leads to another

NOTE: Thus far my research did not yield values for the areas markede "Not determined." I hope to continue such research in the future.

I believe that our most significant work as teachers is to help students to understand and to develop different perspectives that contribute to how we do language. We should help them find ways to understand how language use impacts the construction of their own identities. I propose that African American rhetoric and African American feminist rhetorical practices can be placed at the center to facilitate this movement. African American strategies are around us everyday in the news and entertainment alike. In fact, according to Smitherman, African American rhetoric is perhaps more global than any other at this historical moment. One hears it equally in the United States as one hears it in Germany and Japan ("Keynote"). We cannot dismiss these strategies as only "racial." They are a critical part of American traditions and our popular culture. And African American rhetorical strategies are being recognized as such in other countries, even if our own home culture has been perhaps slow to do so.

In fact, I would argue that even a brief look at African American rhetoric reveals its power. African American rhetoric, and particularly African American feminist rhetoric, has a long history of mediating between nondominant and dominant rhetorical strategies. Given the visibility of African American language, particularly in entertainment and the popular youth culture that reaches many ethnic groups, African American rhetoric seems familiar to students. Yet African American and non-African American students alike are unfamiliar with examining the thought, meaning, and language of African American rhetoric used to define self as a personal and societal political strategy. At times, students and teachers alike resist examining such a history. Yet in working through this resistance to acknowledging the power and place of African American feminism, students giving these rhetoric strategies a close scrutiny will discover their own voices—as have my students—the self-authorized voice or writerly self, social responsibility, and call and response.

As Morrison offers, we must make sense of the feminist existence; we must journey, re-create, revision. My early feminist foundation allowed me to consider these other possibilities of African American rhetoric for a feminist rhetorical practice in the classroom. My experience with how African American feminist rhetorical strategies impact all students illustrates its effectiveness in facilitating the opportunity for them to find their writerly selves in the context of social responsibility to the content, to themselves as writers, and to their audiences.

WORKS CITED

Amistad. Dir. Steven Spielberg. Perf. Anthony Hopkins, Morgan Freeman. Universal Studios, 1997.

Comfort, Juanita Rodgers. "Becoming a Writerly Self: College Writers Engaging Black Feminist Essays." *College Composition and Communication* 51.4 (2000): 540–59.

Cooper, Anna Julia. "Womanhood a Vital Element in the Regeneration and Progress of a Race." *The Norton Anthology of African American Literature*. Ed. Henry Louis Gates and Nellie Y. McKay. New York: W. W. Norton, 1997.

Dunbar, Paul Laurence. "We Wear the Masks." *The Norton Anthology of African American Literature*. Ed. Henry Louis Gates and Nellie Y. McKay. New York: W. W. Norton, 1997.

Equaino, Olaudah. "The Interesting Life of Olaudah Equiano or Gustavus Vassa, the African." *The Norton Anthology of African American Literature*. Ed. Henry Louis Gates and Nellie Y. McKay. New York: W. W. Norton, 1997.

Finding Forrester. Dir. Gus Van Sant. Perf. Sean Connery and Rob Brown. Columbia/Tristar Studios, 2000.

Gates Jr., Henry Louis, ed. *The Classic Slave Narratives*. New York: Mentor, 1987.

Gates Jr., Henry Louis, and Nellie Y. McKay, ed. *The Norton Anthology of African American Literature*. New York: W. W. Norton, 1997.

Gates Jr., Henry Louis. *The Signifying Monkey*. New York: Oxford University Press, 1988.

Gilyard, Keith. "The Social Responsibility That Writing Is." *Let's Flip the Script*. Detroit, Mich.: Wayne State University Press, 1996. 21–27.

———. *Voices of the Self*. Detroit, Mich.: Wayne State University Press, 1991.

Gray-Rosendale, Laura. "Once upon a Theory: Cracks in the Authoritative Chronicles of the Contact Zone." *Questioning Authority*. Ed. Linda Adler-Kassner and Susanmarie Harrington. Ann Arbor: University of Michigan Press, 2001. 153–67.

Guerra, Juan C. "The Place of Intercultural Literacy in the Writing Classroom." *Writing in Multicultural Settings*. Ed. Juan C. Guerra, Carol Severino, and Johnnella E. Butler. New York: Modern Language Association, 1997. 248–60.

Hairston, Maxine. "Diversity, Ideology, and Teaching Writing." *Cross-Talk in Comp Theory*. Ed. Jr. Victor Villanueva. Urbana: National Council of Teachers of English, 1997. 659–75.

Hemphill, Essex. "Conditions." *The Norton Anthology of African American Literature*. Ed. Henry Louis Gates and Nellie Y. McKay. New York: W. W. Norton, 1997.

Higher Learning. Dir. John Singleton. Perf. Omar Epps, Laurence Fishburne, and Kristy Swanson. Columbia/Tristar Studios, 1995.

hooks, bell. *Teaching to Trangress*. New York: Routledge, 1994.

Lisle, Bonnie, and Sandra Mano. "Embracing a Multicultural Rhetoric." *Writing in Multicultural Settings*. Ed. Juan C. Guerra, Carol Severino, and Johnnella E. Butler. New York: Modern Language Association, 1997. 12–26.

Miller, Richard E. "Fault Lines in the Contact Zone." *College English* 56.4 (1994): 31–40.

Morrison, Toni. *Toni Morrison: Lecture and Speech of Acceptance, Upon the Award of the Nobel Prize for Literature*. New York: Alfred A. Knopf, 1994.

Nash, Diane. "Inside the Sit-Ins and Freedom Rides: Testimony of a Southern Student." *Speech and Power*. Ed. Gerald Early. Vol. 1. Hopewell, N.J.: Ecco, 1993. 361–71.

Powell, Kevin. "The Word Movement." *Step into a World*. Ed. Kevin Powell. New York: John Wiley and Sons, 2000. 1–12.

Powell, Malea. "Blood and Scholarship: One Mixed-Blood's Story." *Race, Rhetoric, and Composition*. Ed. Keith Gilyard. Portsmouth, N.H.: Boynton/Cook, 1999. 1–16.

Pratt, Mary Louise. "Arts of the Contact Zone." *Profession* 91 (1991): 33–40.

Richardson, Elaine. "A Linguistically Diverse Approach to Teaching Written Standard American English." TYCA Midwest Conference 2000. Wayne County Community College District. Detroit, Mich., 2000.

Rickford, John Russell, and Russell John Rickford. *Spoken Soul*. New York: John Wiley and Sons, 2000.

Royster, Jacqueline Jones. *Traces of a Stream*. Pittsburgh: University of Pittsburgh Press, 2000.

Scollon, Ron, and Suzanne Wong Scollon. *Intercultural Communication*. Malden, Mass.: Blackwell, 2001.

Smitherman, Geneva. "Keynote." *American Ethnic Rhetorics*. Pennsylvania State University, 2001.

———. *Talkin That Talk*. New York: Routledge, 2000.

Walker, Alice. *In Search of Our Mothers' Gardens*. New York: Harcourt Brace Jovanich, 1983.

Chapter Twelve

Looking to East and West

Feminist Practice in an Asian Classroom

CHNG HUANG HOON AND CHITRA SANKARAN

INTRODUCTION

We approach feminism as a social and political movement, which works to bring about gender equity through consciousness raising and through discovering the means to redress the wrongs of a patriarchal society. However, we are aware that (1) Singaporeans in general, and our students in particular, are not too aware of sex discrimination within Singaporean society, such being the power of naturalized assumptions and behavior, and hence the need for consciousness-raising in our context;[1] (2) local feminists are overly cautious and very concerned about operating within systemic constraints, and in extreme cases, even resort to acts of semi-conscious self-censorship. This has a direct impact on efforts to redress the existing gender inequalities in Singaporean society, and hence also actively impedes the attainment of a more equitable society.

BACKGROUND OF OUR COURSE

As feminist scholars teaching in a university context, our feminism course is one way of cultivating a feminist consciousness among our students. Our syllabus and course activities are inevitably influenced by our beliefs, our perceptions of what is needed or is lacking in our students, and by the nature of the systemic constraints under which we have to operate. In this chapter, the aims and the challenges of offering such a course in the Singaporean university curriculum are dealt with from a feminist ethnographic point of view. This viewpoint is feminist in orientation and ethnographic in its approach as we reflect on our own instances of feminist praxis in our classroom. Our observations take into consideration our shared experience of the past three years teaching together the course Feminist Theory and Feminist Discourse. This chapter will highlight the differences engendered by the fact that this is a unique Asian classroom where Asian mindsets comingle with First-World comforts and in the economic sense at least is unhindered by the problems that shackle women in other Asian countries. Our discussion will give emphasis to specific points of fissure and fracture whenever they occur.

TEACHING FEMINIST THEORY AND FEMINIST DISCOURSE: A VIEW INTO THE SINGAPOREAN CLASSROOM

The most significant fact about our course is that it is not a traditional rhetoric and composition class where often teaching feminist theory is subsumed under the goal of teaching students to write. Instead, Feminist Theory and Feminist Discourse is a final year course that is offered to graduating majors in English language and literature. The primary goal is to explore and analyze feminist concepts with students. This freedom from the constraints of composition pedagogy is in many ways liberating, but it is also deeply challenging in our cultural context. Foremost among these challenges is the actual enrollment. Because our course is neither compulsory nor even among the slew of encouraged electives, there is always the anxiety that there might not be a sufficient number of students to justify offering the course. However, contrary to our fears, since its inception, there has never been a dearth of students, and in fact our stipulated number of sixty usually gets filled.

Why is the course generally popular? That it is one of the very few courses in the university on gender issues is one likely reason. We also like to think that word about our liberatory methodology has got around and that students want to experience something different from the usual run-of-the-mill courses. Also, very often, students at the honors level who want to pursue a research thesis related to gender issues have found that this course provides a strong foundation. Moreover, there exists a curiosity about feminism among some students who enroll in our course. We have students coming to us before the semester begins with queries such as: "What is feminism? What is the course about?" When we provide them with a brief explanation, they are often sufficiently intrigued to enroll in the course. There are yet other (less interested) students who enroll because our course meets a general elective requirement for the purpose of graduation. There are thus many reasons why students enroll in the course, and although interest is not always *the* reason, we note that quite a number develop an interest in feminist issues.

Given that our course is one of a few courses related to women's issues offered within the university curriculum, an immediate question we put to ourselves was, What did we want to impart to our students? Or, more ambitiously, not withstanding Brumfit's statement that a syllabus "can only specify what is taught; it cannot organize what is learnt," we asked ourselves, What do we want our students to have absorbed by the end of the course, given that this may be their only contact with a feminism course in the university (76)? The challenge was how to impart in the course of a thirteen-week semester first, at the very minimum, fundamental feminist principles when our students have little or no background in feminism; second, to attempt a measure of consciousness raising leading to greater feminist awareness.

While we did not want to assume prior knowledge on the students' part about the subject, we *did* want to make sure that students go away with a decent foundation in feminist theory to enable them to pursue the relevant issues at higher levels. For this reason, we consciously looked for ways to convey ideas and introduce materials not just within the classroom but outside it as well. Our first moment of "epiphanic truth" occurred when we realized that given our Asian positioning our pedagogical struggles began at the relatively basic level of curricular construction.

Given Singapore's unique economic and ideological location in that it is balanced precariously between an essentialist Asian ethic that is aggressively promulgated at all levels by the ruling People's Action Party, and a phenomenal economic success that leaves the nation facing many problems relating to a First-World economy (such as a dwindling and aging population), Singaporeans are constantly pulled between East and West. There is evident at all levels of Singaporean governance this looking to East and West to formulate policies—forging Western ideas to an Asian, local ethic. Even in designing a feminism course we had to contend with this problem. While we needed to introduce students to established (Western) proponents of feminist theory, we also wanted to ensure that Asian feminist thinkers did not go without mention. This concern has fed directly into shaping the course packet, which sees us striking a difficult balance between employing mainstream feminist texts (such as Beauvoir, *The Second Sex*, and Friedan, *The Feminine Mystique*) and nonmainstream texts (e.g., works by Singaporean women in Leong, *More Than Half the Sky*). On the one hand, we could not afford to ignore the global developments in feminist thought and praxis; on the other hand, we needed to relate these ideas to the Asian context to demonstrate their relevance. Our course description for students reflected this double concern:

This course is in two parts. The first part aims at introducing students to the works of some prominent feminist scholars, thus familiarizing students with the history of and the more contemporary trends in feminist thought and scholarship. The second part of the course concentrates on specific texts, and students will be guided in the application of a feminist reading or critique of these texts. Through such an introduction to both the theories and the practical critique in contemporary feminism, it is hoped that students will gain a critical understanding of this fast-growing field.

Another equally sensitive issue was balancing theory and practice. Given the problematic nature of the "white versus rest" debates within feminism, which seem to imply that white feminism generally occupies a privileged, often elitist position as opposed to black and Asian feminisms, we felt that the responsibility rested with us to ensure a balance and not to feed into these dichotomies. Therefore, *how much theory and whose theory, how much practice and whose practice* became extremely crucial and problematic issues.

A central problem we faced is a lack of infrastructural support and sociopolitical reinforcement of gender issues in our society. In Singapore, given that gender has never been problematized, there exists a general lack of a rhetoric that encourages overt sensitivity to gender politics in our social context. In fact, the impression is that gender is *not* a problem, and the problematic of a woman's place in society is a nonissue. This indeed seems to us a very singular circumstance. Generally speaking, with most feminist/women's studies accounts, the discourse seems to point to the problems that emerge in trying to reinforce the balanced and academic nature of the discipline to a class filled with enthusiastic, not to say fanatic (feminist) ideologues (see Patai and Koertge). But strangely, our problem seemed to be the opposite. Most of our students seemed frankly apathetic about feminism as a concept, the rest wary, while the rare few are moderately enthusiastic. It behooves us to understand the reasons for the existence of this overall apathy. To do this, we require an overall understanding of the sociopolitical context of Singapore.

THE SINGAPOREAN CONTEXT

Singapore (population 3 million) has been an independent nation since 1965. It has developed rapidly from an insignificant city-port situated at the margins of an empire to a cosmopolitan island-state with one of the highest per capita incomes in Asia. Environmental planning and urban development have transformed our landscape. The home purchase scheme has benefited 90 percent of Singaporeans. There are affordable health care and good education systems in place.

Women have contributed actively to and benefited from Singapore's progress. The female labor force participation steadily climbed to 51 percent in 1997 (Wong and Kum), and the situation has been improving yearly. Singaporean women have lower maternal mortality rates, lower fertility rates, and much higher use of contraception than any of their Asian counterparts. In education and training, the participation of Singaporean women is comparable to the best in the world. Statistics reveal that women here have a negligible illiteracy rate of 3.8 percent (Department of Statistics). School enrollment is even between boys and girls. Thus, in terms of educational opportunities and job options Singapore is equal to any developed nation.

All these factors contribute to the spurious notion of absolute equity of opportunity and prevalence of universal meritocracy, a view that is contested only by a few members of the majority Chinese race, but understandably by more members of the minority races such as the Malays and Indians, and by a few women, all of whom are usually viewed as disgruntled people eager to blame the system for their own shortcomings. Overt instances of gender discrimination, such as the preference for men over women in professional courses such as medicine,[2] or discrepancies between the benefits that accrue to male over female employees or to married over single women, are usually justified through the ethic of the Asian family perspective. The Asian perspective, the public rhetoric emphatically asserts, looks at the overall good of the family unit. Therefore, the gains, it is often argued, should be viewed from this collective perspective and not from a spurious "Western, individualistic" perspective. This rhetoric is by and large accepted without contestation because the general level of wealth and a smooth, orderly civic life ensures that the people do not get unduly fractious about minor inequalities, beyond grumbling about it occasionally. Consequently, Singaporeans are largely unaware that gender discrimination is deeply entrenched and needs to be addressed at several levels.

Thus, it is not an exaggeration to say that the majority of the students who enroll in our course enter with frank apathy or a deep-rooted skepticism, if not actual wariness, about feminism. However, it is interesting to note that despite their lack of consciousness and knowledge of feminist concepts, students are yet very keenly aware of the negative publicity that feminism generates. For example, students often ask us if our course is a male-bashing course. Also, they seem to have associated feminism negatively with radical/militant feminists and bra burning. In addition, there seems to be a general avoidance of the label *feminist*. If one is a feminist, one is thought of as somehow antifamily and therefore somehow not quintessentially Asian. Of course, we do have some thoughtful students who worry over how they can reconcile feminist goals with their conservative existences without "rocking the boat." This is indeed a very real issue: most of us live in traditional Asian family contexts that do not comfortably accommodate feminist ideas. Despite Singapore's cosmopolitan exterior, we still live in social networks that favor paternalistic values (such as femininity over feminism for one). In the thirteen-week time constraint, this becomes an even bigger problem as we attempt to find ways to address these ideological problems and to facilitate reconciliation between theory and practice.

FEMINIST PEDAGOGICAL PRACTICE, SYSTEMIC CONSTRAINTS AND CONSEQUENCES

One way of demonstrating the value of feminist concepts and practice has been through following feminist classroom praxis. Therefore, we lay emphasis on a nonhierarchical and nonauthoritarian style of teaching that foregrounds the instructor as a learner embarking on a shared journey of discovery with students in the class (Maher and Tetreault; McLaren; Bunch and Pollack). In the spirit of feminist pedagogy where the pedagogues have viewed themselves as "creative agents for change" (see Morley and Walsh) we have striven from the beginning to develop an authentic liberatory praxis in our classroom. We believe that this dialogic exchange is a key move in encouraging students to take ownership of their own learning, to voice their own experiences in relation to the issues raised in each class, thus giving space to anyone who cares to participate in the exchange. While this method of teaching is by no means revolutionary, in the Singaporean context where classroom cultures remain largely authoritarian, such a simple gesture contributes to breaking traditional molds of classroom practices. Our students' feedback over the years praises such an approach especially after the predominantly monologic sessions that they customarily encounter in the university environment.

However, despite our concerted efforts at liberatory education, and despite the fact that students seemed to like it, strangely, not much was changing except at superficial levels. In other words, "this pedagogy of possibility" was not opening up any further possibilities. It seemed that our efforts were thwarted by the reactionary attitude of our students who evinced an unwillingness to speak up in class and to participate in our liberatory efforts. It took us a while to understand that perhaps foremost amongst several complex reasons for their reactionary ways was the educational ethos in our society.

The education system is subject to the direct scrutiny of the Singaporean government. As is often articulated in political rhetoric, in a resource and land scarce Singapore, people are our only recourse, and for Singapore to survive, we need to educate the population and cultivate talent in the country. For this reason, education takes a high priority in domestic policy concerns. The result generated over the years is an education system that is planned to the last detail with nothing left to chance.

A Singaporean child entering the school system is subject from the first to a carefully planned curriculum that exacts close to 100 percent of the child's energy. Hurdles begin as early as lower primary school in Singapore (U.S.

equivalent, first through third grade). In primary four students take a streaming exam that determines their suitability for different educational tracks. At the end of primary six they have to take a public exam, the Primary School Leaving Examination (PSLE) that determines the secondary school (seventh through tenth grade) they go to. Because secondary schools are ranked according to their performance and have a PSLE grade entry requirement, and because it is rare that a child from a low-ranking secondary school gets into the three local universities, it is imperative that a Singaporean child gets into the best secondary schools to get a head start. In lower secondary (seventh and eighth grades) students once again take a qualifying exam that determines who qualifies for the coveted triple science stream (i.e., premed), the double science stream, the subscience, or the arts stream. After four or five years at a secondary school, the students take their Cambridge O level examination, a national exam that has its origins in the U.K. education system. Their performance determines whether they qualify to go to junior colleges (equivalent to eleventh and twelfth grades, again ranked) that prepare students to enter university or a local technical college.

The levels of anxiety and stress generated by this system on students and parents is, to say the least, phenomenal. It is understandable therefore, that a student, one of a very small and very elite cohort, who has crossed all these hurdles and makes it to the local universities, should rightfully feel that he or she has "arrived" and can afford to take life a little easier thenceforth.

What is more important however, is that in such a culture, what we generally get is a passive participant in activities not of his or her own making. Our students are the final, time-tested products of this rigorous system, and by the time they enter the university, they are either inveterate followers of rules or seasoned test takers, often, both. Our classrooms can be like silent tombs, filled with highly intelligent students in their early twenties who have made it through a highly competitive educational system and are among the top 10 percent of school-leavers. However, they are more interested in knowing how to obtain their *A* grades than scrambling to share their views about specific issues. This passivity, we felt, symptomized by their reluctance to speak out in class, is the result of an educational system that has located students in a passive rather than an active space.

Their reluctance to speak could also be due to the deeply ingrained notion of teachers as knowledge-givers rather than as knowledge-sharers. Therefore, students very often wait to hear our views rather than voice theirs. Perhaps also, tertiary students by this stage have internalized the view that their ideas are not sought, that their opinions are not valued, and that speaking out might even get them into trouble. This is not to say that they are not capable of forming informed opinions. On the contrary, the few who do actually take us seriously when we earnestly solicit their ideas have insightful things to say. But these indeed are few and very often (though not invariably) from the small coterie of male students, compared to "the silent majority" (i.e., the female students). Contrary to documented views of feminist pedagogues elsewhere who talk about how female students welcome and value the space that women's studies forums offer to articulate their views, the majority of our female students are silent.

Here it is useful to consider the ways in which a cultural context shapes education and how this in turn could impact on discussions of gender issues. One current event that in fact directly links both is the recent controversy over the wearing of the *tudung* (Muslim women's head dress) to school.[3] Fathers of four primary school girls (aged between four and six) refused to permit their daughters to attend school without a headscarf. However, the government would not relax the rules to permit this. The official stand was that this infringes on public space, which is perceived as a sacred multicultural space that should be used to strengthen multiracial integration and not to promote group-related agendas. The moral to be drawn for feminist discourses is that the airing of specific group-related issues such as those related to gender or class which do not stress national integration will not be tolerated in public fora.[4] There is also the possibility that our students feel that gender concerns are not legitimate concerns to be voiced in public spaces such as the classroom.

Intrinsic to our problem therefore was the question of voice. In order to make sense of our problem we looked to poststructuralist feminist ideas of power and oppression. Writing on releasing oppressed student voices from silence to speech in classrooms, Mimi Orner observes: "Historically, the demand by academics and other powerful groups for an 'authentic' people's voice or culture to be heard has been received by disenfranchised groups with a great deal of suspicion. Why must the 'oppressed' speak? For whose benefit do we/do they speak?" (76). Basing her argument on Foucauldian notions of power as relational, woven in networks, Orner queries traditional notions of classrooms as "safe places" for the oppressed to speak up. Paulo Freire often talks about the "culture of silence" when oppressed groups come face to face with authority, even when that authority espouses radical or emancipatory politics. In fact, G. Spivak sums up the problem succinctly when she asks, "Does the demand for student voice welcome selective inhabitants of the margin in order to better exclude the margin?" (107). This draws our attention to the possibility that sometimes the micropolitics of emancipatory classroom practice may appear to operate similarly to the macropolitics of dominant governance.

Was this then our problem? Were our students *afraid* to speak up in class? Did they view themselves as inhabiting "oppressed" spaces? However, this did not seem to tally with what we know: that with increasing prosperity, the average Singaporean youth is more materially and ideologically self-assured than ever before. The majority of our students most definitely did not view themselves as "oppressed" or "marginalized." For one thing, students of Chinese ethnicity (the major ethnic group in Singapore) tend to constitute 90 to 95 percent of the class makeup.[5] Thus though one cannot rule out the possibility of power dynamics operating within any group, it would have surprised us if we had discovered that the majority of students *feared* speaking up in our classroom. As mentioned earlier, our student feedback (solicited online, anonymity guaranteed) is extremely supportive and appreciative of our pedagogical methodology. Also, if it was fear that motivated silence in classrooms, then this should have been reflected in our overall curricular context that also encouraged academic participation through various written media. For in addition to lecture and tutorial sessions, we introduced our students to other avenues where they could express their views on various issues.

For the purpose of course assessment, students had to work through two auto-tutorials and a term paper project. Auto-tutorials that occur independently, without the presence of the tutor, are sessions that solicit students' independent views on a range of feminist issues through short assignments. For example, on one occasion, we asked students to analyze Charlotte Perkins Gilman's story "Circumstances Alter Cases."[6] On another occasion, we asked for students' written responses to Camille Paglia's argument on women and rape. Through these short exercises, we provided students with additional opportunities to air their views about specific feminist concerns such as rape and responsibility. In all instances, the responses were intelligent and sometimes deeply thought provoking.

We also had a term paper project for the course that provided an extended venue for students to formulate their own topic of discussion. Usually ten to twelve pages in length, students were required to submit an essay discussion on any feminism-related topic of their choice by the end of the course. Our students worked on a variety of topics such as the representation of women in advertising in Singapore, the status of women in Japan, and the portrayal of women in Indian movies. Some delved into specific theories, but others avoided theories and concentrated instead on analyzing texts.

The use of the Integrated Virtual Learning Environment (IVLE) software made available by the university enabled us to engage in online discussions about course issues with students. It is interesting that when we set up an electronic chat forum for the class and stated vaguely that class participation, which would include participation in the e-forum, would be graded, we had a number of students participating enthusiastically in the e-chat room with fairly contentious opinions being flaunted. But this was not reflected in a corresponding classroom verbal participation. Thus, it seemed that the students were not afraid to be identified for their contentious views in various written forums be it auto-tutorials, term papers or even e-forums. So again fear or a consciousness of oppression did not prompt their silence in classrooms. Also, whenever they felt the need to register their opinions in order to enhance their grades, they never hesitated, even if these were in the more permanent written medium. But they were at all times reluctant to speak up in class. Combating this apathy became our increasing preoccupation.

We therefore ask our most pressing question now: Why are our students not interested in engaging in debate in our classrooms? If they are so ingrained in passive spaces, would they be able to participate so actively in other written forums and offer sophisticated views about feminist concepts? If they saw themselves as the oppressed and feared punitive action, would they associate their names unhesitatingly with contentious and polemical opinions through their written assignments and e-forums? The answer to both of these queries is no, which takes us back to the question, Then what brings about this overriding indifference in our classroom?

Our concerted efforts at making sense of our predicament led us to explore Freire's notion of *conscientizacao* (1972) or "conscientization." Conscientization, as Robert Mackie points out, in the Freirean context "corresponds to highly permeable, interrogative, restless and dialogical forms of life" (96). Inherent in the notion of conscientization is the development of critical consciousness. As Jane Kenway and Helen Modra observe, "there is a world of difference between consciousness-raising and the development of critical consciousness" (156). While the value of consciousness raising about gender discrimination cannot be overemphasized and is rightly identified as one of the central liberatory goals that feminist pedagogy aims to achieve, it should by no means be confused with the development of critical consciousness (138–67). Freire's "critical consciousness" facilitates the analysis of the contexts in which problem situations occur leading to the possibility of enabling people to transform their lived realities. This difference between consciousness raising and conscientization we felt was at the center of our problem of student apathy.

Given the present lived reality of the Singaporean sociopolitical context, the transformative possibilities of conscientization seem to be highly idealistic, perhaps impossible. We surmise that our students, highly intelligent as they are, have reasoned themselves into locations of least resistance with the least need for expending energy. To them, engaging in a heated debate about the possible transformations that a feminist consciousness could effect would appear, in the final analysis, wasteful! As such, they reserve their energies for activities that would fetch them better grades and exhibit indifference and apathy toward everything else. Thus, they engage actively in written fora not necessarily because they want their opinions heard but because they know the quality of their responses will be assessed and graded. This entirely utilitarian attitude is the only one that seems to make sense to them. We have thus a more profound problem on our hands than a mere lack of feminist consciousness. We wondered what we could do as feminist scholars and teachers to combat this sense of hopelessness, to convey to students the transformative possibilities of a feminist consciousness even in our context.

IMPLICATIONS FOR A FEMINIST PRAXIS

The fundamental need then seemed to be to inculcate a critical consciousness in our students. For this, it is crucial that students understand that every act of social transformation has its origins in small individual changes spreading outward into the wider social realm. Only when individual effort is recognized will there be greater motivation for individual exertion. In fact, apathy results when individuals feel strongly that the lone "I" cannot possibly make a difference in the world, and hence such affirmation of individual effort is absolutely necessary.

Freire describes liberatory education as the "struggle to change structures" (27). What we need is to construct what is known as "cointentional education," where we, together with the students (both participants of a shared reality), need to learn to unveil that reality together. Through this process we need to recreate our knowledge structures. For this, we need to pursue not the traditional "banking education" that Freire identifies (chapter 2) but a problem-posing one. This kind of education, which would demand dialogical relations between student and facilitator, would have to be radically reconfigured. First, the students need to be placed in an active location right from the start. We intend for them to be involved right from the stage of curricular construction, struggling with us to make the course meaningful to all of us. We hope to start with a course description and a skeletal curriculum and then leave the space for the students to construct enough of it to make them feel an active responsibility for it. If we involve them in actively planning and constructing the course (within certain systemic constraints), they would gradually move from their passive positioning to an active one. Thus, more time could be spent discussing topics selected by the students. This would then be the first step toward inculcating a critical consciousness in our students. If we can make them understand through these pedagogic strategies that no reality transforms itself except by the active intervention of individuals, then we would be achieving our goals—not dramatically, not overnight, but gradually and purposefully. Hence, the twin concerns of consciousness raising and cultivating critical consciousness should be our focus. Only then can we hope to bring to light dormant power struggles within and outside the classroom and attempt real changes.

EPILOGUE: CONSUMING GLOBAL THEORY; PRODUCING LOCAL THEORY

Even as we struggle to make our course relevant to our students, we realize that our greatest hurdle is global feminist theory. We cannot do without global theory because it gives us the history, the text and context, and the intellectual sustenance vital to our endeavors. Yet it effectively distances feminist concerns from our own immediate experiences. Let us demonstrate this with two examples. One student working on Betty Friedan's ideas about the alienation experienced by suburban women in America wanted to link it to a similar alienation evident in some Singaporean women. However, she found that beyond a point Friedan's ideas cannot be applied in the local context because a Singaporean woman could feel a similar isolation because her sense of identity and intrinsic worth, like her American sisters, go beyond what she can routinely achieve in the domestic sphere. There are significant differences that bring about the dissatisfaction. Unlike the American homemaker, many Singaporean women still live in an extended family context, with support from siblings, parents, and sometimes grandparents. Yet these supportive (and cloistered) conditions can stifle a woman's sense of engagement with the wider community. Thus, similar emotions could be brought about by radically different factors.

Another example pertained to Adrienne Rich's classic text on motherhood, *Of Woman Born*. When a student attempted a study of Singaporean mothers and tried to apply Rich's ideas, she soon discovered that the space occupied by a Singaporean mother is very different from the space occupied by the mother in the American context. The kind of enclosed space that isolates a mother and child in some Western societies that Rich describes is definitely not typical of the Singaporean context. Singaporean Chinese, Malays, and Indians alike locate motherhood in a communal space within the extended family and see the experience of mothering as a cooperative undertaking. The Asian mother in most instances might feel crowded, resent the intrusion and the lack of privacy but would rarely feel a sense of isolation in the experience of mothering, such being the nature of extended Asian family networks.

What these examples demonstrated to us was that while influential Western theorists may have important theoretical lessons for us, there are significant differences that emerge in the application of these theories in our context. This alerts us to the fact that we have to be very sensitive about how we present global feminist theories to our students. We need to caution them about their limited relevance in our local context, important as these ideas are in mainstream feminist scholarship.

In general globalism versus nationalism is a problematic issue in Singapore. In a multicultural but relatively cohesive Singaporean society, upward mobility through merit and application is seen as an attainable goal by most Singaporeans. The national rhetoric—that nothing can stand in the way of the success of a hard-working Singaporean of either sex—is generally considered as reality by the majority of youth of all races. Therefore, the rhetoric of global feminist theory with its emphasis on fragmentation and discrimination and the call for activism does not strike a chord with most young Singaporeans, because women are visible at all levels of society.

Given our demographic reality—that we are a small island constantly buffeted by winds of social and economic changes not of our making (Indonesian civil war that threatened our social stability; recent US recession that wrought economic turmoil)—Singaporeans have a healthy postmodern skepticism about any kind of grand global movements that inflict themselves willy-nilly on our lives. Our stand on global movements is ambivalent to say the least: we realize our dependence on them, yet we desire to be free of them. This in effect dictates our own relationship to feminist global theory. We cannot ignore it, but we have to ensure its adoption does not result in alienating local affinities and sensibilities. Our starting point to resolve these problems could perhaps follow Martin and Mohanty's envisioning collective struggle as beginning from an acknowledgement that "unity—interpersonal, personal and political—is necessarily fragmentary, not given, but chosen and struggled for—but not on the basis of sameness" (208–09).

Classroom practices that facilitate the movement between global feminist concepts and local women's concerns need to be nurtured. Our cointentional educational practices would serve us well in this endeavor. Identity would then be perceived as "nonessentialized and emergent from a historical experience" (hooks 54), as a necessary stage in a process, a process, not an arrival, that makes complex and multiple subject positions possible. We need to cognize our multiple subject/object positioning that negotiates our peripheral yet (in some ways) privileged locations with a more progressive yet contested global feminist location, without dichotomizing either. An acknowledgement in the best traditions of poststructuralist feminist epistemology "accepts that knowledge is always provisional, open-ended and relational." Progressing toward this would be our testing ground. In this slow onward struggle we hope to refine our pedagogic practices and adapt our consumption of global feminist theory by modifying it to local needs. In its turn, global theory must learn to temper continually its pronouncements by being cognizant of situated locations in the periphery such as ours. This would, we hope, lead to a unique brand of feminist pedagogic practice which nevertheless would be of relevance to countries test-teaching feminism elsewhere.

NOTES

1. In Singapore, we do not have a well-established feminist tradition. Hence, terms such as *consciousness raising* are not familiar to many Singaporeans. Therefore, consciousness raising entails both introducing students to this concept and also overtly identifying areas of discriminatory practices that students are not necessarily aware of, despite their lived reality.

2. This issue of quota restriction imposed upon women entering medical school is only now being seriously reviewed at higher levels of governance.

3. See "*The Straits Times* Reports on The Tudung Issue" in the following issues of *Straits Times* online: 30 January, 4 February, 12 February, 15 February, 2002.

4. There seems to be two kinds of spaces/voices: private and public. The public voice is perceived as one that tries to emphasize unity between the different national groups thus encouraging national integration; but the private voice speaks up for group interests within the nation.

5. Singaporean society is made up of a multiracial, multi-religious mix even though the Chinese are the dominant group. The question of racial marginalization or exclusion is seldom a question in the school system and we can say with confidence, is never a question in our feminism classroom. Hence, we do not find ourselves perusing a class list and worrying about the racial distribution in the class because the numbers are reflective of the country's demographics. However, we do notice that males tend to be a minority in this course.

6. Gilman's story demonstrates that the same set of facts are viewed differently when the person concerned is female rather than male.

WORKS CITED

Brumfit, Christopher. "Function and Structure of a State School Syllabus for Learners of Second and Foreign Languages with Heterogeneous Needs." In *General English Syllabus Design,* ELT Document 118, Oxford, UK: Pergamon Press in association with The British Council, 1984.

Bunch, Charlotte and Sandra Pollack, eds. *Learning Our Way: Essays in Feminist Education.* Trumansburg, New York: Crossing Press, 1983.

De Beauvoir, Simone. *The Second Sex.* New York: Vintage, 1952.

Freire, Paulo. *The Pedagogy of the Oppressed.* Harmondsworth, Middlesex, UK: Penguin, 1972.

Friedan, Betty. *The Feminine Mystique.* New York: Norton, 1983.

Gilman, Charlotte Perkins. "Circumstances Alter Cases." *The Yellow Wall-Paper and Other Stories.* Ed. Robert Shulman. Oxford: Oxford University Press, 1995.

hooks, bell. "The Politics of Radical Black Subjectivity." *Zeta Magazine* (April 1989).

Kenway, Jane and Helen Modra. "Feminist Pedagogy and Emancipatory Possibilities." *Feminisms and Critical Pedagogy.* Ed. Carmen Luke and Jennifer Gore. London: Routledge, 1992.

Leong, Liew Geok. *More Than Half the Sky.* Singapore: Times Books International, 1998.

Luke, Carmen and Jennifer Gore. "Introduction." *Feminisms and Critical Pedagogy.* Ed. Carmen Luke and Jennifer Gore. London: Routledge, 1992.

Mackie, Robert, ed. *Literacy and Revolution: The Pedagogy of Paulo Freire.* London: Pluto Press, 1980.

Maher, Frances and Mary Kay Thompson Tetreault. *The Feminist Classroom.* New York: Basic Books, 1994.

Marin, Biddy and Chandra Talpade Mohanty. "Feminist Politics: What's Home Got to Do with It?" *Feminist Studies/Critical Studies.* Ed. Teresa de Lauretis. Bloomington: Indiana University Press, 1986.

McLaren, Peter. *Life in Schools: An Introduction to Critical Pedagogy in the Foundations of Education.* New York and London: Longman, 1989.

Morley, Louise and Val Walsh. *Feminist Academics: Creative Agents for Change.* London, Washington: Taylor and Francis, 1995.

Orner, Mimi. "Interrupting the Calls for Student Voice in Liberatory Education: A Feminist Poststructuralist Perspective." *Feminisms and Critical Pedagogy.* Ed. Carmen Luke and Jennifer Gore. London: Routledge, 1992.

Paglia, Camille. *Sex, Art, and American Culture.* New York and Toronto: Vintage Books, 1992.

Patai, Daphne and Noretta Koertge. *Professing Feminism: Cautionary Tales, from the Strange World of Women's Studies.* New York: Basic Books, 1994.

Shor, Ira and Paulo Freire. *A Pedagogy for Liberation.* Westport, Conn.: Bergin and Garvey, 1987.

Spivak, Gayatri Chakrovorty *In Other Worlds: Essays in Cultural Politics.* New York: Routledge, 1987.

The Straits Times Interactive, http://straitstimes.asia1.com.sg/home.

Wong, Aline and Leong Wai Kum, eds. *Singapore Women: Three Decades of Change.* Singapore: Times Academic Press, 1993.

CONTRIBUTORS

M. DIANE BENTON teaches at Eastern Michigan University in Ypsilanti and at a private high school in Ann Arbor, Michigan. For ten years she taught at Washtenaw Community College. Now she teaches first-year composition classes and African American and American literature as well as technical and business writing courses. Her interests include African American rhetoric and literature, cultural rhetorics, curriculum design, and multigenre curricula. She holds master's degrees in the teaching of writing and educational psychology. She has twenty years of experience working in business and industry.

LINDA S. BERGMANN is associate professor at Purdue University. Linda has published over fourteen articles on various genres of writing, teaching writing, and directing writing programs, and she has conducted a wide variety of workshops on writing and teaching writing at colleges and universities. Her most recent publications include "WAC and the Ethos of Engineering: Conflict and Accommodation," in *Language and Learning across the Disciplines* and "Addressing Gender Issues in the Engineering Classroom," co-authored with Connie Meinholdt (psychology) and Susan Murray (engineering management), in *Feminist Teacher*.

STUART H.D. CHING is assistant professor of English and assistant director of liberal studies at Loyola Marymount University. He teaches courses in composition, Asian Pacific American literature, and children's literature. Ching's publications include articles and stories in journals and anthologies such as *Language Arts, Writing on the Edge, The New Advocate, Fourteen Landing Zones, The Best of Honolulu Fiction,* and *Growing Up Local: An Anthology of Poetry and Prose from Hawaii*. His research on memory also includes essays forthcoming in *The New Advocate* journal of children's literature, and in the composition anthology *The Subject is Story*.

JOANNE DETORE-NAKAMURA is a self-described equity feminist, who piloted the first women's history month celebration, designed and offered the first women's literature course, and designed and facilitated the first gender/diversity faculty and staff training courses at Brevard Community College in Melbourne, Florida. At BCC, she was a tenured, full professor, a former department chair, and a finalist for Distinguished Educator who taught composition and literature courses from 1995 to 2002. Her teaching and work in women's history has been recognized by her inclusion in several additions of *Who's Who Among America's Teachers* and in the *Who's Who of American Women 2002* edition. Her creative work has been published in such journals as Purdue's *Voices in Italian Americana* and York University's *Journal of the Association of Research on Mothering* (ARM). Additionally, she has given a number of papers on women's literature at the Virginia Woolf Conference, the 20th Century Literature Conference, the Irish Studies Conference and the Midwest MLA, among others. She was a university fellow at Southern Illinois University at Carbondale where she attained her Ph.D. in American Literature and Women's Studies, winning a number of research awards, including one for the most promising dissertation proposal, which recognized her groundbreaking theory called "the friendship plot" in contemporary women's novels. Her most recent research interest is mothering and motherhood. Currently, she is coediting an anthology of original essays about working mothers and childcare issues throughout the twentieth century, and presented the work-in-progress at an ARM conference in Toronto this year. She shares her life with her husband and their four-year-old daughter in the Daytona Beach area. She began a new chapter of her life this fall when she gave up her tenure status at the community college to accept a tenure-track position at Embry-Riddle Aeronautic University, where she is assistant professor of humanities and social sciences.

LAURA GRAY-ROSENDALE is associate professor of English specializing in rhetoric and composition, former chair and current cochair of the Commission on the Status of Women and director of a summer bridge writing program at Northern Arizona University. She teaches graduate and undergraduate classes in cultural studies and visual rhetoric, the history of rhetoric, gender studies, and literacy theory. Along with over twenty articles and book chapters, Gray-Rosendale has published *Rethinking Basic Writing: Exploring Identity, Politics, and Community in Interaction* (2000) and *Alternative Rhetorics: Challenges to the Rhetorical Tradition* with Sibylle Gruber (2001). Her new book, *Radical Relevance: Essays toward a Scholarship of the "Whole Left"* with Steven Rosendale, is forthcoming (SUNY Press, 2004). Gray-Rosendale is also completing a textbook on rhetorical analysis, argumentation, and popular culture studies for freshmen composition students (McGraw-Hill Publishers, 2004).

SIBYLLE GRUBER is associate professor of English and director of composition at Northern Arizona University. She is the editor of *Weaving a Virtual Web: Practical Approaches to New Information Technologies* (2000). She also co-edited *Alternative Rhetorics: Challenges to the Rhetorical Tradition* with Laura Gray-Rosendale (2001). Gruber's work on cybertheories, feminist rhetorics, composition, and cultural studies can be found in journals such as *Computers and Composition, Computer Supported Cooperative Work, Journal of Basic Writing, Works and Days, The Journal of the Assembly on Computers in English,* and *The Information Society,* and books such as *Feminist Cyberspaces: Essays on Gender in Electronic Spaces,* and *Global Literacy Practices and the WWW: Cultural Perspectives on Information Distribution, Interpretation, and Use.*

GIL HAROOTUNIAN teaches at Syracuse University and serves as an advisory editor and writer for the literary quarterly *Ararat.* She is a Fulbright senior lecturer and researcher whose current projects investigate the transnational use of American English in new democracies. Harootunian edited *The Personal Narrative: Writing Ourselves as Teachers and Scholars* (1999) and authored *The Fatal Hero: Diana, Deity of the Moon, as an Archetype of the Modern Hero in English Literature* (1996; 2nd edition 1998). She has published in various literary and academic journals, her most recent contribution forthcoming in *In the Writing Studio: Designing Assignments for Student Learning* (SU). Her research interests also include the intersections of feminist theory and the use of contingent labor in the academy, her latest perspectives on this issue just having been published in a conversation of letters in *The Chronicle of Higher Education.*

CHNG HUANG HOON is assistant professor at the Department of English Language and Literature and at the American Studies Center, at the National University of Singapore. Her research interests are in feminist theories and discourse and gender discrimination and the law, with particular focus on the U.S. Supreme Court. Her publications include a monograph, *Towards Multidisciplinarity: The Case of Judicial Language* (this is a book published by the Department of English Language and Literature, National University of Singapore, 1996), and her most recent article, "In the Beginning There Was Myra: The Role of Language in the Construction of Gender and Power Relations in the Judicial Setting" (1998). She is preparing her first book publication on law and gender discrimination, to be published by John Benjamins, Amsterdam.

ROSE KAMEL is professor of English at the University of the Sciences in Philadelphia. Her publications include *Aggravating the Conscience: Jewish-American Foremothers in the Promised Land* (1989) and articles and chapters on feminist theory in literature, including "Before I Was Set Free: The Creole Wife in *Jane Eyre* and *Wide Sargasso Sea,*" in *The Journal of Narrative Technique*

(Winter 1995) and "Written on the Body: Charlotte Delbo's *Auschwitz and After*," in *The Journal of Genocide and Holocaust Studies* (Spring 2000). Her current research interests lie with Sylvia Plath and the diaries of Hannah Senesh and Etty Hillesum, and she has published articles on these subjects in *The Northwest Review of Books* (Spring 1981) and *Women's Studies Quarterly* (Fall/Winter 1989).

VERONICA PANTOJA is a doctoral student in rhetoric, composition, and linguistics at Arizona State University, where she has served as a teaching associate in the Department of English and a research associate in the Center for Learning and Teaching Excellence. Her research interests include computer-mediated teaching and learning, composition studies, and faculty development. She recently co-edited *Strategies for Teaching First-Year Composition* with Duane Roen, Lauren Yena, Susan K. Miller, and Eric Waggoner.

BRADLEY PETERS coordinates the Writing across the Curriculum Program and directs the University Writing Center at Northern Illinois University. He teaches courses in cross-disciplinary rhetorics, composition, professional writing, tutoring, and rhetoric/composition theory. Publications include essays in Keith Gilyard's *Race, Rhetoric, and Composition* (Heinemann Boynton/Cook, 1999); John Tassoni and William Thelin's *Blundering for a Change* (Heinemann Boynton/Cook, 2000); Linda Adler-Kassner and Susanmarie Harrington's *Questioning Authority* (University of Michigan Press, 2001).

DUANE ROEN is professor of English and director of the Center for Learning and Teaching Excellence at Arizona State University. His research interests include gender and written language, collaboration, audience, and writing across the curriculum. He has published the following books: *Composing Our Lives in Rhetoric and Composition: Stories about the Growth of a Discipline* (with Theresa Enos and Stuart Brown, 1999), *The Writer's Toolbox* (with Stuart Brown and Robert Mittan, 1996), *A Sense of Audience in Written Discourse* (with Gesa Kirsch, 1990), *Becoming Expert: Writing and Learning across the Disciplines* (with Stuart Brown and Robert Mittan, 1990), and *Richness in Writing: Empowering ESL Students* (with Donna Johnson, 1989).

CHITRA SANKARAN is assistant professor at the Department of English Language and Literature, National University of Singapore. She authored *The Myth Connection: The Use of Hindu Mythology in Some Novels of Raja Rao and R. K. Narayan* (Allied Publishers, 1993), and she has published articles in *World Englishes, Journal of Commonwealth Literature, Journal of South Asian Literature, World Literature Written in English,* and various book chapters in feminist theories and postcolonial studies and comparative East-West literature. Chitra is currently at work on a course text on postcolonial studies for the Open University, UK, and she is engaged in translation studies and researching comparative East-West literatures.

EILEEN SCHELL is associate professor of English and writing at Syracuse University, where she is also director of graduate studies in composition and cultural rhetoric. She is co-editor of *Moving a Mountain: Transforming the Role of Contingent Faculty in Higher Education and Composition Studies* (with Patti Stock, 2000) and author of *Gypsy Academics and Mother-Teachers: Gender, Contingent Labor, and Writing Instruction* (1997). She has published widely in academic journals on feminist issues such as "The Costs of Caring: 'Feminism' and Contingent Women Workers in Composition Studies," in *Feminism and Composition Studies*, ed. Susan Jarratt and Lynn Worsham (MLA 1998).

SHELLY WHITFIELD has dedicated the past four years to teaching English in high school and community college classrooms in Texas and Arizona. She recently received her master's degree in English curriculum and instruction from Arizona State University, where her studies focused on composition and assessment. Other research interests include comparative composition instruction, critical theory and teacher education programs, and teaching with technology. Shelly is studying at the University of Leeds, where she is looking at teaching critical theory (coupled with reader-response theories) to secondary students.

INDEX

feminism *(continued)*

empowerment, 61
ethnography, 145, 216
ethos, 131–141
fairy tales and, 134
history, 72–73
interrogation of, 11–13, 16
labor conditions and, 147
liberal, 3
materialist, 31–41
multiple, 1–2
poststructuralist, 6–7, 227
radical, 5–6, 47–48, 50, 219
socialist, 4–5
teaching, 15, 138–139, 141, 145
theory,
Freire, Paulo, 51, 224–225

gender
boys' prison, 202–206
ethnography and, 149–151
literature and, 120–121
male students, 17, 53, 58–59, 95–96,
98, 107, 113, 118–119, 121–123,
133–147, 149–151
male teachers, 16–17, 89–100,
106–107, 137–140
politics, 216–218, 222
genre, 119
ethnography, 143–156
persuasion (Aristotle), 132. *See*
assignments
globalization, 15, 21, 35–36, 39–41, 41f,
118, 211, 217
global feminist theory, 226–227

harassment
administrative policies, 65–84
heterosexuality, 47–48, 60–61
hierarchy, 67–68, 77–78, 126, 164–166,
182–183
homosexuality, 47–49, 60–61, 97,
111–113, 205

journals, 52–54, 119, 134, 203

literature, 216
fairy tales, 134
medicine and, 118. *See also* African
American, 21, 54, 99, 124,
153–154, 195–213

Marxism, 15, 31–41
post-Marxism, 31. *See also* Freire,
Paulo, 51, 224–225
medicine, 18, 89–100, 117–126, 228f

Native American, 211

oral communication, 109
oral history, 20, 183, 188–189

persuasion (Aristotle), 132
practice
based teaching, 12, 13–14, 138–141,
143–145
theory and, 17–19, 45
prison, 202–206

race, 186
ethnography and, 153–154
Euro-American, 118, 124, 133–134,
196–197, 209–212, 218
Italian American, 47–48, 56–58
students and, 38, 153–154. *See also*
African American, 21, 54, 99,
124, 153–154, 195–213; Arabic,
211; Asian, 20, 21, 125, 211,
215–227; Native American, 211
religion, 4, 46, 203, 222

science, 18, 89–100, 117–126, 221. *See
also* engineering, 17–18, 103–115 and
medicine, 18, 89–100, 117–126, 228f
service learning, 53
silence, 13, 19, 60–61
subject (position), 7; 17, 50, 118–119,
125–126, 152–153, 155, 164, 168,
197–199, 205, 221, 225, 227

teaching
feminist, 17, 18, 52, 110, 138–139,
141, 145, 169–172, 220